WILL PFEIFER

"The Avengers" 1930s

Iron Man
Errol Flynn

Captain America
Jimmy Stewart

Thor
Nat Pendelton

Black Widow
Barbara Stanwyck

Nick Fury
Paul Robeson
(uncredited)

Hulk
Edward G. Robinson

Spider-Man
Mickey Rooney

Falcon
Bill Robinson
(uncredited)

Scarlet Witch
Marlene Dietrich

Vision
Robot from "The
Phantom Creeps"

War Machine
Dooley Wilson
(uncredited)

Dr. Strange
Warren William

Ant Man
Harry Earles

Wasp
Daisy Earles

Black Panther
Rex Ingram
(uncredited)

Thanos
Eugene Pallette

Starlord
Clark Gable

Gamora
Theresa Harris
(uncredited)

Rocket
Asta from
"The Thin Man"

Groot
Tree from "The
Wizard of Oz"

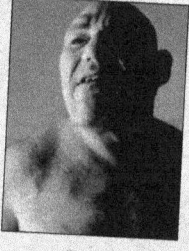
Drax
Maurice Tillet
a/k/a "The
French Angel"

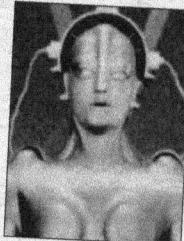
Nebula
Maria robot from
"Metropolis"

Loki
Groucho Marx

Red Skull
Boris Karloff

Typography by **MARK SIMONSON**

PUBLISHER'S LETTER
BY MICHAEL GERBER

EROS AND THANATOS
A few stray thoughts on Love and Death

Recently I got an email from a famous Boomer satirist who shall remain nameless. "Your comedy is sadly propaganda," Nameless said. "Count me out. I really enjoyed what you were up to, how sad for this bullshit."

"Shut up, Dad!" I wanted to reply. "I learned it from you!" But instead I was polite. Instead I patiently explained why *Bystander*'s editorial mix has temporarily become more political, and why it's likely to stay that way until (God willing) January 21, 2021.

The American Bystander exists to provide a outlet for the most interesting comic writers and artists working today, and to update the grand literary tradition of print humor magazines. To do these things, it must reflect its time. Since November 2016, I have received a torrent, a deluge, a cataract of Trump-based humor and cartoons, 99% of which is rejected out-of-hand. But when you look at over 1000 submissions per issue, even 1% is a lot.

Of course, I could ignore my contributors. I could make *Bystander* a vacation, a respite from woes both foreign and domestic. How wonderful that sounds, how restful. So much more pleasant to read. So much more pleasant to *edit*. I'm sorely tempted…

…and then I think of Ralph Ginzburg.

MICHAEL GERBER (@mgerber937) is Editor & Publisher of *The American Bystander*.

Ralph Ginzburg was a publisher back in the 60s and 70s. If you remember him at all, it's for the political magazine *Avant Garde*, or the hardcover "sex and love magbook" *EROS*. This high-toned, design-forward, mail-only quarterly was beautifully art-directed by Herb Lubalin. I had a copy of *EROS* (Summer 1962) which I referred to regularly as I created the high-toned, design-forward, mail-only quarterly *American Bystander*.

In Summer 1962, my grandfather was a young executive type, happily married, living in Connecticut with his wife and three boys. Since he's not here to defend himself, let's say Gramp was given that copy of *EROS* by a disreputable friend, was horrified by its contents, then took to his manly sickbed, too incapacitated by migraines to burn it immediately, as he doubtless intended. All I know is, I discovered it in his basement around 1980 and, in the tradition of adolescent boys everywhere, I swiped it.

You won't believe this, but I wasn't swiping it for the porn. As you can see online, *EROS* was incredibly tame, horrifyingly tame, much tamer by far than any issue of *The National Lampoon*.[1] Back in 1962, *EROS* treated sex like NORAD treated nuclear warheads: a necessary, regrettable, dangerous fact of modern life whose destructive power nevertheless exerted a dark fascination. *EROS* doesn't show people having sex, or even having fun; it shows a society frozen to the waist by sublimation, frustration, and the mendacity caused by both. To which any sensible human being must say: *fuck that*.

[1] *EROS* is here: http://eros.110west40th.com/

No, I stole that magbook because I was (and am) fascinated by the Kennedy brothers. The issue in question had an article called "We All Love Jack" about the magnetism JFK exerted on female voters. Turns out that Attorney General Robert F. Kennedy was as interested as I was in that article, but for a slightly different reason. Anxious to keep an ever-growing number of cats in an ever-growing number of bags, RFK toyed with the idea of suing Ginzburg right then and there for obscenity. But he didn't, figuring that a lawsuit might only draw attention to all his brother's stray magnetism.

So RFK, a smart man, and still a little closer to his Roy Cohn side than his Aeschylus one, waited a couple of issues. Sure enough, in Winter 1962 *EROS* published a "photographic tone poem" starring a black man and a white woman. Now *this* the Justice Department could work with! And they *worked* with it, holy shit did they ever.

Like I said, you can see this danger to American democracy online, but to give some idea of what we're talking about, here's that article's scorching-hot intro:

"On the following eight pages, *EROS* proudly presents a photographic tone-poem on the subject of interracial love. This is presented with the conviction that love between a man and a woman, no matter what their races, is beautiful. Interracial couples of today bear the indignity of having to defend their love to a questioning world. Tomorrow these couples will be recognized as the pioneers of an enlightened age in which prejudice will be dead, and the only race will be the human race."[1]

Obviously *that* couldn't be allowed in the public print; so a Kennedy loyalist in Congress branded *EROS* "part of an international Communist plot," and ol' Ralph Ginzburg was hauled into court. He bucked it and bucked it. Three years later, he went in front of the Supreme Court and lost, in part it seems because he looked, well, grubby? And also Jewish. (To me, he just looks like a guy named "Ralph.")

Oh sure, the magazine was protected by the First Amendment, the Justices said, but Ginzburg's mailing advertisements, which were *not* protected, emphasized the magazine's titillating sexual content, and were therefore "obscene."

It was an odd ruling, but all appeals were for naught; so in 1972, as *Playboy* reached its highest monthly circulation, Ralph Ginzburg entered the Federal Pen at Leavenworth. He got out eight months later, right around the time *Deep Throat* began to set box office records, and *SCREW* published nude photos of Jackie O. (RFK was unavailable for comment.)

If Trump and his Republicans manage to transform American society in the ways they seem determined to, these kinds of stories will become common again. Justice randomly applied. Political animus hiding behind morality. Scapegoating, hypocrisy, the well-connected getting away with it and the rest of us getting it in the neck. More to the point, modern comedy—the anti-authoritarian, taboo-busting, *free* type of humor that's been America's most beloved export for sixty years—that will wither and die, because the cultural and legal conditions it needs will no longer exist.

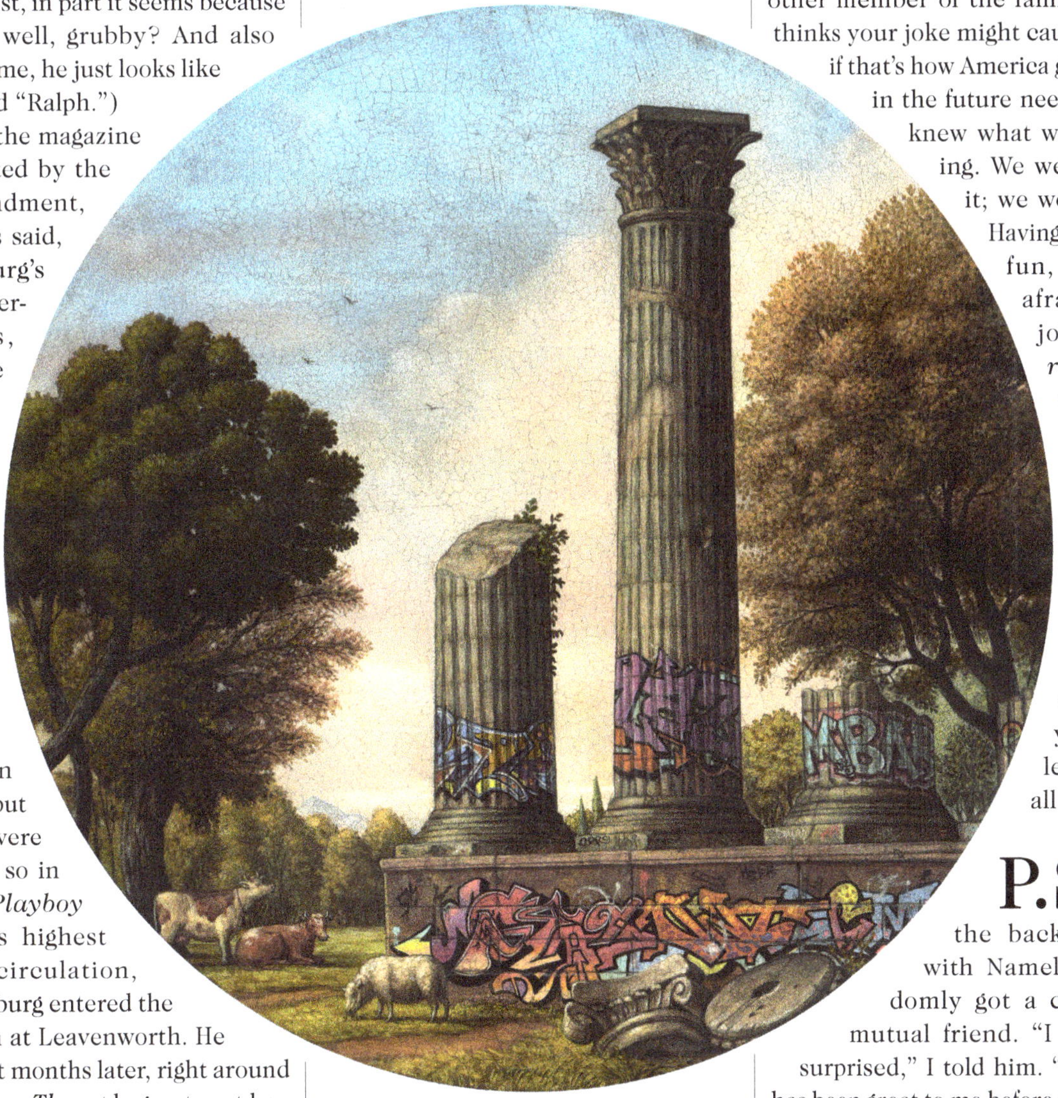

And it will be easy, so easy. Big publishers and TV networks, we know they'll cave. Outfits like Netflix and Amazon might hold out for a while, but only until the FCC finds the right nut to squeeze. The internet's most vulnerable of all: Just hold ISP's and big tech companies legally responsible for "offensive" content, and watch the filtering and takedowns begin. Maybe it'll go state-by-state, or maybe all at once. New media, same old censorship.

So I *have* to publish these articles now, in case nobody can publish them later. I *have* to press the boundary now, so if it does collapse—if in 2023 a cartoon or humor piece might get you eight months because it's "inflammatory" or "libellous" or "obscene" (maybe because it references a powerful politician doing something shady, and some other member of the family dynasty thinks your joke might cause trouble) if that's how America goes, people in the future need to see we knew what was happening. We were fighting it; we were *awake*. Having fun, poking fun, and not afraid. Every joke—every *reader*—was a seed designed to sprout later, when sanity returned. All that might not mean so much to you, Nameless, but it's all I've got.

P.S. Following the back-and-forth with Nameless, I randomly got a call from a mutual friend. "I was really surprised," I told him. "[Nameless] has been great to me before." The friend begged me to send the email, and after initially demurring (I didn't want to make a Federal case out of it), I did so.

"Not our boy," he said confidently. "You got phished." Wow, could it be? There *was* a Gmail alert on it. I Googled the address; it exists nowhere on the internet. The closest match was the Twitter handle of an Irish sports photographer, and an executive in Dublin. Neither are subscribers to *Bystander*.

So...enjoy the issue, comrades?

(I hope the rest of you do, too!) **B**

---

[2] If you ever wondered what it would be like if Gene Rodenberry wrote a *Penthouse* letter, now you know.

MARC BURKHARDT

TABLE OF CONTENTS

DEPARTMENTS
Frontispiece: "The Avengers: 1930" **by Will Pfeifer**..............1
Publisher's Letter **by Michael Gerber** 2
Hey Fellers! Do Your Bit **by Ross MacDonald** 86

GALLIMAUFRY
Risa Mickenberg, Steve Jones, Ian Baker, Ilana Gordon, Tom Chitty, Rob Kutner, Lars Kenseth, Phil Witte, Rebecca Clifton & Lance Hansen, Stephen Knight, Tyson Cole, Lydia Oxenham, Bob Eckstein, Mike Shiell, Luke Roloff, Melissa Balmain, George Booth, Patrick Kennedy, Alex Watt, Stan Mack.

SHORT STUFF
Days at Sea **by Rick Geary**...................................5
A Thrown Cup **by M.K. Brown**...............................7
The End of the Beginning **by Megan Koester**.........23
Owning the Libs By Suffering in Hell **by Alex Schmidt**........24
Serfs at the Gate **by Matt Garczynski**.....................26
My Sopranos Cameo **by Laurie Rosenwald**...........28
Unlocking the Door **by Jay Ruttenberg**..................30
An Email for the Lotion I Just Ordered From Amazon
  by Sarah Hutto 32

FEATURES
Wigglesworth **by Brian McConnachie** 35

The AMERICAN BYSTANDER
#11 • Vol. 3, No. 3 • June 2019

EDITOR & PUBLISHER
Michael Gerber
HEAD WRITER
Brian McConnachie
SENIOR EDITOR
Alan Goldberg
CONTACTEE Scott Marshall
ORACLE Steve Young
STAFF LIAR P.S. Mueller
INTREPID TRAVELER
Mike Reiss
AGENTS OF THE SECOND BYSTANDER INTERNATIONAL
Craig Boreth, Matt Kowalick, Neil Mitchell, Maxwell Ziegler
MANAGING EDITOR EMERITA
Jennifer Boylan
CONTRIBUTORS
Melissa Balmain, Ian Baker, Tracey Berglund, George Booth, M.K. Brown, Marc Burckhardt, David Chelsea, Tom Chitty, Rebecca Clifton, Tyson Cole, Joe Dator, Bob Eckstein, Ivan Ehlers, Meg Favreau, Chuck Finkle, Shary Flenniken, Matt Garczynski, Rick Geary, Ilana Gordon, Sam Gross, Tom Hachtman, Lance Hansen, Todd Hanson, Ron Hauge, Sarah Hutto, Steve Jones, Ted Jouflas, Patrick Kennedy, Lars Kenseth, Megan Koester, Stephen Knight, Stephen Kroninger, Peter Kuper, Rob Kutner, Sara Lautman, Mike Loew, Stan Mack, Merrill Markoe, Risa Mickenberg, Lydia Oxenham, Will Pfeifer, Jonathan Plotkin, K.A. Polzin, Andy Prieboy, Luke Roloff, Laurie Rosenwald, Jay Ruttenberg, Alex Schmidt, Cris Shapan, Mike Shiell, Jim Siergey, Mahendra Singh, Edward Sorel, Rich Sparks, Nick Spooner, Ed Subitzky, D. Watson, Alex Watt, Phil Witte.
THANKS TO
Kate Powers, Lanky Bareikis, Jon Schwarz, Alleen Schultz, Molly Bernstein, Joe Lopez, Eliot Ivanhoe, Neil Gumenick, Mary McCullough, Thomas Simon, Greg and Patricia Gerber and many, many others.
NAMEPLATES BY
Mark Simonson
ISSUE CREATED BY
Michael Gerber

Vol. 3, No. 3. ©2019 Good Cheer LLC, all rights reserved. Proudly produced in California, USA.

FEELING LOST AND LORN, I BOOKED MYSELF ON A SINGLES CRUISE.

MY FELLOW PASSENGERS WERE RADIANT WITH THE HOPE OF NEW LOVE...

AND ONLY THE FAINTEST HINT OF DESPERATION.

ONE LADY WAS QUITE PERSISTENT IN HER ATTENTIONS TO ME.

IT SEEMED LIKE THERE MIGHT BE REAL POSSIBILITIES BETWEEN US.

SO I WAS SHOCKED TO LEARN THAT SHE HAD BEEN MURDERED IN HER CABIN.

EVERY PASSENGER NOW BECAME A SLEUTH.

CRUCIAL CLUES LAY HIDDEN ABOUT THE SHIP.

BEFORE LONG, A GROUP OF SUSPECTS WAS ASSEMBLED...

MYSELF AMONG THEM!

BUT WE COULD NOT RETURN TO PORT, FOR THE OCEAN'S LEVEL HAD RISEN DRAMATICALLY.

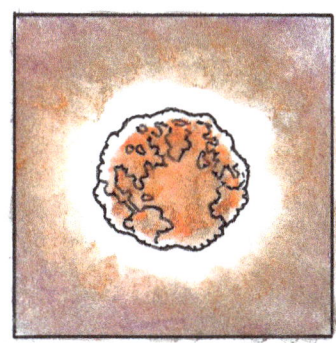
DUE TO WORLD CLIMATE CHANGE.

I NOW SPEND MY DAYS, ALONG WITH MY FELLOW PASSENGERS...

WATCHING A FESTIVAL OF CLASSIC HOLLYWOOD FILMS.

SPECIAL GUEST: JANE POWELL!

Donald Trump's KGB File *by Michael Gerber* 41
  Found! *by Steve Young & Mike Loew* 43
  Donald the Trumple *by Larry Doyle & Jim Siergey* 47
On Throwing Things Out
  by Merrill Markoe & Andy Prieboy 57
Hero of the Beach? *by K.A. Polzin* 60
The World's Longest Joke *by Ed Subitzky* 61
Lou Hirshman, American Caricaturist
  by Stephen Kroninger 62
The Tinseled Eyesore of Iniquity *by Ted Jouflas* 66
It Came From Inner Space: TRUUMP! *by Peter Kuper* 67
The Necroworld *by Todd Hanson* 74

OUR BACK PAGES
Gertrude's Follies: "Two Passes to Paris"
  by Tom Hachtman & Sam Gross 79
What Am I Doing Here?: West Africa
  by Mike Reiss 81
P.S. Mueller Thinks Like This *by P.S. Mueller* 83

CARTOONS & ILLUSTRATIONS BY
Ian Baker, Tracey Berglund, George Booth, M.K. Brown, Marc Burckhardt, David Chelsea, Tom Chitty, Joe Dator, Larry Doyle, Ivan Ehlers, Peter Elwell, Chuck Finkle, Shary Flenniken, Rick Geary, Sam Gross, Tom Hachtman, Lance Hansen, Ron Hauge, Lou Hirshman, Peter Kuper, Sara Lautman, Mike Loew, Stan Mack, P.S. Mueller, Will Pfeifer, Jonathan Plotkin, K.A. Polzin, Laurie Rosenwald, Cris Shapan, Jim Siergey, Mahendra Singh, Mark Simonson, Rich Sparks, Nick Spooner and D. Watson.

"It happens every time Ernestine gets her period."

COVER

Our cover is from the fiercely kind and capable **Mike Loew**, who spun a half-baked idea I mocked up in my bathroom into something grand. In this *fecockte* era, everybody needs a Mike Loew, a person you can ramble at semi-coherently ("It's gotta look like a mass-market paperback, a spy thriller, British probably, from the late '70s, but no later than 1982...") who laughs and improves and *understands*. Kudos, Mike, and if there's more Gerberian rambling in your future, well, it's your own darn fault.

ACKNOWLEDGMENTS

All material is ©2019 its creators, all rights reserved; please do not reproduce or distribute it without written consent of the creators and *The American Bystander*. The following material has previously appeared, and is reprinted here with permission of the author(s): Ross MacDonald's cartoon "Hey Fellers! Do Your Bit For the Homeland" was originally published in *The Virginia Quarterly Review* in 2008. But everything else? Far as I can tell, it's all brand spanking new, folks.

THE AMERICAN BYSTANDER, Vol. 3, No. 3, (ISBN 978-0-578-53802-0). Publishes ~4x/year. ©2019 by Good Cheer LLC. No part of this magazine can be reproduced, in whole or in part, by any means, without the written permission of the Publisher. For this and other queries, email *Publisher@americanbystander.org*, or write: Michael Gerber, Publisher, *The American Bystander*, 1122 Sixth St., #403, Santa Monica, CA 90403. Subscribe at www.patreon.com/bystander. Other info can be found at www.americanbystander.org.

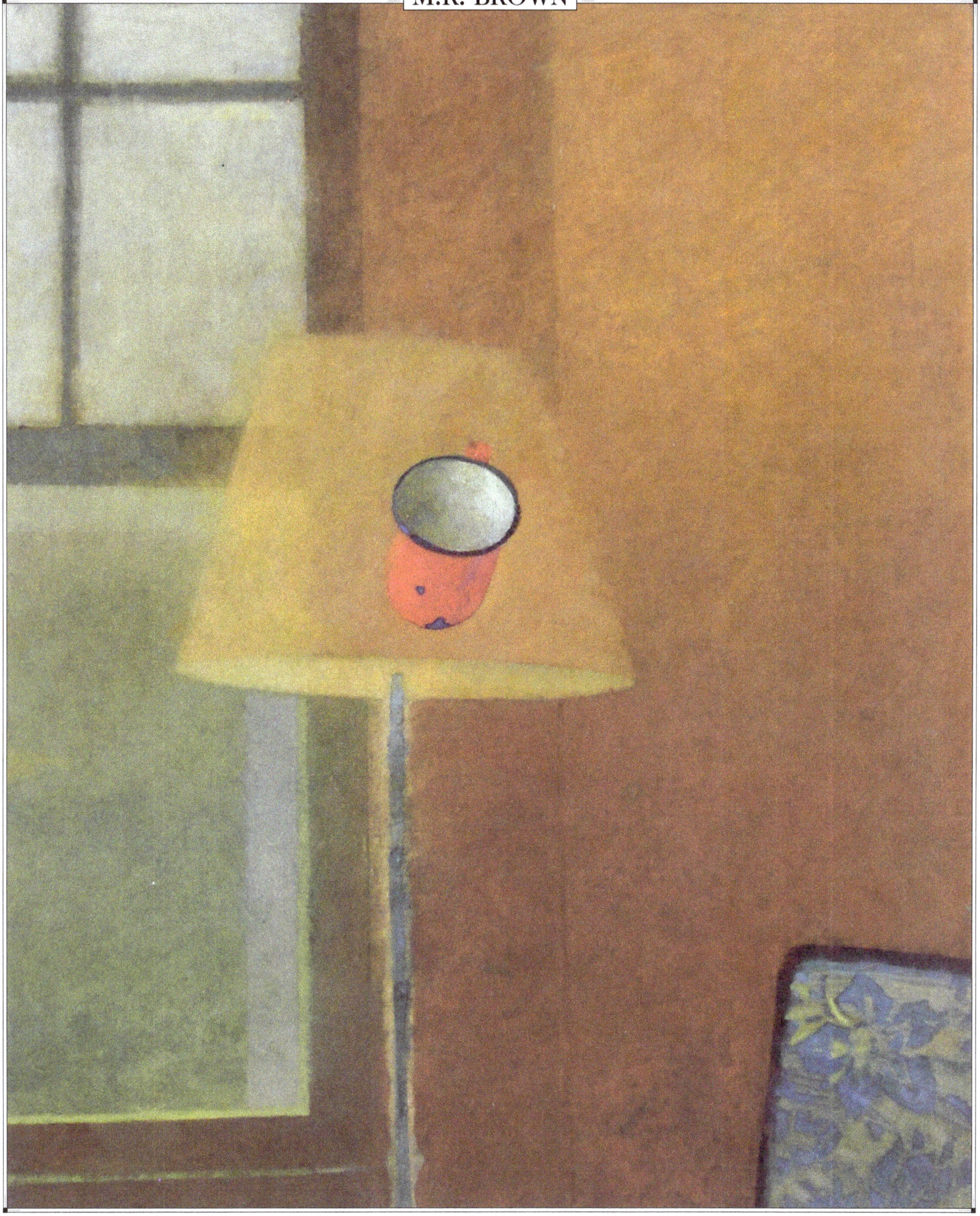

MEG FAVREAU

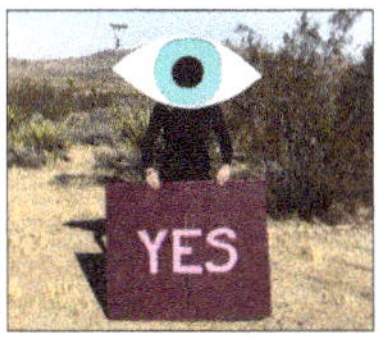
YES

THE EYE *is a* **BENEVOLENT FORCE**. **THE EYE** does not **NEED TO BE UNDERSTOOD**. **THE EYE** *can simply be* **APPRECIATED**, *like a* **FLOWER** *or a* **DRUM SOLO**...*If it* **LOOKS LIKE A DUCK** *and* **SWIMS LIKE A DUCK** *and* **SENT YOU A BIRTHDAY CARD**, *congratulations: You are* **FRIENDS** *with a* **DUCK**...**FELLAS!** *Isn't it* **CRAZY** *how* **LADIES** *always keep their* **SKELETONS** *inside of their* **BODIES**? *And* **LADIES!** *Isn't it* **WEIRD** *how* **FELLAS** *are always having a* **COMPLICATED RELATIONSHIP** *with* **HUMAN MORTALITY**? *It's like we're all just* **PEOPLE** *trying to* **CARVE A TENDER LIFE** *for* **OURSELVES**, **WORKING FOR A BETTER FUTURE** *and trying to keep our* **BONES INSIDE**. *(Twitter:* **@THE_EYE_FRIEND**.*)*

SPOTLIGHT

BY RON HAUGE

I LOST 87,000 LB.

(...and counting, obviously)

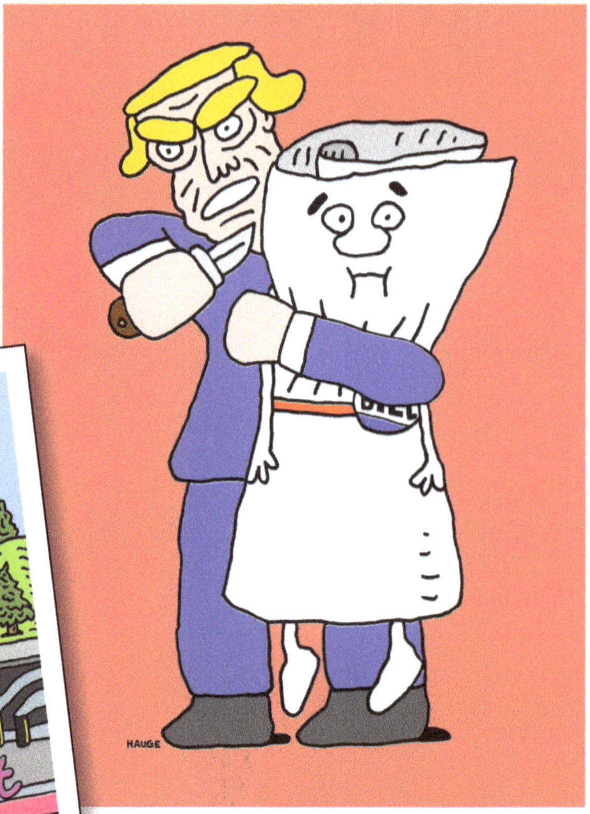
HAUGE

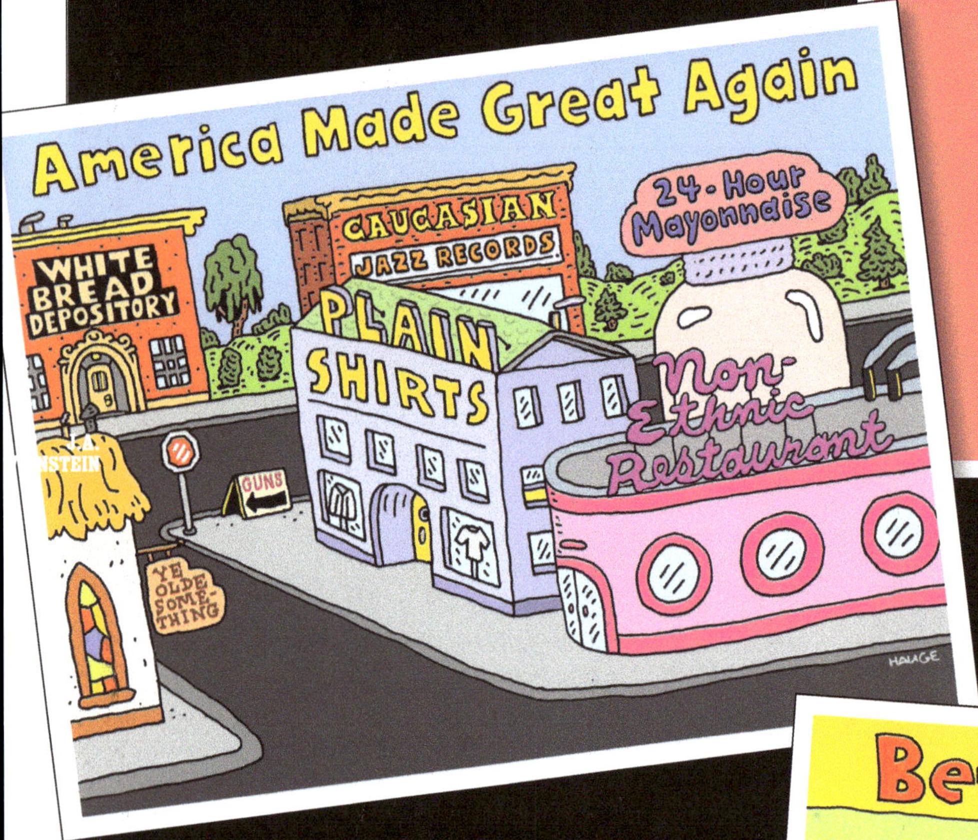
America Made Great Again
WHITE BREAD DEPOSITORY
CAUCASIAN
JAZZ RECORDS
24-Hour Mayonnaise
PLAIN SHIRTS
Non-Ethnic Restaurant
GUNS
YE OLDE SOME-THING
HAUGE

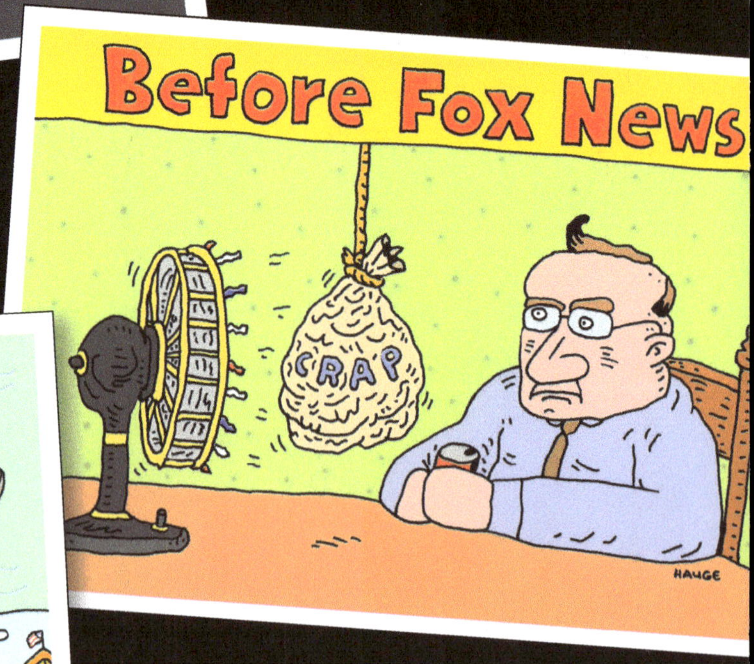
Before Fox News
CRAP
HAUGE

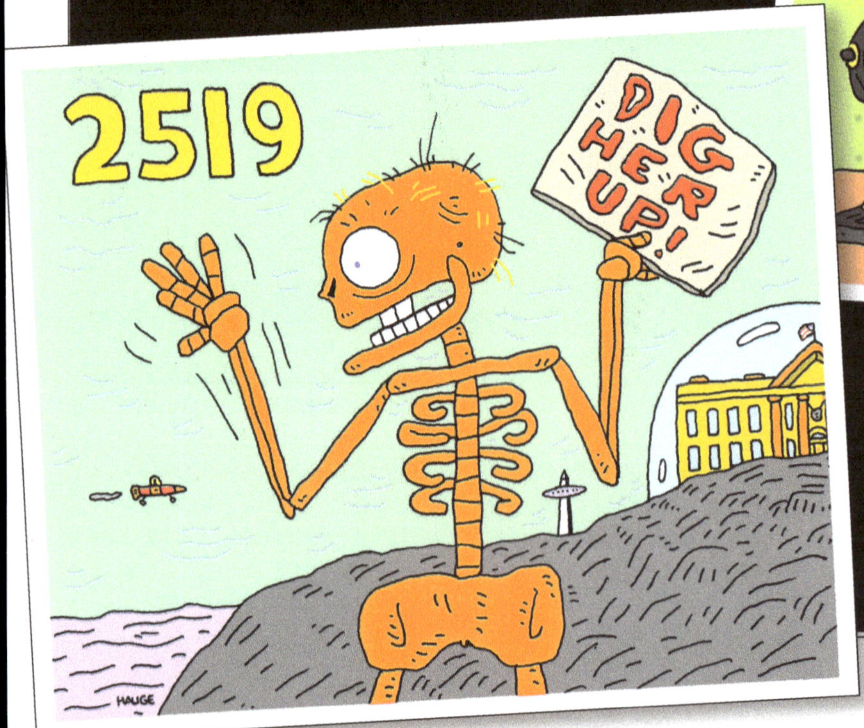
2519
DIG HER UP!
HAUGE

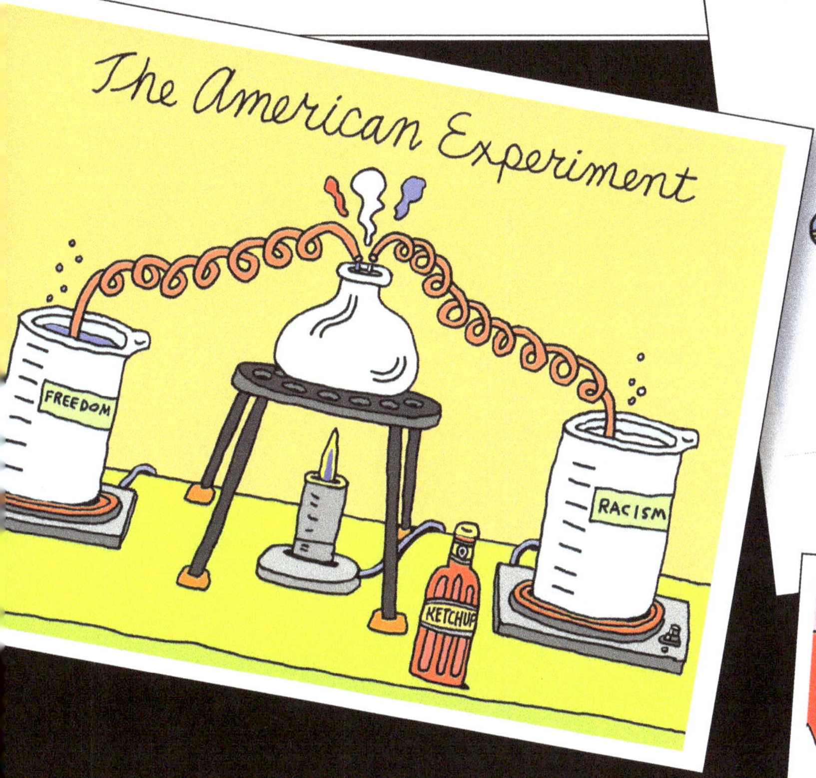
The American Experiment
FREEDOM
RACISM
KETCHUP

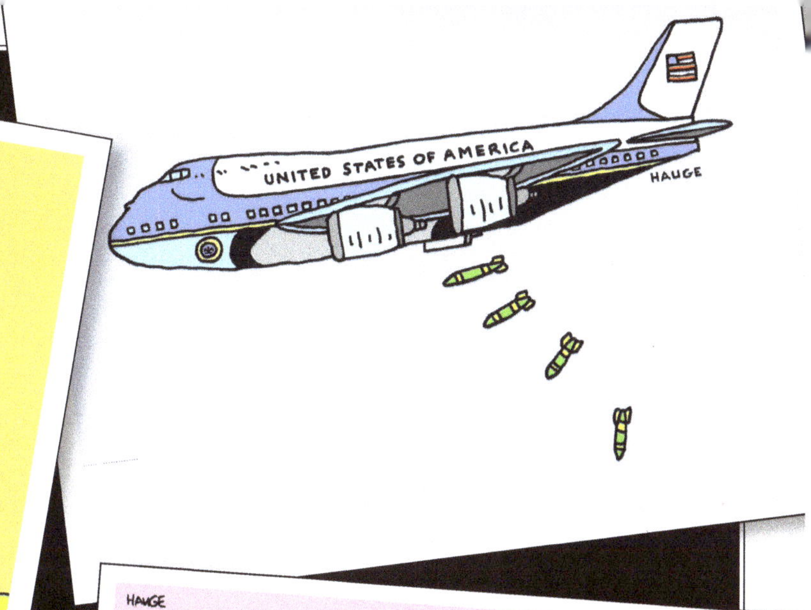
UNITED STATES OF AMERICA
HAUGE

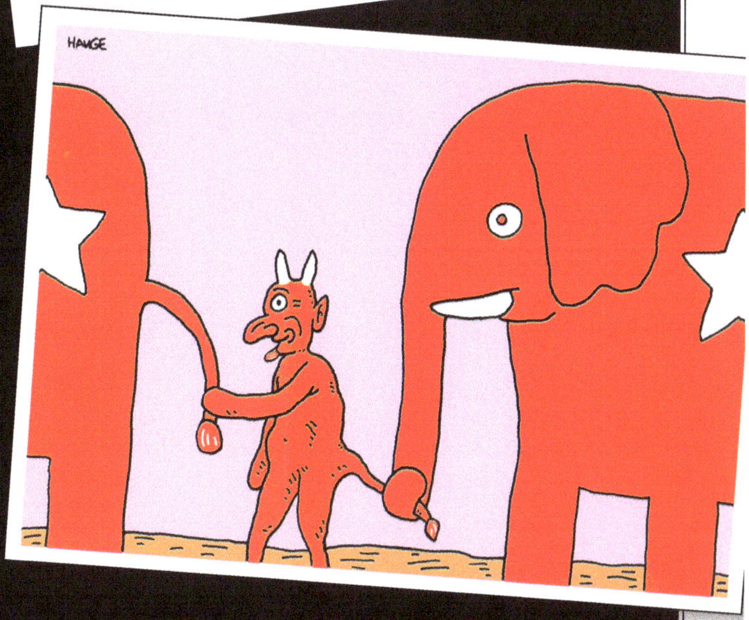
HAUGE

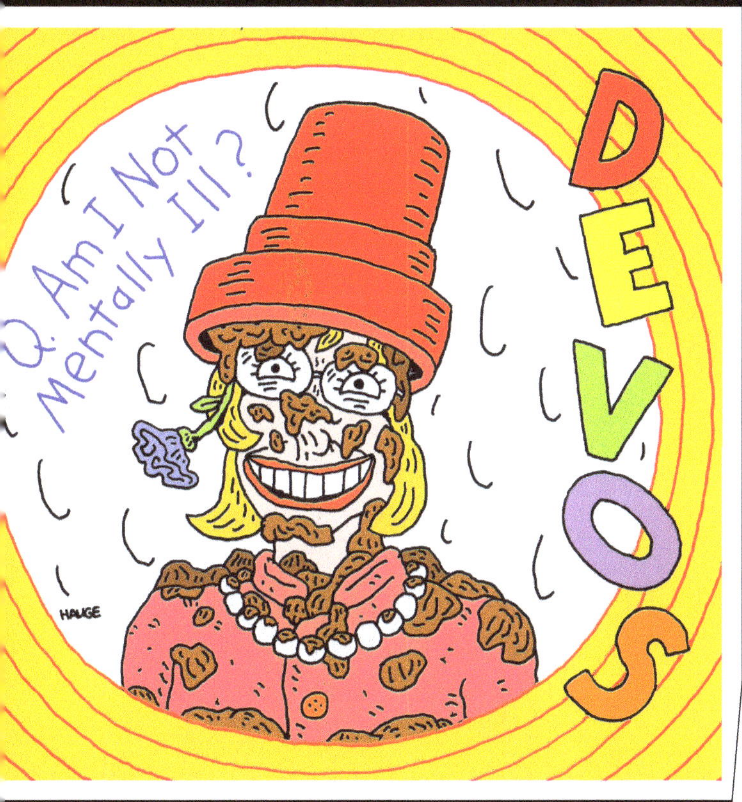
Q. Am I Not Mentally Ill?
DEVOS
HAUGE

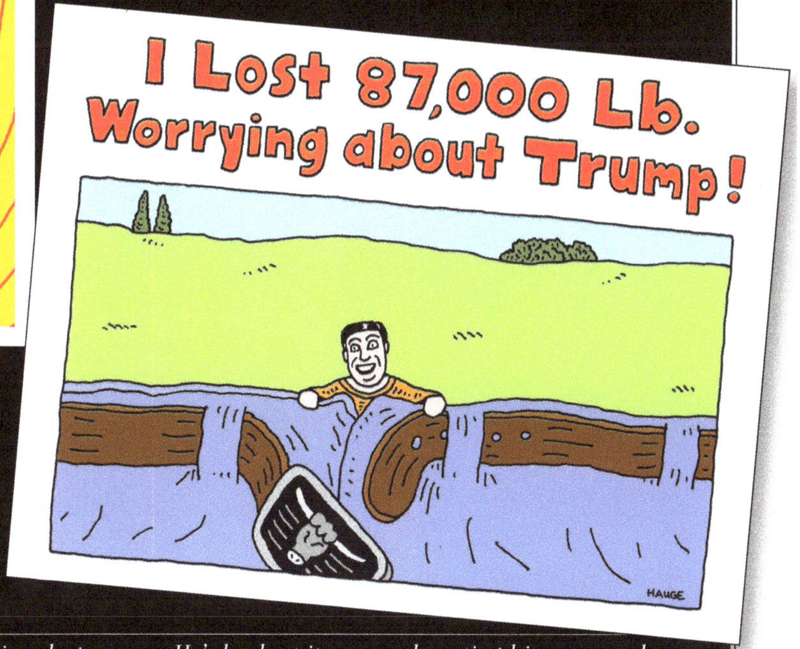
I Lost 87,000 Lb. Worrying about Trump!
HAUGE

RON HAUGE'S *cartoons first appeared in a bygone era. He's back at it now and posting his new work on Instagram: @ron_hauge.*

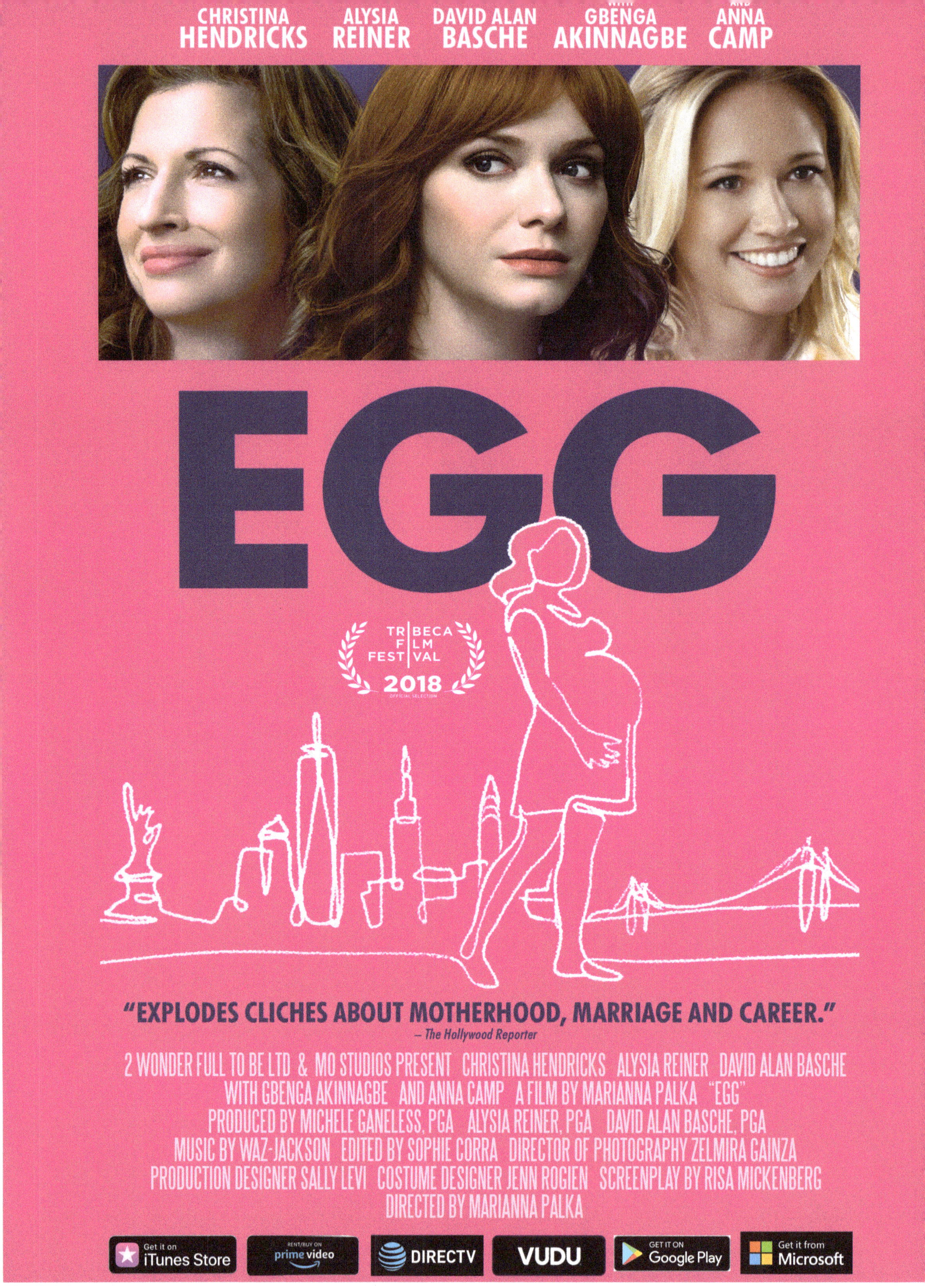
CHRISTINA HENDRICKS
ALYSIA REINER
DAVID ALAN BASCHE
GBENGA AKINNAGBE
ANNA CAMP
EGG
TRIBECA FILM FESTIVAL 2018
"EXPLODES CLICHES ABOUT MOTHERHOOD, MARRIAGE AND CAREER."
– The Hollywood Reporter
2 WONDER FULL TO BE LTD & MO STUDIOS PRESENT CHRISTINA HENDRICKS ALYSIA REINER DAVID ALAN BASCHE
WITH GBENGA AKINNAGBE AND ANNA CAMP A FILM BY MARIANNA PALKA "EGG"
PRODUCED BY MICHELE GANELESS, PGA ALYSIA REINER, PGA DAVID ALAN BASCHE, PGA
MUSIC BY WAZ-JACKSON EDITED BY SOPHIE CORRA DIRECTOR OF PHOTOGRAPHY ZELMIRA GAINZA
PRODUCTION DESIGNER SALLY LEVI COSTUME DESIGNER JENN ROGIEN SCREENPLAY BY RISA MICKENBERG
DIRECTED BY MARIANNA PALKA
Get it on iTunes Store
prime video
DIRECTV
VUDU
GET IT ON Google Play
Get it from Microsoft

Gallimaufry

"Sober or blotto, this is your motto:
keep muddling through."
P.G. Wodehouse

KAMALA HARRIS GOES TO A RESTAURANT.

Why do you ask if we want "freshly ground pepper"?
[...]
Why do you never offer *other* spices to be ground at the table?
[...]
Let me repeat the question another way: Why is pepper being so aggressively promoted?
[...]
How much would you estimate all of this free pepper costs annually?
[...]
I see. Yet why are so many people constantly trying to *give pepper away?*
[...]
You're going to every table. Why can't other spices seem to break the stranglehold that pepper seems to have?
[...]
So you don't know where this whole thing began or who's reponsible, but you're offering the pepper and someone here is in charge of the pepper, and someone is responsible for making sure *every patron in this restaurant* is offered freshly ground pepper. Am I correct?
[...]
Are there any consequences if you don't offer freshly ground pepper?
[...]
What are the other responsibilities of the person who walks around grinding pepper on peoples' dishes?
[...]
And is that a designated role?
[...]
Do you like pepper?
[...]
Yet you're the one with the pepper mill. Would you put pepper on rigatoni?
[...]
Seems like something you should be able to answer.
[...]
Okay. Did a salesforce sell the idea to this restaurant?
[...]
Was it *American?*
[...]
Can you tell me exactly how pepper, a spice, got itself linked with salt, a mineral which according to doctors is necessary for life?
[...]
It's a simple question.
[...]
Unlike Morton's or Lawry's, there is no brand name pepper. Yet it is marketed to the point of omnipresence. This puzzles me. Do you think there is a conscious strategy here to conceal the entity or entities behind pepper?
[...]
Is "S&P" connected in any way to the S&P 500?
[...]
Not to your knowledge. Could this potentially be a branding opportunity for the salt-pepper consortium?
[...]
Who controls the salt-pepper consortium?
[...]
Are you sure there is no salt-pepper consortium? Yes or no please.
[...]
In your opinion, is pepper addictive?
[...]
What's the difference with "getting people to develop a taste" for something and fostering an addiction?
[...]
A dependency. An unhealthy, immoderate desire. A craving beyond all bounds of logic.
[...]
You're "not sure." But you, personally, don't like pepper.
[...]
No, I wouldn't like any pepper.

—Risa Mickenberg

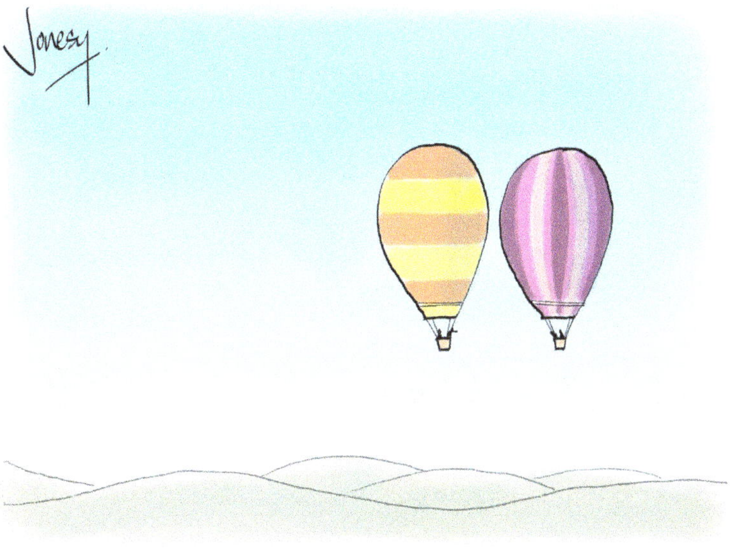
Jonesy

"No, you *back up!"*

TO THE CLASS OF 2019.

Congratulations! You made it!

I have good news: you live in the freest, best country in the world, where anybody can do anything they set their mind to—trust me on this; I'm what they call "a self-made man." But

"Say when."

nobody's going to give you anything; you're going to have to do it yourself. Even I, with all my accomplishments, can't do it for you. All I can do is share my own experience, and let you draw your own conclusions.

My resolve to succeed was forged in the underground bank vaults where six-figure payments were deposited annually into my childhood account. My grit and perseverance are the hard-won byproducts of years spent watching others exert themselves vigorously on the tennis courts. I come by my work ethic honestly, which is to say that I purchased it from an immigrant for a fair market value.

I was born to humble beginnings; I overcame my early limitations as Baby With No Discernible Motor Skills to emerge, transformed, as Man With Some Degree Of Control Over His Executive Functions. And I did it entirely on my own, without any assistance from my butler, Kent.

I started at the bottom, managing a tiny 52-unit apartment complex my father gave me and rapidly worked my way up to larger real estate holdings, that he also gave me.

But a Self-Made Man knows it's not enough to simply construct an empire. A Self-Made Man takes an already existing one, deflates the valuations of those assets for tax purposes, then inflates those same assets to get big loans — then he rebrands it as an entirely new business, which promptly goes out of business.

Is that a failure? Some might call it one—small people, envious people. A Self-Made Man doesn't care. A Self-Made Man must be willing to self-destruct, chasing that American Dream.

I chased it first from the backset of a chauffeured Lincoln Towncar, and later from behind the wheel of a 2003 Mercedes-Benz SLR McLaren. I never paused at stop lights. I yielded to no one. I accrued an impressive number of parking tickets, that I continue to not pay.

You see, I understand that the government doesn't make money—it just takes it. Money that you work hard for. No one has worked harder than me. Property manager, landlord, author, motivational speaker, litigant—on paper I've done them all.

Now, obviously, there are people with inherited privileges. Don't pay any attention to them; they'll never know what it's like to be a Self-Made Man. Because it's how you make it that really counts. I entered this world naked but for the designer clothes on my back. I scaled the corporate and social ladders with no help from anyone, except the four burly men I hired to hold the rungs steady. I wasn't born with a silver spoon in my mouth; I employed state-of-the-art CGI technology to digitally insert it after the fact.

People ask, "Did you struggle?" Well, does a yacht float? Is gold an excellent hedge against inflation? Are private jets a baseline necessity? Is caviar made from squishy fish treats? Are off-shore bank accounts tough to keep track of? Do peacocks make the best pets? Are AirPods intended to be disposed of after a single-use? Can $50 dollar bills double as toilet paper? Was prep school a total drag? Are taxes optional? Do private islands make good anniversary gifts? Is "prenuptial agreement" the most sensual phrase in the English language?

So yeah—I struggled; everyone does. But the difference between a Self-Made Man and everyone else is this: a Self-Made Man self-makes it look easy.

I remember the exact moment I realized I had Self-Made It. I was at the summit of Mount Everest, having ascended on the backs of local Sherpas who were built for this sort of thing. As the largest Sherpa cradled me in his arms, dangling me over the mountain's edge so I might take in all that I had accomplished, I said to myself, "Self, you've really made it."

I'd like to leave you with two final thoughts:

The first is an affirmation I rely on in moments of difficulty. It goes, "I am a Self-Made Man. I am proud to stand on my own two feet, secure in the knowledge that they are protected by $10,000 shoes."

The second is a warning. I am a Self-Made Man and if you approach me after this speech to solicit advice or job opportunities, these four burly men will have you arrested.

In closing, I'd like to thank the Board of Trustees for paying me to be here. Congratulations again to the Class of 2019 and as you go off into the world, please remember that I am a Self-Made Man and I paid an assistant minimum wage to write this message on my behalf.

Congratulations again to the Class of

2019. I believe you have the potential to do great things. Work hard, dream big and when you inevitably stumble, blame it on your butler, Kent.

—Ilana Gordon

ADVANCE PRAISE.

"*Dishonorable Intentions* is a literary tour-de-force, from a singular voice in letters."

—Howard Kulkin, author,
All of Momma's Lies

"*All of Momma's Lies* is incandescent, indelible storytelling from a literary master."

—Elizabeth Stringer, author,
Dishonorable Intentions

"*What The Groundskeeper Saw* is an instant classic, which will undoubtedly be cherished for generations."

—Howard Kulkin, author,
Don't Wake Me, I'm Dying

"*Don't Wake Me, I'm Dying* is a true masterpiece, which will probably be cherished for generations."

—Elizabeth Stringer, author,
What The Groundskeeper Saw

"Stringer's latest is incomparable, addictive, absorbing… I'm sorry, 'probably?'"

—Howard Kulkin, author,
Desperation Gulch

"Once again, Kulkin is perfectly attentive to every detail, except for inviting so-called 'friends' to his book launch parties."

—Elizabeth Stringer, author,
Bitter—Party Of One

"Brimming with poise and grace—unlike a certain person acting like an ass after too many mimosas at the *Don't Wake Me, I'm Dying* event."

—Howard Kulkin, author,
Liver Damage

"A genius on the order of Toni Morrison, Karl Ove Knausgaard, or Joyce Carol Oates—who all insisted my impression of you was hilarious!"

—Elizabeth Stringer, author of
Bucktoothed Know-It-All

"'In the blue twilight, the blue candle flickered bluely'—how's that for an impression, you hack?"

—Howard Kulkin, author,
I Have 'Woman' Issues

"A literary impresario, whose skills for mimicry are only matched by his excellent taste in subjects to emulate."

—Elizabeth Stringer, author,
Time To Up Your Meds Again, Howie

"Three-time PEN nominee, Chair of Creative Writing at University of Phoenix, Man Booker Prize medium-listed… oh wait, that's me, not typing monkey Elizabeth Stringer.

Mea culpa!"

—Howard Kulkin, author,
Awards Mean I'm A Real Writer, Right Mother?

"'Eep eep oop oop. I shall now repair to this rock to scratch my genitals and fling fecal matter'… is something more likely to be said by Howard Kulkin."

—Elizabeth Stringer, author,
Murderer Who Turns Out To Be Male Novelist

"An incomparable stylist whose nature descriptions are perfectly apt description of herself."

—Howard Kulkin, author,
Nailed It!

"Beautifully accurate in describing himself, but unfortunately unable to say what I am."

—Elizabeth Stringer, author,
Nuh-Uh!

"A stalwart piece of literary glue to whom all influences stick, unlike the more staid rubber of a me."

—Howard Kulkin, author,
Yah-Huh!

"Once again, Howard Kul-Kan't raises critical questions like, 'Does this bother you? I'm not touching you.'"

—Elizabeth Stringer, author,
I'm An Older Sibling

"Stringer makes us stop and wonder, 'Why do we keep turning on each other, when it's the publishing industry whose diminishing attention to the mid-list forces us to fight over scraps?'"

—Howard Kulkin, author,
Just Read Like Half a Review of a Noam Chomsky Book

"Kulkin is right. Why not stand strong

INSIDE BASEBALLS
PETRIFIED BONE CORE
CLONED FROM THE BABE'S CHIN D.N.A.
CORRUGATED
MINOR LEAGUE BASEBALL CARDS
FOLDED BY EXPERTS
WHOTHEHECK McNOBODY
THIN LAYER OF
PREMIUM HOT DOG FLESH…
…INFUSED WITH
Warm Beer®
PEANUT AND CRACKERJACK NOSTALGIC GLOB™
Cracker Jack
SONIC AMPLIFICATION TUBE
ACTIVATED BY BAT CONTACT
LEAGUE SANCTIONED SOUND DISTORTION SETTINGS:
WHISTLE
FIZZ
SCREAM
WORLD SERIES TICKET MÂCHÉ
FROM GAMES NEVER PLAYED
E.G. Nos 5-7, 1963
GLOB™ BASE REGULATIONS VARY:
NATIONAL LEAGUE
OXYGENATED RIB GREASE
AMERICAN LEAGUE
QUEBEC PURE MAPLE SYRUP
TOM CHITTY

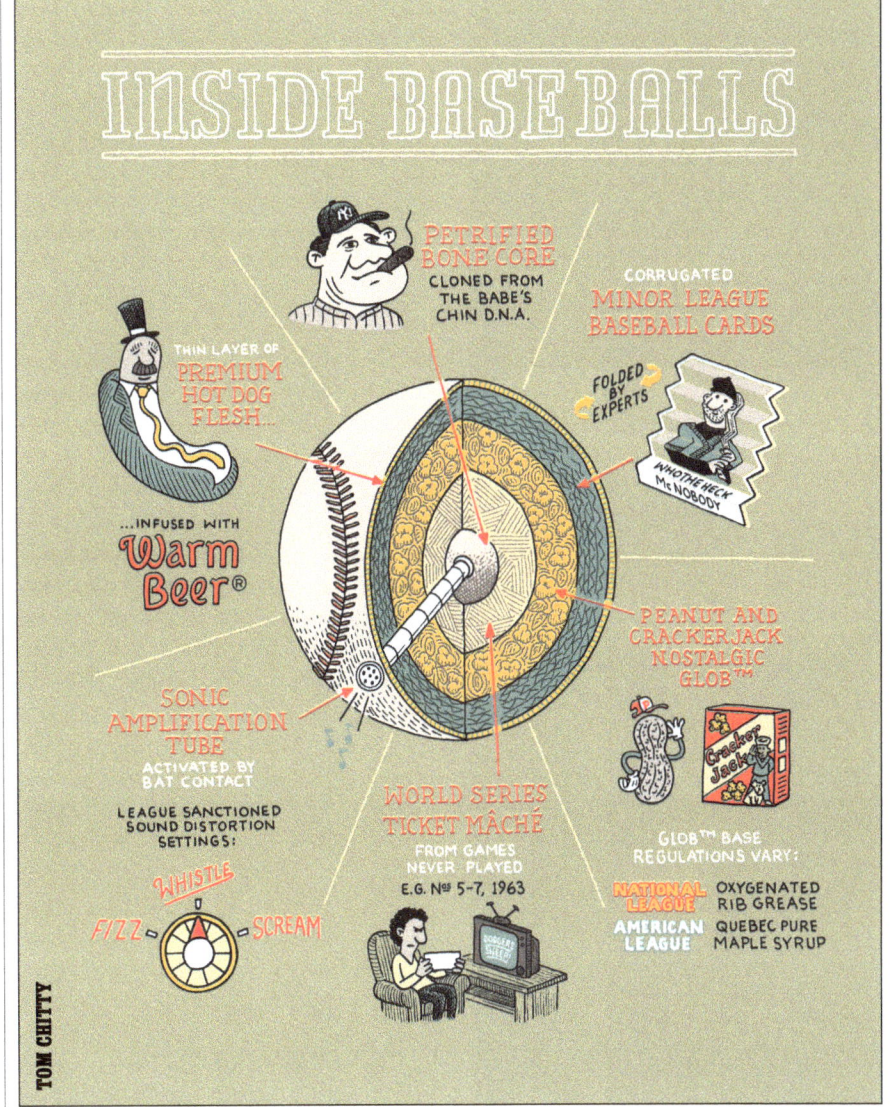

THE WORST OF MEN

by Lars Kenseth

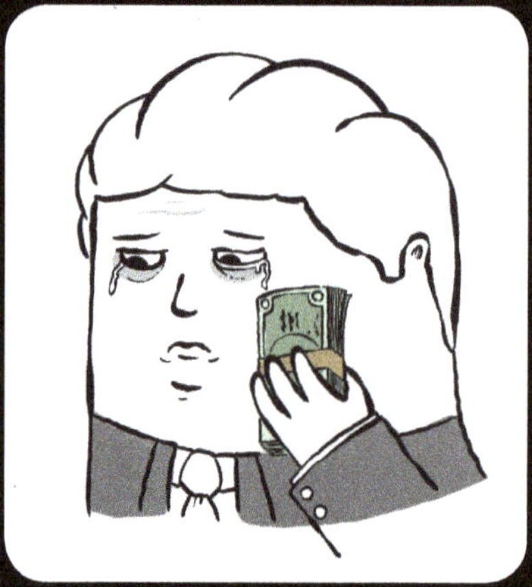

Hey. I'm that super wealthy friend that's surprisingly dead inside. Let's take a ride in my Tesla Model X while I unburden myself of all the elaborate escape fantasies I've been hiding from my wife. Yeah, life has been tough lately. My gardener got grass clippings into the wishing well out back, so naturally that ruined my week. I'm so sad all the time. God, I feel old. Maybe I should pick up guitar again? Did you know white privilege is a myth? I'm actively terrible.

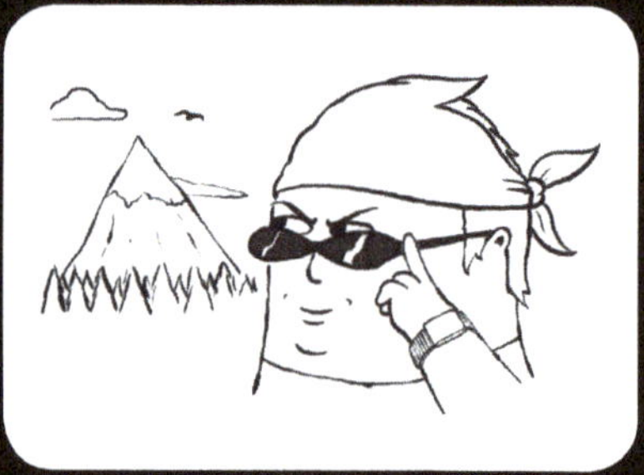

Sup? I'm that guy who saw *Free Solo* and was like, yeah, I'm doing this now. It must be the first thing I've ever done because I never stop talking about it. I've spent so much money at REI the cashier asked if I was okay. I wear a bandana in public. You'll overhear me say stuff like, "It's all about the climb" and, "I'm in a relationship with Mother Nature." You hope that one day I'll just walk into the woods and never come back but I always do. I am just no good.

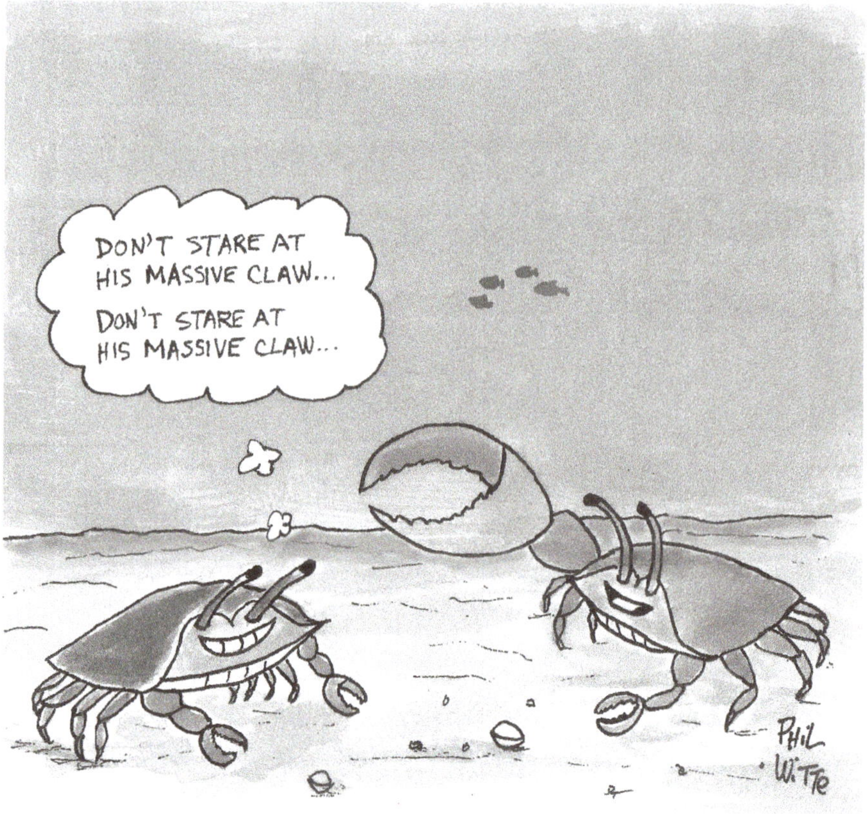
DON'T STARE AT HIS MASSIVE CLAW...
DON'T STARE AT HIS MASSIVE CLAW...
PHIL WITTE

together against the forces of capitalism that systematically destroy artists? Let us join forces and show the world that we the creators rise above money."

—Elizabeth Stringer, author, *All of a Sudden Getting Kind of Weirdly Political*

"Stringer raises excellent points—which we shall add the manifesto that will be unveiled by the Creators' Solidarity Group, this Tuesday night at McLaren's (after trivia night)."

—Howard Kulkin, author, *Yeah, All My Dates' Eyes Just Kinda Glaze Over When I Start Ranting*

"Kulkin's moving words fill me with tender, painful regret that I can't make Tuesday. *Dishonorable Intentions* just got optioned by Netflix. SEE YA SUCKA!"

—Elizabeth Stringer, writer, upcoming Netflix series, *Teenagers Gettin' Awkward About Sex Stuff!*

—Rob Kutner

ATTENTION BILLIONAIRE CANDIDATES!

Well, you're obviously qualified. Unfortunately, people who are sadly not billionaires will try to trick you by asking confusing questions like how much a box of Cheerios costs. This handy quiz features common questions non-billionaires face. Pick the most electable answers, and you, too, can become a leader of the common man!

1. How much is a Little Caesar's Hot And Ready Pizza?

a. The price is irrelevant. It's delicious!"

b. "Less than a billion dollars, so I can definitely afford it."

c. "If my AI-enhanced assistant Googled correctly, six dollars."

2. You've been invited to a wedding, but can't afford a gift. What do you do?

a. "When I hit ten yogurts, maybe Yogurtland will give me cash instead."

b. "Have one of my artist friends—like Damien Hirst—do an installation for them. Personalized gifts are always better anyway."

c. "I'm not going to any weddings until my gay friends can legally marry. Oh, they can? In that case, I attend the wedding, then mail them their local newspaper with the words 'You own this now' scrawled across it."

3. You've decided to take a "stay-cation." How do you spend it?

a. Punching up my resume while driving for Uber and delivering for Caviar so I can afford daycare.
b. With Richard Branson and Mariah Carey, fishing off of Richard's blimp.
c. Stay-cation? Oh, I see what you did there. That's not really a thing, is it?

4. How often do you frequent Dollar Tree?
a. Two to four times a week, give or take.
b. Funny, that's what I used to call my trust fund.
c. You mean my genetically engineered hibiscus, which blooms U.S. currency in $20 and $50 denominations, and is kept in a heavily fortified, subterranean greenhou—I mean, "whenever I am looking for top quality merchandise at a cheap price, naturally."

5. What are the dimensions of a Little Caesar's Hot And Ready Lunch Combo?
a. Four 3.5x7-inch slices. That's half of a 14-inch Deep Dish square pie! (Comes with a 20 oz. Pepsi!!).
b. Funny story: the first time I tried pizza I was in Lake Como with Khloé Kardashian.
c. Wait—is it pizza? I've just analyzed it and found it is 47.5% "inorganic material."

6. You are the hunter in a "Most Dangerous Game"-type scenario. What bait would you use to lure your common, yet cunning prey?
a. Affordable healthcare
b. Little Caesar's? You seem to be fixated on that. It's a tie-in, good thinking.
c. Hmmm, my money tree would be pretty irresistible...Oh dammit!

7. Do you even know what a "Cheerio" is?
a. It's the name brand version of my favorite Dollar Tree cereal: "Circle-ohs."
b. What Richard Branson says when you're boarding his blimp.
c. Cheerios is an American brand of cereal manufactured by General Mills, consisting of pulverized oats in the shape of a solid torus. Of course I know what they are, because I am a human entity.

8. Little Caesar's is out of Hot And Ready Pizza. What do you order?
a. Well, I only have $6 for food today. But it looks like most of the menu is pretty cheap—oh wait! Here they come with more Hot And Readys!
b. Artisanal thin crust gluten-free pizza with shaved white truffles. (What I ate with Khloé.)
c. Nothing. My new iGut prototype metabolizes all necessary vitamins and minerals from my own hair and fingernail clippings, creating a closed system viable indefinitely.

Answer: Please don't become President.

—*Rebecca Clifton and Lance Hansen*

A PARTY MOST MURDERED.

Parties at remote island mansions off the coast of England are supposed to be total ragers—an assumption the guests

Hey buddy, I'm a hipster guy with a silly little mustache. I wear tee shirts with the neck all stretched out and I speak so soft only bats can hear me. You think I'm a really smart, kind person, so you set me up on a date with your friend and then she informs you that I'm actually a column of spiders surrounded by human skin. We shall never speak of this again. Why don't we hang out as much anymore? I miss you! Banish me to an island solely populated by crabs.

Hi! You know what I love? An intelligent, wide-ranging exchange of ideas. By that I mean, I like to argue and get really loud until I win. I do this neat trick where you ask me to keep it down, but I get even louder. I don't see the big deal, we were just talking. You aren't afraid of a little debate, are you? You say that I keep cutting you off, but how can I win at word fighting if I let you talk? I'm the reason there should be long-term storage for people.

Quack. I'm the bossiest duck at the park. I just run around the pond, quacking at other ducks. I say some pretty sexist stuff, but you'd never know because you don't speak duck. You wish that one of those awful kids who scare the ducks would chase me, but they never do. Seriously, I am just a bad egg.

I'm genial, funny—really a pleasure to be around. Sure, I'll exchange personal information with you. So funny, I never meet anyone cool at these things and 9/11 was an inside job. Too late, I have your name and phone and e-mail. Yeah, I've done all this research about it and it was the CIA or Lyndon Johnson. That's cute, you taking me to that football field filled with evidence to the contrary, it's very compelling. But not as compelling as this 2008 YouTube video filmed in a bathroom by an alcoholic structural engineer. I am a sucking black hole.

"You're flying a little bit right now, aren't you?"

of Lord Albert began to seriously doubt, after his ancestral home revealed only one secret staircase and precisely no haunted heirlooms. Stranded until the arrival of the morning boat, the enervated and increasingly stroppy guests succumbed to a tedious game of bridge… until this was mercifully interrupted by a woman's scream.

The group rushed to the foyer, where they found the body of former guest Barbara Marple, bludgeoned to death with a heavy silver candlestick.

"Who did this horrible thing?"

"We must call the police!"

Ever the competent host, Lord Albert calmed his guests. "Nonsense," he said. "We'll split up and search for clues. Duchess, you go with Sir Edward, and Edith, you--"

"I did it!" George raised his hand. "I was married to Barbara, but she left me for my valet. I thought I could get away with her murder, but I didn't anticipate the suffocating guilt. Albert, I'll reimburse you for the rug."

The rug was indeed ruined, but Lord Albert hardly noticed. "Damn it, George!" he said crossly. "You couldn't let us try to solve the mystery for, like, 10 minutes?"

"I didn't want to ruin the party."

"The murder was the party!"

Lightning flashed, revealing the horror on everyone's face.

Lord Albert continued. "I only invited people who had a hateful history with another guest, hoping that Nature would then take its course."

The Duchess' mouth fell open. "You planned for us to kill each other?"

"Not all of you," Lord Albert said. "Just one murder would do. It would take three, maybe four hours, to solve it, then I'd give an eloquent speech explaining the whole thing in great detail. It was to be high drama, with pauses and everything…" He shot a bitter look in George's direction. "Now Mr. Penitent here blows his load in fifteen seconds. What in blazes am I supposed to do with these party favors?"

The annoyed peer grabbed one of the gift bags near the door, and yanked out a t-shirt. It read *I Survived the Grant House Mystery of '32*.

The Duchess broke the embarrassed silence. "It's unusual to be sure, but I for one think this makes for a most exciting party," she said. "I've never attended anything like it, and that includes the night the Prince of Wales chloroformed his stableboy."

"I'd much rather attend a party to kill and be killed than see and be seen. I'd be the talk of the town!" Edith laughed at the thrill of it. "Though I suppose now that the plan is revealed, the party is spoiled."

"Oh no, I couldn't murder anyone now," Sir Edward agreed. "Not when everyone is expecting it."

A crack of thunder startled the guests.

"That's just my gardener beating large sheets of metal." Lord Albert was slumped into a chair, despondent. "Seems silly now, but I thought it would add a nice texture."

"Oh Albert, I do hate to see all your planning go to waste," the Duchess said. "There must something else we can do to entertain ourselves."

"I know!" Edith clapped her porcelain hands together. "We could play charades!"

"Charades, yes!" Sir Edward said. "Why, it's a mystery in movement."

"I appreciate what you're doing, but it's no use," Lord Albert moaned. "George ruined my party and my rug. We'll just have some dinner and talk about foxhunting until a respectable hour has passed. If you'll excuse me, I must go tell cook to put George's name on the cake."

As Lord Albert sulked off, the guests glumly returned to their card game. That there was a custom cake seemed to make things even worse, somehow.

Moments later, they heard a gunshot followed by a crash.

Once again they rushed; this time to the parlor, where they found the butler standing over a tray of shattered brandy glasses and the body of their host.

"Who could have done such a thing?" Edith gasped.

"We must solve Albert's murder," Sir Edward said.

"For his party's sake," the Duchess agreed.

While the guests scattered throughout the manor in search of clues, the butler knelt next to his master. Lord Albert was not quite almost dead.

"My dear Jenkins," Lord Albert sputtered softly, "why did you do it?"

"My life's purpose is to anticipate your every need, my lord. And what you need now is an evening's entertainment for your guests."

"Jenkins, you are a marvel," Lord Albert said, flickering. "Please… frame… George." And with that the host died, but his party remained very much alive.

It was the talk of the season.

—Lydia Oxenham

I'M THE MAN JOGGING WITH MY SHIRT OFF.

Hello! I am the man jogging in public with my shirt off. Just wanted to say, hi. As if my naked chest wasn't already greeting you.

In fact, I think I've seen you before. Yeah, you kinda glanced at me, my pectorals glistened at you, then you veered sharply away from me. Hello again!

I love to run around places with my shirt off. I'm a healthy person, too.

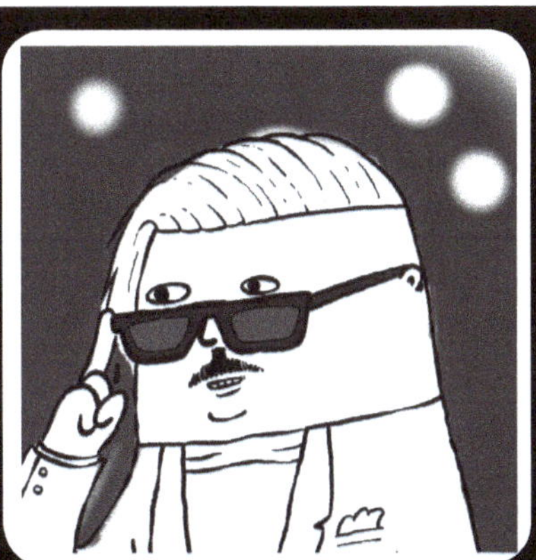

Hey bud, haven't seen you in a while! I'm that guy with the weird disease that makes my eyes lock onto a a woman's parts whenever one walks by. Let's have some drinks and catch up, maybe someplace with a lot of foot traffic so we can never make eye contact. You barely know me, but I think we're really close. I keep telling you how alike we are and that fills you with existential dread! I belong at the bottom of the ocean.

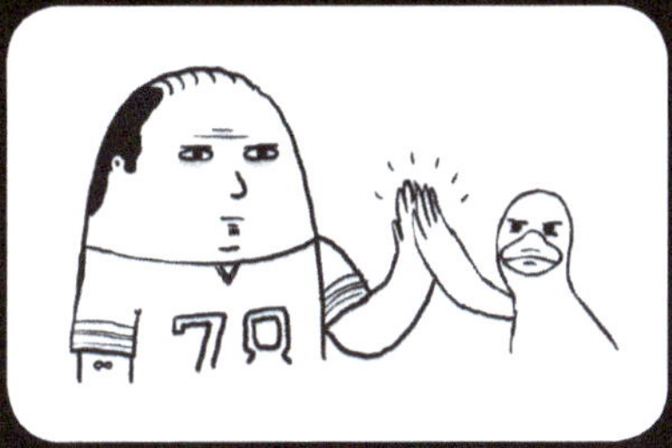

70

Yo, I'm just a guy's guy telling it like it is! Don't like it? There's the door! My spirit animal is Jordan Peterson and my body pillow looks like Adam Carolla. I'm sorry, does that "offend" you? Gee, I didn't realize that men can't talk anymore. Get a grip, snowflake. When we're not hitting the bars, Bossy Duck and I egg male nurses outside the teaching hospital. I'll never be loved. **B**

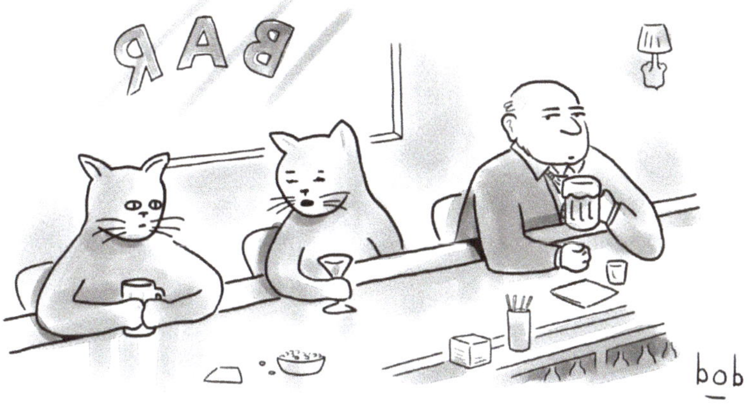

BAR
bob

"What part of 'neutered' don't you understand?"

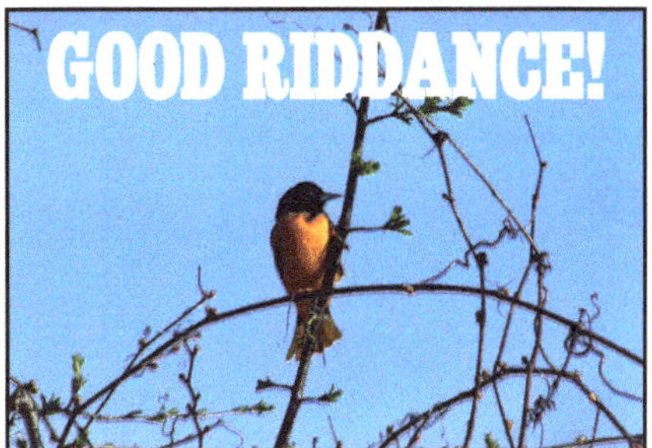

GOOD RIDDANCE!

To celebrate the ongoing right-sizing of our biosphere, we highlight the long-overdue extinction of Nature's takers, flora and fauna unwilling to pull their weight. This issue's deadbeat is ***Gergson's Warbler***, who thought that singing, being pretty, and pollinating the occasional fruit tree entitled it to a habitat. Well the joke's on you, asshole! Go peddle your hippie bullshit on ***some other planet!***

That bird's name was Gary. He liked pie and doo-wop, and suffered from seasonal depression.

Though I don't have a six-pack, I have a sixteen-pack. There are more ripples on my torso than in the ocean. And these are my nipples. See?

It's funny, occasionally people ask me, "Why is your shirt off?" or "Please put your shirt on," or "I'm not running with you, I'm running *away* from you, psycho!!!" And it's always the same answer: because it's just so natural.

There's nothing more natural than derobing in public to expose the pageantry of your waxed chest. Think of all the suitable places; the beach, the locker room, the Garden of Eden, Chipotle—where does it end!?

My pectorals? You must know more about my unfettered pecs? Well, since you asked. My pectorals are vegan. They brew their own beer. They volunteer downtown. They're good people. I think you'd like them.

Ever streak through an active beehive just to feel alive? I actually feel like a swarming bumblebee sometimes, and nature is my flower. And I'm just buzzing all over, stinging people with my friendly nipple pollen.

Sometimes I get a "runner's high," and it doesn't go away. But my mind goes away, way away, to Nude Island, where it's no shirts allowed.

My unclad back is as rugged as the Appalachian Mountains. When I go for my morning jog, gusts rush through its canyons, cougars hunt their prey—uh oh, now the humans want to hunt the cougars? No they don't, not in my mountain range's house. In my mountain range, cougars run wild, with their shirts off.

Yeah, romping around town like an American Ninja Warrior with a blank expression on my face as to say "Hey, this is normal life" has instilled in me a real confidence. I've been able to take on new interests like powerwalking and steroids.

I swear we've met, but I just can't place you. Do you live somewhere? Do you just try and mind your own business? Maybe I saw you at the health food store? Maybe I brushed my lubricated skin against yours while spelunking the isles like Tarzan 2.0?

Guess what? I have a tattoo of a dolphin with an over-prominent dorsal fin, he's captaining a speedboat, and then spouting out his blowhole is a little talk bubble that says "NO SHOES. NO SHIRT. NO LOITERING. LEAVE THE PREMISES. NO PROBLEM." and I'm riding him bareback with nothing but a sombrero and a loaded bazooka. Check it out, it's right here on my butt.

I see you're wearing conventional length shorts. I am not. It restricts my thighs from swishing through the air. Nothing's more important than the vagility of my thighs. Go ahead, touch my thighs. Don't be shy. Pet them. They're smooth. My thighs are bald eagles soaring free, majestically declaring, "Hey, I'm on top of the world and I have a perfect tan, pass me a bionic smoothie, it's time to party." These unfurled thighs of mine, oh, if they could talk. They probably wouldn't, because they're doers not talkers. But if they did, they'd be motivational speakers and spiritual gurus who weren't afraid to raid your personal bubble and fall in love with you and start a family, only to start a second secret family, though this time really do it right. Ya know? Seriously, go ahead and touch them.

Truth is, life's just too short to clothe the entire length of your body. And too long not to experiment with a lewd gang of exhibitionist, and too medium to burden yourself with knowing the difference between public and private property, and too itchy to wear a shirt when an iPhone armband is sufficient.

You know what I'm saying. Well, hey, this was great. I'm so glad I ran into you again. Be sure to follow me on the 'gram, and I'll be sure to creep up on you in the park!

—Luke Roloff

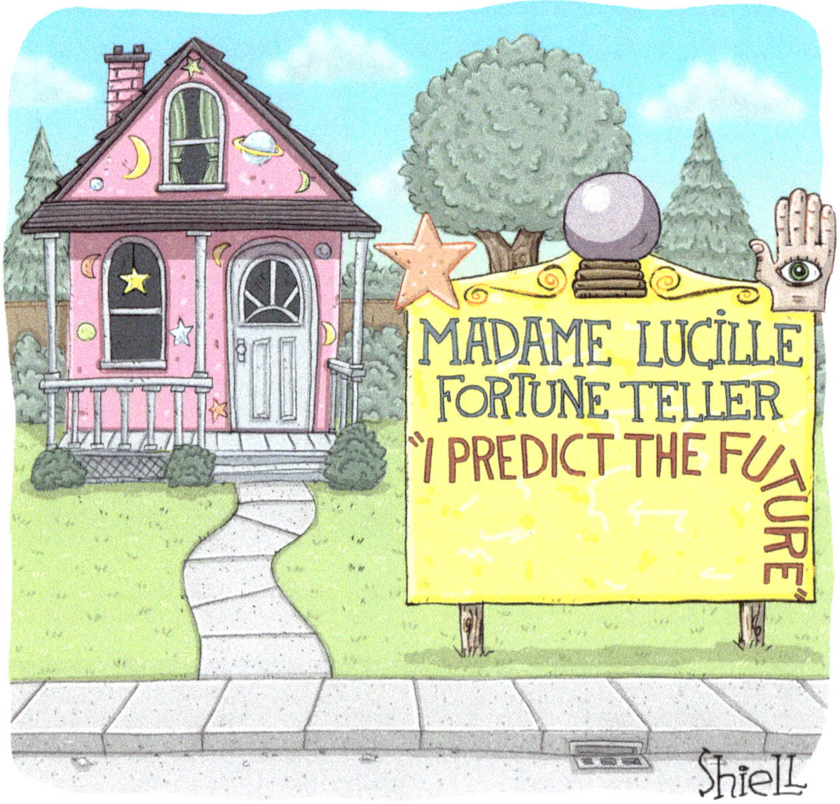
MADAME LUCILLE
FORTUNE TELLER
"I PREDICT THE FUTURE"
Shiell

DEAR ZACHARY.

I have changed the locks, and you know why. The facts, if I may. When first we agreed to share this rehearsal studio—I with my experimental electronica act, Borginborg; you with your garage punk outfit, Donnie & the Dicks—we settled on a fair arrangement. Borginborg would have use of the space Mondays, Wednesdays, and Fridays; the Dicks got Tuesdays, Thursdays, and Saturdays. We would alternate Sundays. (I still have the spreadsheet calculating how to divide Sundays evenly over the course of twelve months of varying numbers of weeks.) You would collect your band's share and give it to me, and I in turn would pay our landlord, Arman Broghosian.

This arrangement worked well for two months. Then you began paying

THE LITTLE MERMAID'S SECOND THOUGHTS

Stupid human—such trouble to save,
then so clueless about what I gave
and gave *up*: my lost flukes! How they'd wave!
And my voice! How it used to enslave
Kraken hunks at an ocean-floor rave!
Now I'm stuck, like a whale in a cave,
eating "cake" (not the kelp that I crave),
and I can't get these legs to behave.
Worst of all? I'm expected to shave.

—Melissa Balmain

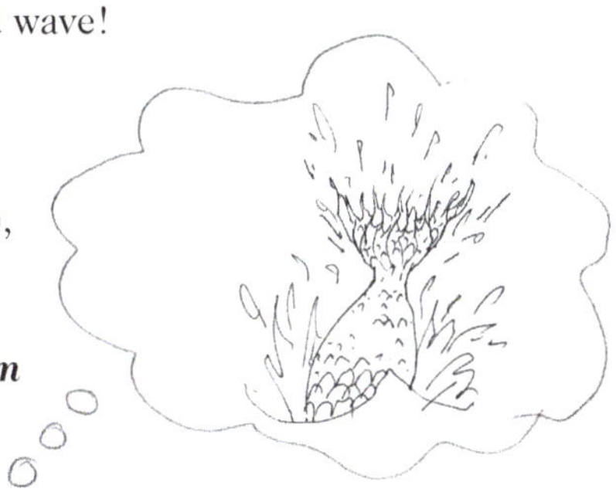

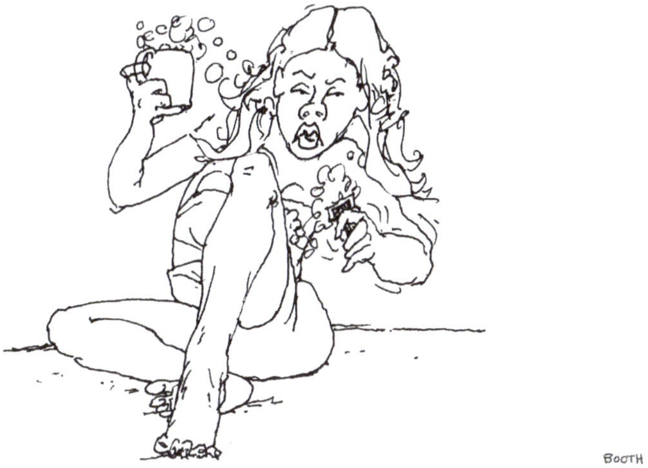
BOOTH

me late or only in part. Where was the money? Your litany of excuses included "I forgot it," "I used it to buy blow, some of which I will totally give you," and "I had to buy my fucking kid baby food, you heartless asshole." It has now been seven months since I have seen any money from you, at all.

Cut to last Friday, a day on which Borginborg normally rehearses, but we were scheduled to attend the Local Music Awards, for which we had been nominated in the category of Best Electro, Calypso, or Other. I stopped by the studio to retrieve my best gold lamé suit.

Upon entering the room, I slipped on one of many empty beer bottles on the floor and fell into a puddle of urine and vomit. Clearly, a social gathering had taken place in the room that raged far beyond the bounds of a conventional music practice. Empty beer bottles (those not rolling across the floor) sat atop every amplifier and synthesizer. Even my wine coolers had been consumed—the beverage which you have pointedly mocked in my presence on many occasions. I perceived this instantly, as the (now empty) mini-fridge door had been left wide open.

Covering the wall were Sharpied juvenilia such as "Borginborgs [sic] Sux / Donnie & the Dicks rock your sock offs [sic] BOOM." And why was this writing legible, on walls normally covered in soundproofing? Because, as you surely know, the soundproofing material had been torn from the walls, piled onto the floor, and fornicated upon. A used prophylactic and a woman's hair scrunchie bore witness to the deed.

Zachary, we have known each other for a long time. In seventh grade, I let you copy my answers on every Earth Science quiz. As recently as last year, when we were accosted on the subway by those disadvantaged youths who took exception to your Turbonegro sweatshirt, it was my patient explanation that drew their attention away from you. I earned a thrashing for my efforts, but I was glad to help an old school chum. But at last, my patience is exhausted. You have surpassed Richie Rosotto, of local thugcore purveyors Now You Get Hit, to become my least favorite musician acquaintance. If Richie asked me to split the practice space today, I would gladly assent rather than have you and your band return.

As you can see, your equipment—whatever of it might still be in working order—is lined up neatly in the hallway. Kindly never darken the door of this rehearsal studio again.

Your friend, Barth

P.S. Attached is an invoice for the dry cleaning of vomit stains off my gold lamé suit. Please mail payment at your earliest convenience. A self-addressed stamped envelope is also attached.

P.P.S. In case you were wondering, Borginborg did not win the award. The honor went to a Beat-poetry/posi-core fusion group called Kerouac Kills. Oh, well—wish us luck next year!

—Patrick Kennedy

SUNDAY ROUTINE: ALBERT EINSTEIN

Albert Einstein first silenced the haters with the seminal Annus Mirabilis papers in a 1905 issue of Annalen der Physik, but the German-born, Zurich-educated "think-fluencer" didn't stop there. With over 300 scientific works, Dr. Einstein—who sampled neighborhoods in Brooklyn and Hoboken before settling on a luxury condo in Chelsea, is a star who shows no signs of collapsing.

TIME IS RELATIVE I usually roll out of bed whenever I have to take a leak. My bathroom mirror has all sorts of equations written on it, so I pretty much just leave my hair how it is and start thinkin'. One thing about theoretical physics is that it's one of those gigs you can make your own schedule for. No one really knows what it is, so if you mumble stuff like "$E=MC^2$," the suits will leave you alone. My weekends are chill, like everybody's, but sometimes I just can't turn off the ol' noggin.

SMART START People think because I won a Nobel, I must be eating an acai bowl sprinkled with adderall for break-

STAN MACK'S CHRONICLES

ALL DIALOGUE GUARANTEED VERBATIM

THE SCIENCE OF LOVE

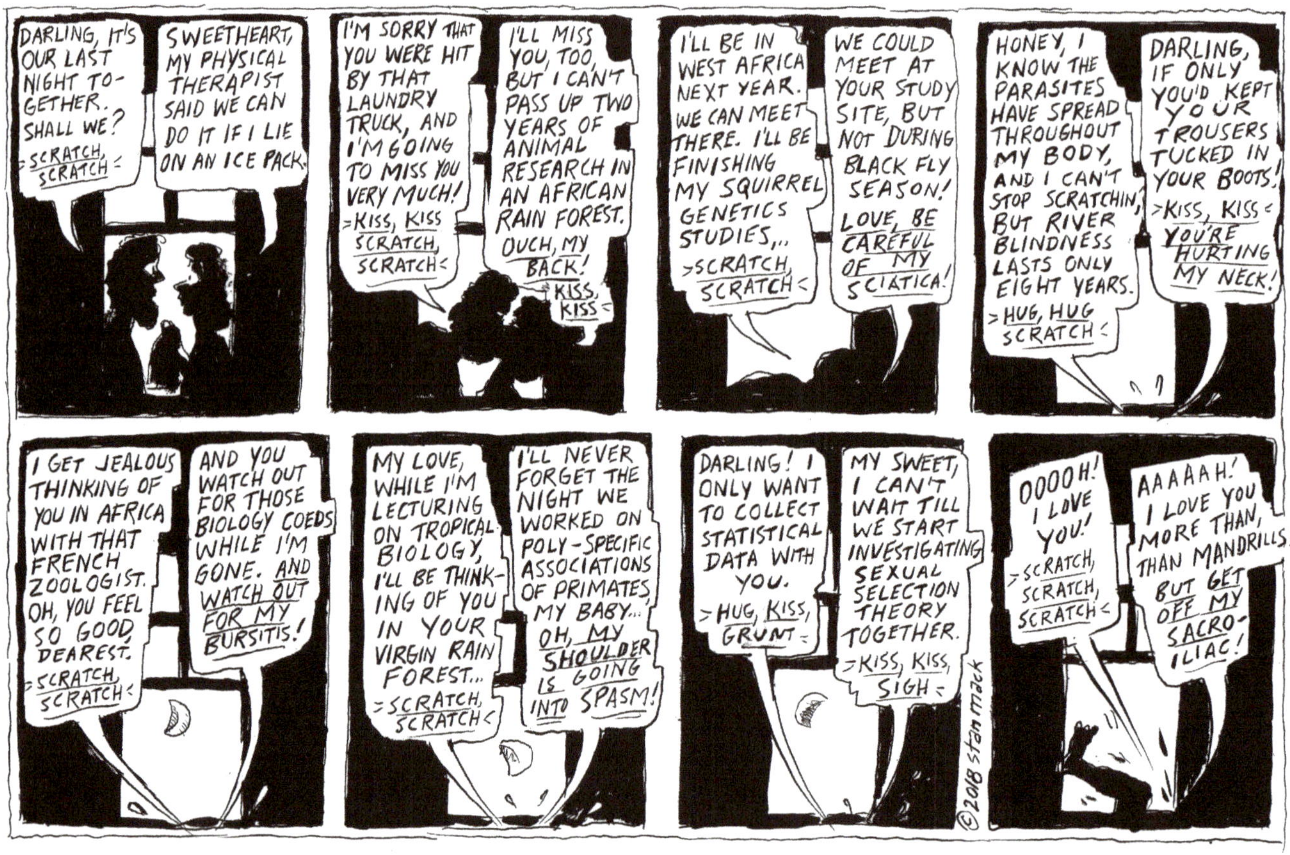

DARLING, IT'S OUR LAST NIGHT TOGETHER. SHALL WE? >SCRATCH, SCRATCH<
SWEETHEART, MY PHYSICAL THERAPIST SAID WE CAN DO IT IF I LIE ON AN ICE PACK.
I'M SORRY THAT YOU WERE HIT BY THAT LAUNDRY TRUCK, AND I'M GOING TO MISS YOU VERY MUCH! >KISS, KISS SCRATCH, SCRATCH<
I'LL MISS YOU, TOO, BUT I CAN'T PASS UP TWO YEARS OF ANIMAL RESEARCH IN AN AFRICAN RAIN FOREST. OUCH, MY BACK! >KISS, KISS<
I'LL BE IN WEST AFRICA NEXT YEAR. WE CAN MEET THERE. I'LL BE FINISHING MY SQUIRREL GENETICS STUDIES,.. >SCRATCH, SCRATCH<
WE COULD MEET AT YOUR STUDY SITE, BUT NOT DURING BLACK FLY SEASON! LOVE, BE CAREFUL OF MY SCIATICA!
HONEY, I KNOW THE PARASITES HAVE SPREAD THROUGHOUT MY BODY, AND I CAN'T STOP SCRATCHIN, BUT RIVER BLINDNESS LASTS ONLY EIGHT YEARS. >HUG, HUG SCRATCH<
DARLING, IF ONLY YOU'D KEPT YOUR TROUSERS TUCKED IN YOUR BOOTS! >KISS, KISS< YOU'RE HURTING MY NECK!
I GET JEALOUS THINKING OF YOU IN AFRICA WITH THAT FRENCH ZOOLOGIST. OH, YOU FEEL SO GOOD, DEAREST. >SCRATCH, SCRATCH<
AND YOU WATCH OUT FOR THOSE BIOLOGY COEDS WHILE I'M GONE. AND WATCH OUT FOR MY BURSITIS!
MY LOVE, WHILE I'M LECTURING ON TROPICAL BIOLOGY, I'LL BE THINKING OF YOU IN YOUR VIRGIN RAIN FOREST... >SCRATCH, SCRATCH<
I'LL NEVER FORGET THE NIGHT WE WORKED ON POLY-SPECIFIC ASSOCIATIONS OF PRIMATES, MY BABY... OH, MY SHOULDER IS GOING INTO SPASM!
DARLING! I ONLY WANT TO COLLECT STATISTICAL DATA WITH YOU. >HUG, KISS, GRUNT<
MY SWEET, I CAN'T WAIT TILL WE START INVESTIGATING SEXUAL SELECTION THEORY TOGETHER. >KISS, KISS, SIGH<
©2018 stan mack
OOOOH! I LOVE YOU! >SCRATCH, SCRATCH, SCRATCH<
AAAAAH! I LOVE YOU MORE THAN, THAN MANDRILLS! BUT GET OFF MY SACRO-ILIAC!

fast. But I'm still "Berty from the Berg" (Kingdom of Württemberg… it's a long story). I'll make myself a full German frühstück featuring sausage, sauerkraut, and that's it. Oh, and some joe, of course! Don't talk to me about the mysteries of the universe until I've had my coffee.

QUANTUM LEAP I have a reputation for being somewhat of a nerd, but if I'm being totally honest, I'm more like a brainy bro. I lift. Pilates. I might not have a jock look, but ask any of the guys I hoop with and they'll tell you. Sure, I use my intelligence (I trash talk in equations), but roundball is one of the few arenas where I can show off the rest of what Gött gave me. When I'm crossing suckers up, clowning them with a no-look, or teabagging pasty fools as I hang on the rim, alls I can say is, *"Wer will als nächstes*, bitches???"

JEANIUS I hate shopping, absolutely loathe it, but the missus says if I wear the same gray suit on our cruise next month, she's ditching me for Brad from Trinidad. What can I say? We love that Royal Caribbean; when your job is to think, it's hella nice to have everything planned out for you. Get two blender drinks in me and I will limbo, so whatever I buy today better not interfere with "how low I can go." The first store I go to has pants in the window, but when I walk in the display tables are filled with hand-carved wooden spoons and books on witchcraft. The beautiful but confused woman behind the counter scowled at me—she could tell I was a man of science. Peace out, Schatzi!

BREW IQ "No problem can be solved from the same level of consciousness that created it." I get a lot of credit for that line, but it really came from my favorite bartender Derek. After 2 a.m. he says the trippiest shit. He's a bigtime beer snob and got me hooked on hoppy ales. Today Derek serves me a limited-release IPA brewed by a kindergarten class from a local charter school. I admire the kids' pluck, but the only thing that stands out is the art on the label. I tell Derek, "It had some flowery notes," and he looks disappointed in me. A balding man who brought his own nachos to the bar takes care of my next round. We get to chatting about life and Theories of Everything (his involve the Bilderbergers), but when I start slurring my words and shit-talking Sir Isaac Newton, I know it's time to go home.

BAZINGA Eventually, I find my way back to mi casa. The wife is asleep on the couch, with the TV on. Since an object will remain at rest until that state is changed by an external force, I lay a blanket over the both of us as gently as possible. My favorite show? The Big Bang Theory. I've seen this episode a million times, but that only makes it funnier. Did Howard just call someone a "Quark block?" This show is too much. I've disturbed my lady with my guffawing (we geniuses really are like that!) and she awakens feeling amorous. Yes, dear reader, I do carnal as well as cerebral; all of us Nobel guys do. I think of the Witch Girl.

BLACK HOLE Finally, some "me" time before bed. Nothing penetrates this next hour or so. It's just me and my big, freakish brain until I pass out. Okay, maybe some Fortnite.

—Alex Watt B

FROM FANTAGRAPHICS UNDERGROUND

A Fistful of Drawings
A Graphic Journal by Joe Ciardiello

A paean to Hollywood, a love letter to the Western, and a tribute to its Italian influences.

In this gorgeous graphic memoir, Joe Ciardiello gracefully weaves together his Italian family history and the mythology of the American West while paying homage to the classic movie and TV Westerns of the '50s and '60s. Featuring Ciardiello's signature sinuous ink line and vivid watercolors, *A Fistful of Drawings* illuminates the oversized characters that dominated the cinematic American West— Clint Eastwood John Ford, John Wayne, Claudia Cardinale, Sophia Loren, and many more.

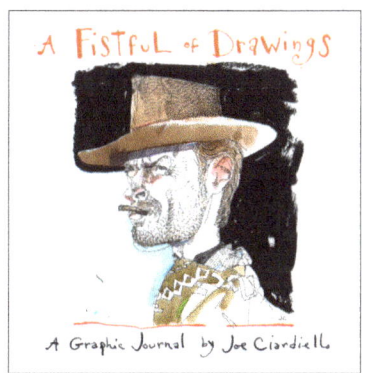

"Joe Ciardiello has been one of America's finest artists for the last generation. Here we finally have his magnum opus: a project that brilliantly blends mid-century culture, the Italian-American experience, and his own personal story into something rare in form, unique in content, and startlingly deep in every nuance. It is a work of genius."

—Steve Brodner
Illustrator/political satirist

ORDER NOW AT FANTAGRAPHICS.COM

A History of the Greatest Magazine of All Time.

THE BOOK OF
WEIRDO
BY JON B. COOKE

Well, that's what the folks over at the *Boing Boing* website called the new, 288-page hardcover, *The Book of Weirdo*. The feller said it was a "deep history," actually. We can attest it *is* insanely comprehensive...

In case you missed the '80s, *Weirdo* was R. Crumb's inspired answer to the "greed is good" Reagan era (and, if you come right down to it, artsy-fartsy comics, as well). Y'know, Robert Crumb: the guy who invented *ZAP Comix*, Fritz the Cat, Mr. Natural... and popularized the phrase, "Keep on Truckin.'" The wacked-out cartoonist who was the subject of Terry Zwigoff's 1994 film documentary... *that* R. Crumb.

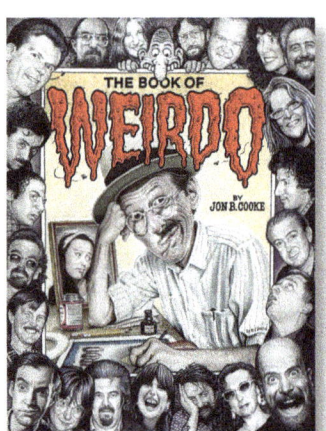

The Original Weirdo
R. Crumb

Anyway, Uncle Bob started and edited this humor comics anthology filled with savagely funny, sometimes puerile stuff. It was often politically incorrect to the Nth degree, and yet it was a haven for "outsider" artists, whether culled from the L.A. and New York City punk scenes, the mini-comics world, and street denizens of Berkeley, plus it welcomed into its pages the stories of a generation of women cartoonists.

WEIRDO

Weirdo lasted for 28 issues, a span when it was used as evidence in a landmark obscenity case, and it was edited by two other zany cartoonists, Peter Bagge and Aline Kominsky-Crumb. Upon its passing, the mag left behind a lingering impression among fellow comix artists. But, outside that crowd, the memory of *Weirdo* started to fade.

Until now.

This May, Last Gasp, the mag's original publisher, has released *The Book of Weirdo*, a 12-years-in-the-making retrospective which the not-easy-to-please Crumb called, "a great book... the definitive work on the subject." With a cover by master caricaturist Drew Friedman (who also provided the introduction), the tome includes recollections and testimonials of over 130 *Weirdo* contributors, plus an informed history of not only the mag, but the entire '80s alt comix scene. In fact, Crumb says, it's a "monumental statement on American culture and life in that dismal decade of Reagan, AIDS, widespread cocaine abuse, and the rise of the Yuppies...."

The opus also features comix by some talented modern-day weirdos too young to have appeared in the mag, and essays by the likes of Ivan Brunetti and others.

But most of all, the book is a tribute to the man much of the comix world calls the greatest cartoonist of all time (who had much of his finest work published in the pages of *Weirdo*).

So get the book, available at better bookstores and comic shops or via the publisher at *lastgasp.com*.

BY MEGAN KOESTER

THE END OF THE BEGINNING

On the other hand, you can finally become President

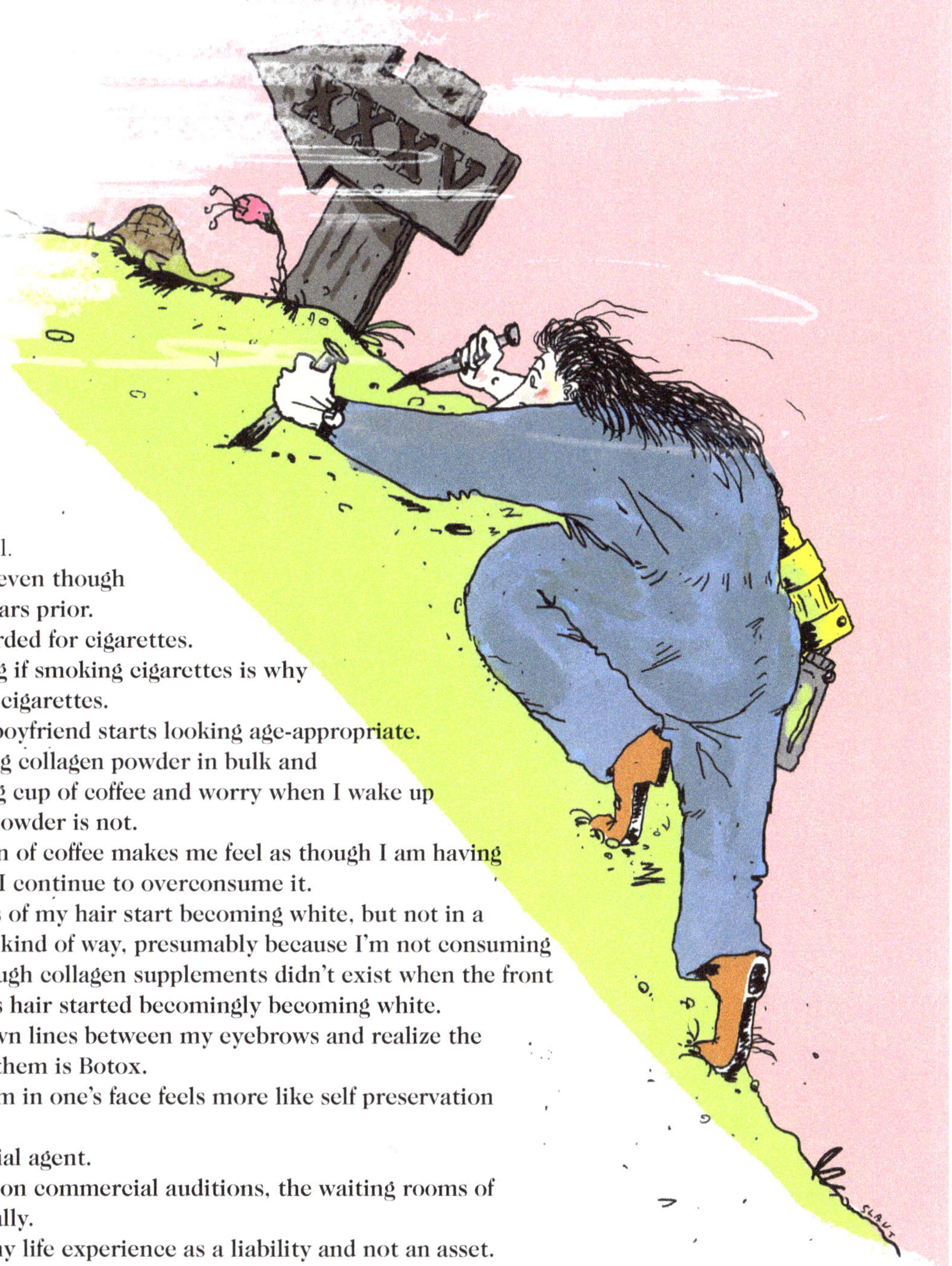
XXXV

Thirty-five

is when it all goes downhill.
35 is when the party's over even though I ceased partying three years prior.
35 is when I stop getting carded for cigarettes.
35 is when I start wondering if smoking cigarettes is why I no longer get carded for cigarettes.
35 is when my 45-year-old boyfriend starts looking age-appropriate.
35 is when I start purchasing collagen powder in bulk and mixing it into my morning cup of coffee and worry when I wake up somewhere the collagen powder is not.
35 is when overconsumption of coffee makes me feel as though I am having a nervous breakdown yet I continue to overconsume it.
35 is when the front strands of my hair start becoming white, but not in a becoming, Anne Bancroft kind of way, presumably because I'm not consuming enough collagen even though collagen supplements didn't exist when the front strands of Anne Bancroft's hair started becomingly becoming white.
35 is when I look at the frown lines between my eyebrows and realize the only way to rid myself of them is Botox.
35 is when injecting botulism in one's face feels more like self preservation than vanity.
35 is when I get a commercial agent.
35 is when I start going out on commercial auditions, the waiting rooms of which affect me existentially.
35 is when I start viewing my life experience as a liability and not an asset.
35 is when I notice all the women playing 35 year olds are 25.
35 is when I start caring about those "under 30" lists.
35 is when Terry tells me that at 40 the bladder starts to fail and I reply "40, really?" and think he's full of shit because he's always full of shit but part of me worries he's not full of shit.
35 is when I realize that in ten years I will be 45.
45 is when I stop caring. But at the moment, I am 35. **B**

MEGAN KOESTER *(@bornferal) is a writer and comedian toiling in Los Angeles. For casting purposes, her adult acne keeps her young.*

#WINNING
BY ALEX SCHMIDT

OWNING THE LIBS BY SUFFERING IN HELL

Does my being in Hell trigger you, Snowflake? I'm a traditional American male. I do not apologize for my conservative values, my belief in one Christian God, or my calls for a white ethnostate. So go ahead: whine about me EARNING MY WAY (heard of it???) to Circle 8. [1/9]

And before you SJWs cry "racist" or "nazi" or "srsly he's in the same circle as actual WW2 nazis", let's get something straight: this is The *Alt* Malebolge. And no, I wont shut up so you can have your "safe space." I can't. The Dark Familiars are using 13th century puppetry rigs to force my hands to tweet 4ever! [2/9]

So u will stay OWNED 😁 Cuz down here there's no #censorship from libturds at Twitter and Facebook and the Chipotle (((Corporation))). So I get to come at you hard, unfiltered, and in the form of a bleeding screaming poplar, [3/9]

Cuz me and my fellow 🔥 Sowers of Memes 🔥 are now a Misery Orchard. In fact I'm GLAD our charter bus to CruelCon (lol c'mon the name's a joke) rolled off an interchange (lol c'mon it's just death). Because when I lived, Ba-cuck Obummer took my guns away, I'm pretty sure. [4/9]

But now I celebrate the 2nd Amndmt all the time. Every hour my penis becomes a Glock, then melts away, then regenerates to do it again AND YES I feel it. Yes, Belphegor makes me watch. But I'm enough of a #RealMan #TradMan #ProudMan to ACCEPT the free market's choice [5/9]

Of flesh-rending genital tribulation. Because this place GETS IT. When I say feminism is brain cancer, they demonstrate literal brain cancer on me 💪 to prove my point. 💪 When I want to yell about Muslims, my yelling goes through two big long curvy trumpets and straight back [6/9]

Into my ears 😎 so I can hear it good. 😎 And whenever I want to boycott Starbucks, 4 tha lulz and 4 a Fox News audition, the folks down here keep me clear of those limo-lib lattes 🎉 by forcing me to hydrate with bile. 🎉 Anyway, enough OWNING YOU so powerfully that [7/9]

I have to keep announcing I'm owning you. I've got better things to do, like saying the Bible proves gay people aren't people while old popes grind my tongue with a sandpaper Leviticus. I'm just gonna be the bigger person, and give myself the last word [8/9]

By threading new tweets on top of the old ones really fast. And that last word is this: no one responds to what I tweet down here because I'm SO right about everything and that's definitely what's happening I win bye bye   haha I win [9/9]

ALEX SCHMIDT
*(@alexschmidty) is a comedy writer, Earwolf podcaster, and **Jeopardy!** champion. His website is alexschmidty.com and he only reads Dante for the articles.*

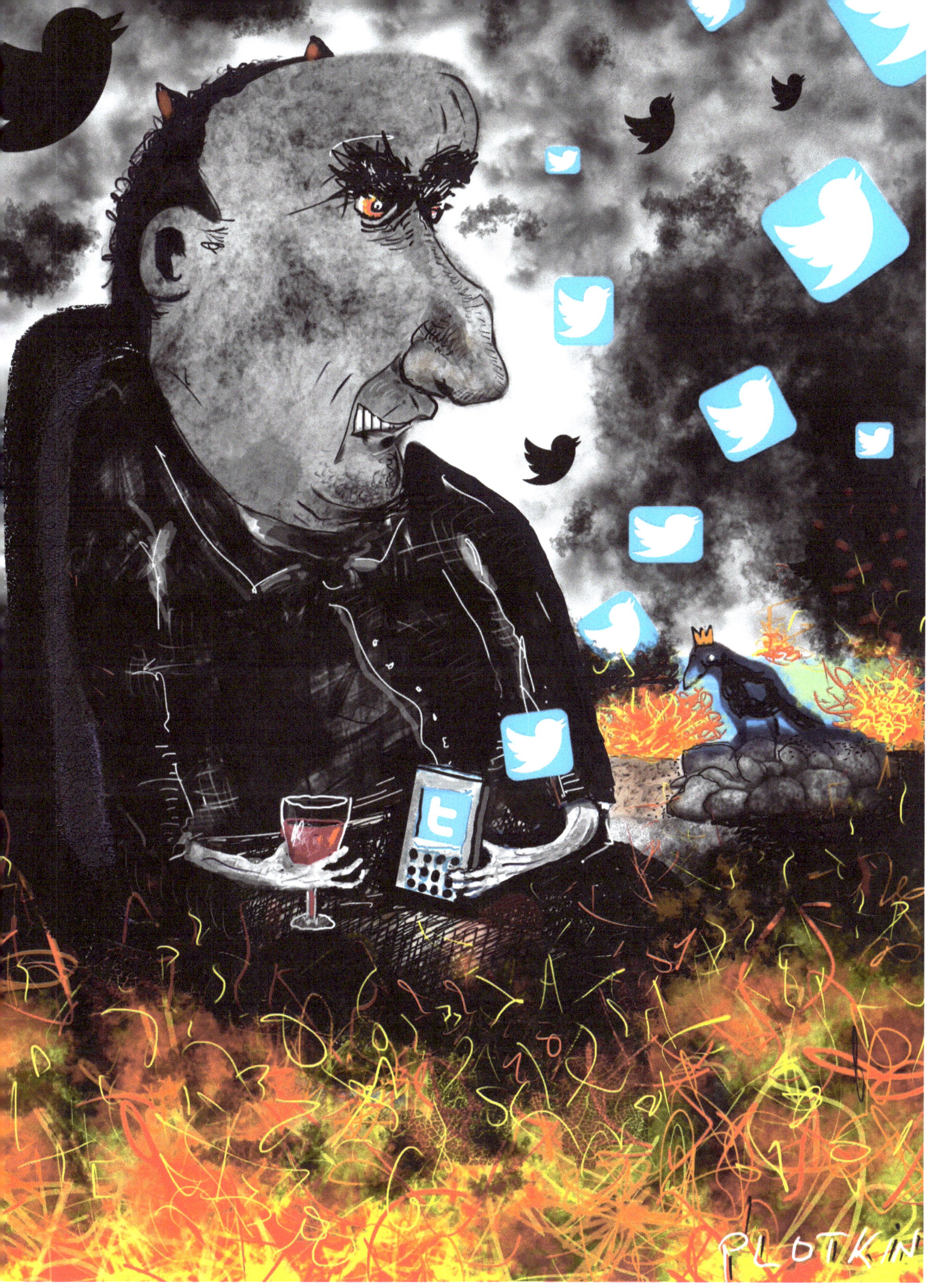
PLOTKIN

SERF'S UP!

BY MATT GARCZYNSKI

Serfs at the Gate

A few words from the 0.00001%

Hey hey, my loyal serfs! Come to thank me for decades of my spectacular lordship? You're just in time. I was about to summon you all to dredge out my septic pit for a cufflink I dropped when I was blasted last night.

By the way, what's with the pitchfork party? You people having another one of your barbaric wedding ceremonies? Sure smells like it—*fyoosh*.

I'm kidding, mostly. You guys are superstars.

An uprising? Right on, fight the power. Hold up. You mean against *me*? Huh. It's kind of out of left field, but—wow. And you're telling me there's nothing I can do or say to avoid my certain death? Seriously. Nothing?

Because in case you didn't know, I can put you in touch with some *extremely* well-connected friends of mine. Remember Prince Pyotr? Tosses fistfuls of rubies from his carriage, loves watching you pounce on each other? He's looking for a fresh batch of peasants, just like you guys, to clear the rats out his wine cellar after his last ones all died of plague. All you have to do is haul out the plague-ridden corpses of the *old* serfs and the job is yours. How's that for a cushy gig? Hauling corpses for a prince! That'd boost you up a rung or two on the social ladder, huh?

Right. I see by the way you're tightening the grip on those bludgeons I might have to sweeten the deal a little. No worries! Here's a thought: let's say I guaranteed your plucky revolt went down in *history*. Y'see, I'm the patron of a very fine oil painter named Nikolai Grek who wouldn't mind sticking around after my tri-weekly portrait sitting to sketch up your little coup for posterity. If you'd all huddle together for him with your razor-sharp reaping tools just like that, and turn those grimaces into big happy smiles, hot dog you're headed for the textbooks!

Heck, I'll even tell him to flesh out those sunken cheeks and ignore the festering wounds incurred from work accidents. Capturing the furious bloodlust in your eyes might be a bit tricky, but I'm sure Niko's up to the challenge.

Whoa-kay! Why don't we back off the flaming torches for a sec? At least till we hear my next pitch? For real, this thing is silk.

Let's see here... Oh! I've got an obscene amount of roast pheasant left over from my Solstice Orgy that still has a semi-tolerable amount of maggots crawling on it. You're welcome to polish that off as a kind of victory banquet, courtesy of your one and only boss man. Lyudmila, maybe when you're done threateningly swinging that mace-and-chain you could break out a couple dozen pig troughs for this hungry crowd? All this carrying on is bound to work up a vicious mob's appetite. Keep this up and I'll have to start letting each family take home *two* bags of grain per season.

Easy with the mace, Lludmila! Almost nicked my perfect jawline there. You know how many cousins it took to make this thing?

How's this for you, peons? I will work for you—cleaning the stables, swinging the pointy wheat stick, all those things you guys love to do. We'll do that for a couple days, just 'til we're even-steven, and then everything can go back to normal. Fine, I'll even replace the humble thatch-roofed church I burned in a drunken rage last week, *and* the village elder I used for fencing practice. That last one will take some time.

Hey, Dragomir? It's kind of hard for me to speak while you're pressing that scythe against my throat. Care to lay off? No? Fair enough.

I know—I could be, like, your jester! Help bring some smiles to those sourpusses. Janusch, my horseshoe guy. I see you over there with the branding iron. Back me up. Tell them how hilarious I am. Like when I come into your shop to get Octavius reshoed, and I pretend to throw your lame legged son Lyubomir into the furnace? This kid, everybody, you gotta see him, just *screams and screams* whenever I grab him by the haunches and hold him so close to the flames it practically singes his greasy little...oh, I see.

Anyhoo! You've heard my offers. Feel free to return to your ramshackle huts, think them over, and get back to me in the morning. We've got a good thing going here—a *great* thing. Once you've had a chance to sleep on it, I'm sure you'll come around. Just remember to be back out in the fields three hours before sunrise. That barley isn't going to thresh itself!

My last words? I guess I never thought about them, Berislav. Why do you ask?

B

MATT GARCZYNSKI (@magznski) *is a Long Island–based writer and activist. He has been named one of the FBI's "Communists to Watch in 2019."*

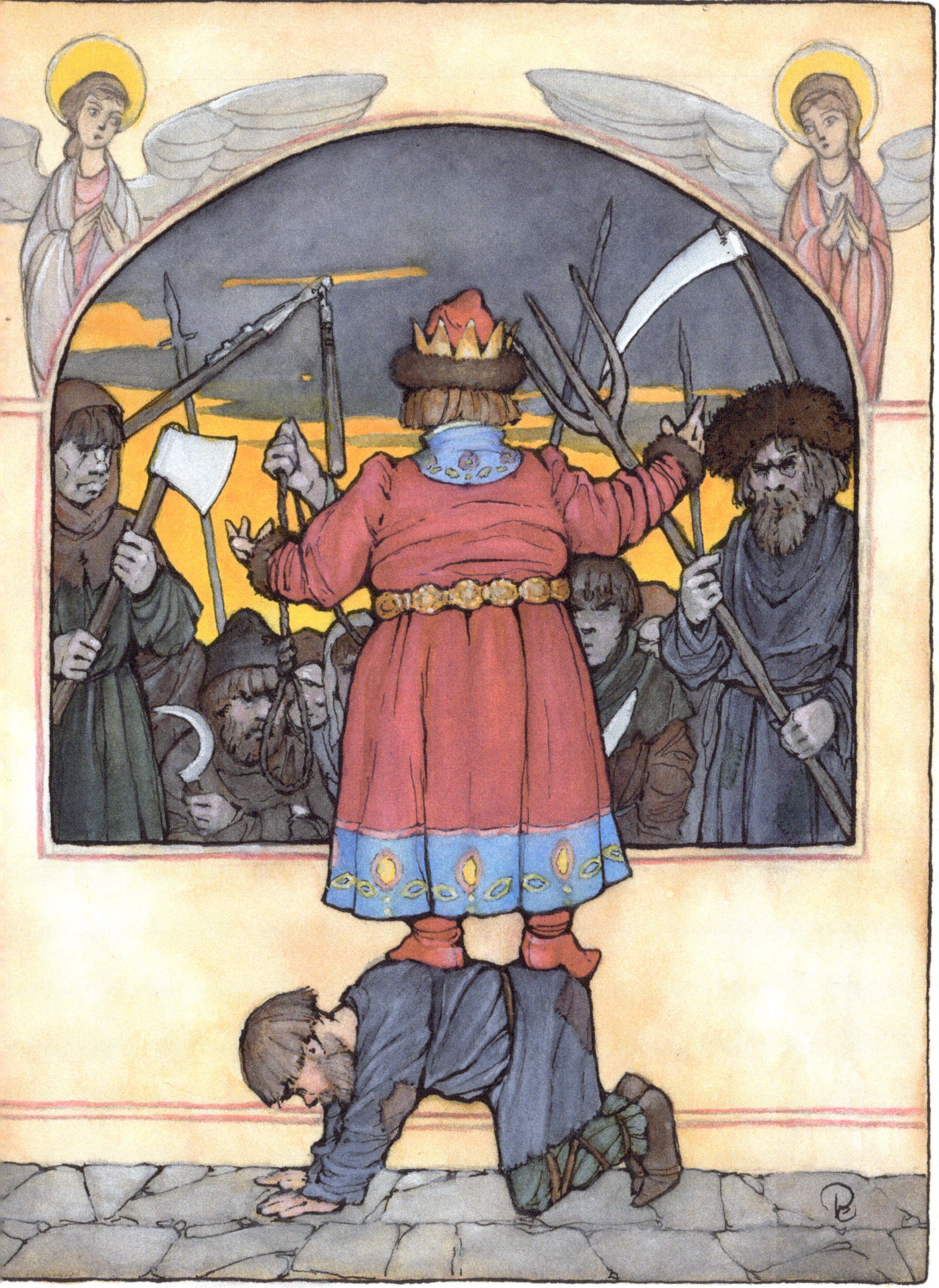

LA DOLCE VITA
BY LAURIE ROSENWALD

MY SOPRANOS CAMEO
FYI, Edie Falco's dog is named "Marley."

On a daily basis, my mailbox is lavishly festooned with a stupefying assortment of invitations. Galleries, book parties, and fragrance launches want me. They want me real bad.

How very dare they assume that I have nothing better to do than imbibe free Aperol spritzes and ingest free Thai meat lollipops? Would I bother to don my stripes and bless their little shindigs with my adorable presence for the paltry reward of a gift bag brimming with Nars Dragon Lady lipsticks, Vahlrona chocolates and a La Prairie White Caviar Illuminating and Replenishing Mask? You're damn right I would.

As an illustrator I don't get out much, so I get out as much as possible, which is all the time. I would gladly attend the opening of a refrigerator.

One night circa 2002, Fate found me at the popular suburban mall formerly known as Soho, at a swanky bash inaugurating some minimalist jewelry emporium. Dashingly out-of-work actors administered turquoise fortune cookies and heady, intoxicating liquids the color of Windex. Inside my cookie I found this tiny cobalt epistle: "You've won a spectacular prize!" This turned out to be a pair of $1400 diamond earrings, which I intend to sell on eBay when I get around to it and yes I know it's seventeen years ago.

My gang ended up at a Japanese restaurant with a showbizzy posse including the pulchritudinous Jade Barrymore and her hunky entourage. The sake seems to have brought out the ham in me, which is pretty close to the surface already. I regaled the table with my saltiest Scandinavian stories.

As pineapple chunks were distributed, an attractive stranger said, "Call me!"

"Sure! Let's be friends!"

"No, about work. I can get jobs for you!"

"Oh! Where do you work?"

"Wilhelmina!"

I said, "What is wrong with you? Are you, by any chance, blind?"

Because Wilhelmina is a topflight modeling agency, and, I am not exactly Victoria's Secret Weapon. The stranger, Marta, said, "No, I represent comics and actors. Send me a headshot."

"But I'm an illustrator!" I said.

Clearly, this woman was bonkers.

A week later, she reminded me. A photographer friend shot my head as a favor. This I sent to Marta, and flew to Gothenburg. For some reason I kinda live in Sweden sometimes.

A year later, Marta called. "The casting director of "The Sopranos" wants to see you."

AVERE CULO! Rocambolesco! Che figata!

I was sent my "side." This is showbiz talk for my page of the script. The part was "Woman." A role I was born to play. I had exactly one line. In a group therapy scene in Melfi's office. I say, "When you say that you make me feel...less than."

I said it to some office woman holding a video camera. Afterwards, I rang for the elevator, turned around, and said, "Can I try again? I really want to "nail it," a beastly Californian expression I'd never used before. Or since.

I got a "callback." That's when they call you back.

This was held at a former commercial bakery in an outer borough. The glamour! The secrecy! SILVERCUP STUDIOS! - where they shoot *Sex in the City*.

There were five of everything. Five *goomars*, with humongous boobs and mighty, mighty hairdos. Five little girls with long black hair, five Hispanic janitors, five Goth chicks with tattoos and piercings. And five unattractive middle aged "Women." My peeps! I waited next to a potential goomar, reading s*Tori Telling*—the autobiography of Tori Spelling.

She said, "Shouldn't you be going over your lines?" I pointed out that I only had one. She answered, "Yeah, but still..."

I said my line to David Chase (the creator of the show) and a large group of intense individuals who frankly scared the *pannetone* out of me.

Maybe they needed an unknown. Maybe they liked my mole. I got the part.

I'd already purchased my return flight back to Sweden on April 15th and they were shooting on the 17th. I changed the ticket to the 18th. My Belgian subletters arrived, surprised to find yours truly *en flagrante locus parenta*. We cohabited. If the Flamands and Francophones could, we could.

At the table reading the cast showed up in reverse order of fabulosity. I was the first one in the room. I placed my coat on a chair, and chatted with Michael Imperioli. I patted Edie Falco's dog, Marley.

LAURIE ROSENWALD
(@rosenworld) is a painter, designer and author of **All The Wrong People Have Self-Esteem**. *You can find her at www.rosenworld.com.*

This was the first episode of the fifth season. They hadn't seen each other since the Emmys!

Gandolfini arrived very late. I sat down where I'd left my coat, and thought "Wow! I'm right next to Bracco, Falco and Gandolfini!"

A second later, somebody tapped me on the shoulder. "Sorry, but this table is for principals only. Would you mind..." Mortified, I ran like the wind to the furthest corner. I read my tiny line. I was dispatched to wardrobe, where an eggplant-colored outfit was selected that expressed a respectable, professional womanliness. I wore a pendant on a chain and carried a tiny handbag. There was nothing in it.

The day of the shoot, I had industrial strength eyeliner applied in the makeup trailer. On my dressing room door was a star, and the word "Woman." Someone knocked. I thought, "This is It!"

But it was not It.

An assistant something informed me the shoot was canceled. Some conflict. She had no idea when they'd reschedule. Anytime that spring. But I was flying to Sweden the following day! I was devastated. I know I'm not the only "Woman" in the world.

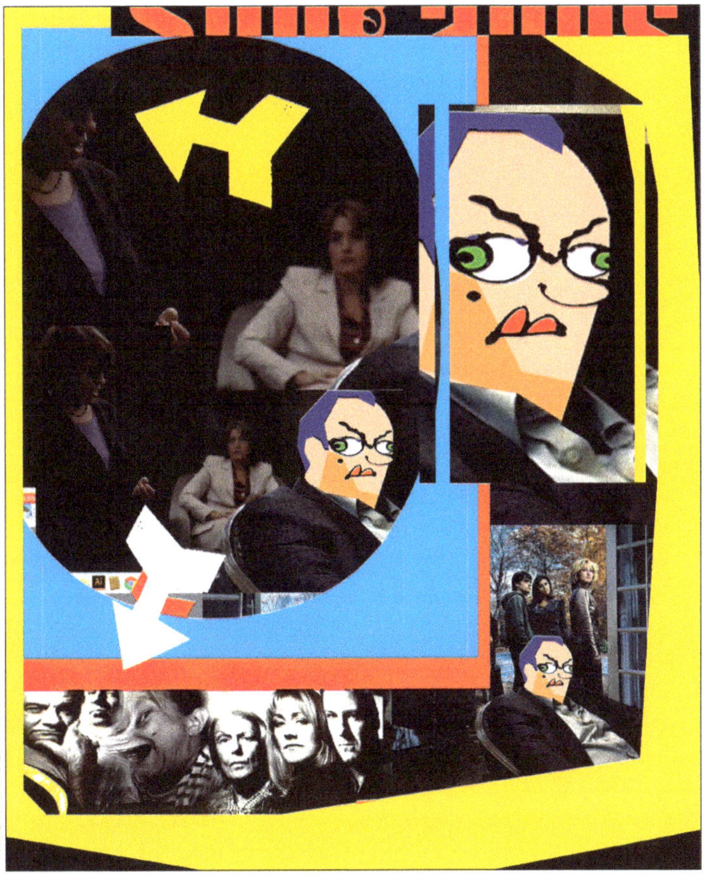

LAURIE ROSENWALD

Right then, my phone rang. It was my cousin Patricia, calling from California.

"Is she dead?"

"Yes."

My mother always loved a dramatic moment.

I didn't go West. When she was sick, I was by her side. Now, I didn't care what anyone thought. I knew there'd be incense, and strong-smelling headachy flowers—and Baha'i's.

I begged Patricia to take charge. I said, "I'll pay for everything. But I won't go."

I hated my mother's home, with its unclean smell of a health food store. She hoarded paper towels and instant noodles. I paid for all of it to be hauled, unseen, and trashed. There was nothing of value. Except for the fact that she'd never, ever, find me again. A Daughter of no Mother. Free at last. Happier ever since.

The day after the aborted Sopranos shoot, I was watching a riveting episode of "Vilse i Pannkakan" at Stefan's apartment in Gothenburg. *Jätteroligt!*

My mobile rang. Marta said, "They're reshooting tomorrow!" I hung up and, without stopping at my place, taxied to Landvetter airport. I had my passport and credit card, but no luggage.

"When's the next flight to New York?"

I paid full fare for the first time ever. The Belgians were surprised. Again.

"Woman" returned to Silvercup. I repeated my line until it became a surreal, tangible object. I could see it.

For the record I think Gandolfini deserved two million an episode. Around then, there'd been a tense controversy about his salary. That night, after the thrilling 12-hour shoot, I had to fly back to Sweden. I was booked to give a lecture at an Illustration conference in Stockholm at noon. At gate 27, I noticed a handsome guy. Handsome the way I like, which is mostly craggy. I never get to sit next to the handsome guy.

But we had the bulkhead seats! Soon we were flirting away like old whores. Polyester blankets, Glenlivet Miniatures and in-flight magazines were piling up—we were flying drunk and happy.

Somewhere over the Atlantic I said, "You're not going to believe this, but I have to work!"

"What?" said handsome guy.

"I have to do a PowerPoint Presentation for a lecture that starts exactly 6 hours from now, and I don't know how!"

"You came to the right place," said Handsome Guy. "Take a nap, give me your Mac, and I'll PowerPoint it for you in ten."

He did. But he deplaned in Frankfurt. *Bluadzakramentkruzifixalleluja!*

Onstage in Stockholm, I wowed 'em. Told the whole story, and apologized for my hair.

The Sopranos never considers spec scripts, but I wrote an episode anyway where "Woman" makes a dramatic return. I make out with "Big Pussy" Bonpensiero in the Bada Bing bathroom, and then get whacked by Paulie Walnuts.

Anyone who would travel 15,000 miles over three days to say one line is capable of every kind of madness. I got $700 per day. Financially, I broke exactly even. For me, this is coming out ahead. *Bada Bling!*

Season Five. Episode One. "The Two Tonys."

Just look for a star-struck "Woman" dressed in eggplant, jet lag, and ecstasy. B

KEY-STROKES
BY JAY RUTTENBERG

UNLOCKING THE DOOR
If you're not portal the solution, you're portal the problem

Thank you for Airbnb-ing with us—here are the keys! The door can be a little tricky until you get the hang of it, so I wanted to pass along some tips.

For the top lock, use one of the keychain's six bronze, round-ended keys. At first glance, all six look identical. You need the one that emits a vaguely bluish hue when held vertically under the hallway light. Another way to tell that you have the correct key: it's the one that doesn't fit comfortably into the lock.

Ignore the other bronze keys. I don't even remember what they are for—they're just on the key chain. Do not put them into the top lock! They will stick inside it, rendering the door unopenable.

After examining the lock, you will be tempted, with every fiber of your being, to insert the key with its edges facing downward. Do the opposite. (IF YOU DID, use a dash of safflower oil to extract the key.) Be careful to insert the key about two-thirds of the way—if it breaks off in the lock, you have pushed too hard. To unlock the bolt, jiggle the key with restrained fervor. Your hand should be shaking at the approximate rate of a coward who is about to give a presentation at work.

The lower lock is much more challenging. Use the oval key with the wan engravings, faded from years of being streaked with tears. Insert it delicately—initially from below, then from above, but always tilted slightly eastward (use "Compass" on your phone). Don't worry if it refuses to slip into the lock right away. It takes some finessing and, depending on the phase of the moon, may need time to ossify.

No jiggling is needed this time—in fact, I would strongly counsel against applying ANY superfluous motion whatsoever, as that may upset the door's alignment. Turn the key clockwise, by which I mean it should be precisely coordinated to your watch's second hand. As you turn, tightly draw the door toward you, like a sleazy businessman shaking the hand of a prospective client; without losing momentum, briefly check in with the divine power of your choice. Once you hear the barely audible click, ease the door open with smooth tact, like a coquettish divorcée repelling a too-eager suitor in the early hours of a date.

On days when the temperature rises above 50 degrees, the floorboards tend to swell, causing the door to jam upon entry. If this is the case, assume a Sumo wrestler stance and, leading with your shoulder, hurl your bulk into the door while emitting a warrior's cry: Hoong-ahhh! A brisk Fonzarelli whack, deftly applied to the door's mullion, can also work, but please bear in mind the 10,000 hour rule.

Because of a past incident, the downstairs neighbors have requested that you not throw the keys in a fit of pique. I add this entreaty to satisfy their legal team, yes, but it remains sound advice. It is imperative to maintain a semblance of serenity. To that end, I find alternate nostril breathing effective when working the lower lock, particularly in the buildup to an anxiety attack. The tapas bar across the street serves an excellent vermut preparado; sometimes it also helps to lubricate the key in their house red. For stronger stuff, try the guy in 5B.

You know how in old cartoons a character will struggle with a door, only to lean on it in frustration and cause it to dramatically swing open? By the grace of God, DO NOT attempt that here.

If you need help, you can try contacting the super, but note that he manages a pair of other buildings—one across town and one in the Dominican Republic—so it can be hard to get ahold of him. Also, he is really bad with keys. The landlord is comatose and his heir is an aspiring monk, but just to be on the safe side, I have included the number of the monastery where the son lives in ascetic seclusion. (His gurus have taken vows of silence, but they know about the situation with the door.) Unfortunately, all reputable area locksmiths have added our apartment to their "do not service" lists. Be aware that, legally speaking, calling them from this address constitutes stalking and is punishable by a brief jail sentence, but I am adding their contact information in case you feel lucky.

In any case, I'm sure you'll figure it out. And enjoy your stay! Instructions for unfolding the futon are on the kitchen counter.

JAY RUTTENBERG edits **The Lowbrow Reader**, *a comedy zine from New York City.*

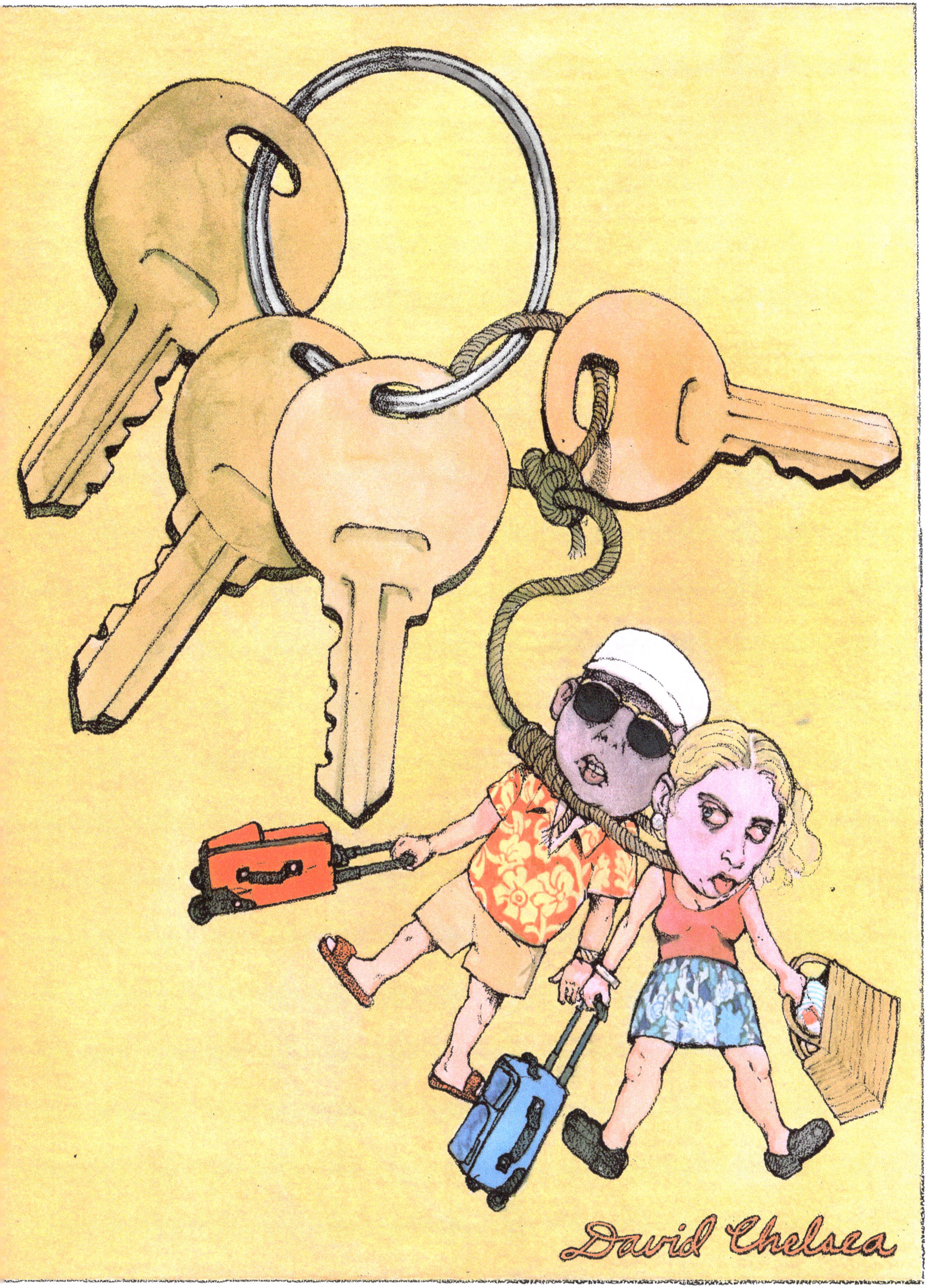
David Chelsea

BY SARAH HUTTO

AN EMAIL FOR THE LOTION I JUST ORDERED FROM AMAZON

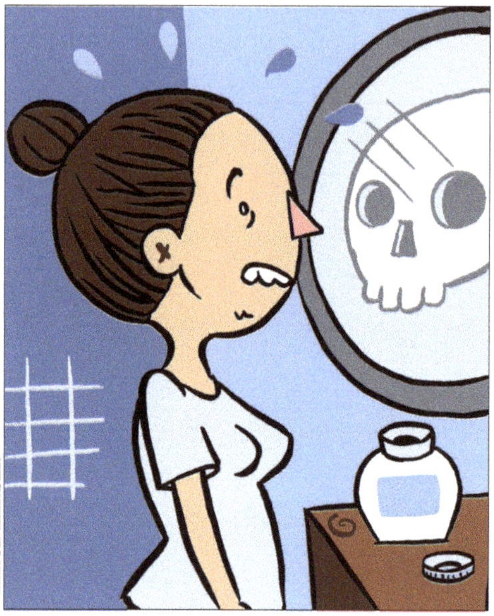
LANCE HANSEN

Hey Sarah,

How you holding up?

We just wanted to let you know that your face lotion was just shipped out of our Tennessee facility about ten minutes ago. You should receive it in two business days.

You can make it that long, right?

We know you ran out last week and that you're probably still tracing your finger along the stark interior of the plastic container before dragging it over your face, as if you might somehow reap the moisturizing benefits of some sort of black magic lotion ritual, but it's just two days.

Surely, two days isn't enough time to send you into an uncontrollable skid of age acceleration, in which the dermal karma of sun exposure and the drug-and alcohol-fueled all-nighters of your twenties suddenly catch up with you all at once, transforming you into the Dust Bowl woman in one weekend.

We know you're just barely hanging on. We know you're standing on the precipice of a steaming crevasse where girlish freshness goes to die. We know that the crustiness has begun to consume you, so that your cynicism and bitterness can no longer be concealed by a cosmetic glow and have taken up permanent residence on your face.

We know that you've become an impromptu alchemist overnight and are now using the unlikeliest of ingredients, hoping to miraculously stumble upon nature's best kept secret, the emollient potency of a ground-up unidentified caterpillar you found outside on a bush (both poisonous, by the way), or attempting to nourish your rough spots with your child's popsicle. We know these experiments have left you sticky, yet inflamed.

Take heart! In two business days, your lotion will arrive, and your weathered face will no longer make that noise when you smile. That noise, which has gotten louder (it's not just your imagination) is the sound of time passing—nay, time passed. It is the sound of forty winters, come and gone, seven presidents, five recessions, twenty-six versions of Windows, and one fluctuating pattern we'll just call "a depression." It is the sound of children, grown into adults. (Well, just older children in your case, but you see where we're going with this). It is the sound of meals cooked, TV binged, sleep missed, brows furrowed, child labor survived, noroviruses endured, financial strain fretted over. It is the sound of a marriage, comfortably worn, yet with a still-adequate amount of ass-tapping.

Yes, the sound of your dry face crackling in the night is the sound of life. Embrace it, Sarah. Embrace the crackling. Because when you've come as far as you have, smiling doesn't need to be silent. Or painless. A smile should remind you, and everyone in the room, that you've seen some shit.

And when your lotion finally does arrive—which it will, as you can estimate by the UPS tracking page left open on your browser—and the decomposition of your face is temporarily stunted once again, just remember: you are but a few unmoisturized days away from the echo of life's truth being visible in that Grand Canyon of unbridled loathing engraved between your eyebrows. The truth is that your face—and we don't mean "your" in the collective sense, but your, as in the face attached to your skull specifically—is but a catcher's mitt for all of the curveballs lobbed by life. Your face, Sarah, YOUR FACE, is the oracle of universal fuckery.

As such, we'd like to extend this coupon for 10% off your next purchase.

Sincerely,
Jeff Bezos.

SARAH HUTTO *(@huttopian) frequently contributes to* **The New Yorker**, **Reductress**, **MAD Magazine**, *and* **McSweeneys**. *Her face is currently on display at The American Museum of Natural History.*

Passing for Human

Liana Finck

Dare to be Different

"PASSING FOR HUMAN IS ONE OF THE MOST EXTRAORDINARY MEMOIRS I'VE EVER READ."
— ROZ CHAST, AUTHOR OF CAN'T WE TALK ABOUT SOMETHING MORE PLEASANT?

"NO ONE DRAWS LIKE LIANA FINCK, AND NO ONE ENCHANTS LIKE HER EITHER."
— STACY SCHIFF, AUTHOR OF CLEOPATRA

A Random House Hardcover

@lianafinck

Wigglesworth

"Quit staring out the window and tend to your labors or I'll box your damn ears, you great, worthless oaf!"

What we did to Wigglesworth was mean. But what he's been doing back has been psychotic. I'll take some blame for starting it.

Bill and I.

Bill Sodarman was my cubie here at Value-Content Plus—an odd name for a niche greeting card company, wouldn't you agree?

The trouble started with Bill being a huge fan of the film *Lawrence of Arabia*. We both were—but Bill could quote the whole movie. He wanted to be Lawrence of Arabia. Whenever he'd head out he'd usually pause in the doorway, punch his fist in the air and demand, "For whom do we ride?"

Then I'd yell, "We ride for Lawrence!" (pronounced "El-Orence.") Sometimes, if spirits were high, other cubies would chime in and we'd all yell, "On to Aqaba!" Then off he'd go, which was usually home for dinner.

That was his bit; my bit was to announce, as I angrily dialed the next client on my call sheet: "These people want their freedom and I'm going to give it to them!"

But in time, it grew stale. We needed something new. Then one day, we heard about a new guy, an illustrator, who recently came to work over in the Art Department. His name was Osgood Wigglesworth.

I don't know why, but I couldn't say it enough. "Osgood Wigglesworth"—it reminded me of some old-timey radio show. Wigglesworth was the underdog who always got screwed over for one specious reason after another, while his boss unloaded savagely on him.

"Have a care, Wigglesworth...Don't think we're not onto you, Wigglesworth...Blast you Wigglesworth, where are those top secret reports? Did you take them to the place of your birth, Wigglesworthtonville?"

Soon, T.E. Lawrence was a memory; now, Bill and I took turns chewing each other out. "Wigglesworth, quit staring out that window and tend to your labors or I'll box your damn ears, you great, worthless oaf."

It was great fun.

Bill and I are in sales. The guts of the joint, we like to think. The Golden Guns, the Death from Above Boys, snug in our F-22 Raptors. We'd bag the prey; they'd skin and clean it. We had rank and influence. People looked up to us. We had a lifetime seats at the cool kid's table. (As if Value-Content Plus had a cool kid's table.)

As I said, we're a niche outfit. Some of our better sellers have been: "Water Awareness Day"; "Great-Great-Grandmother's Day"; "Christmas Is Coming"; "Happy Good Friday"; "Genital Awareness Week"; "We Heard You Put Down Your Ferret, Sorry"; "Your Baby is Certainly Interesting Looking Day"; "Men Who Get Women's Diseases Awareness Month"; "We Heard Your Bike Was Stolen, That Sucks"; "Your Cat's Not Looking Well".

Crap like that. We leave the heavy emotional lifting to Hallmark.

Our supervisor was a shy and uncomfortable man, totally unlike the boss we created for our Wigglesworth saga. Our real boss rarely came around, but when he did, he'd limit his conversation to "How's it going, men?" and "Keep up the good work, fellas." Usually we'd ignore him, or give him a grunt with a forced smile, like: Do you mind? We're trying to get work done here.

On one of these visits Bill had skipped his a.m. meds and was looking pretty manic, and reverted to some standard L. of A. scripture. Our boss never understood any of it—but then, what's to understand? It's just guys at work screwing around and making crap up because we're good at it and the days can get pretty goddamn long around here if you haven't figured that out yet. Though we don't usually make our supervisor the butt of anything, once in a while we'll include him. He seems to love that. On his last visit, he even seemed to be waiting for it, wanting to be included in our merry band.

After an uncomfortable silence, our supervisor asked, "Is there anything...you guys...want to say...to me?" Then, like a football coach expecting the Gatorade bath, he braced himself, squeezing his eyes shut.

Brian McConnachie is Co-founder and Head Writer of this magazine.

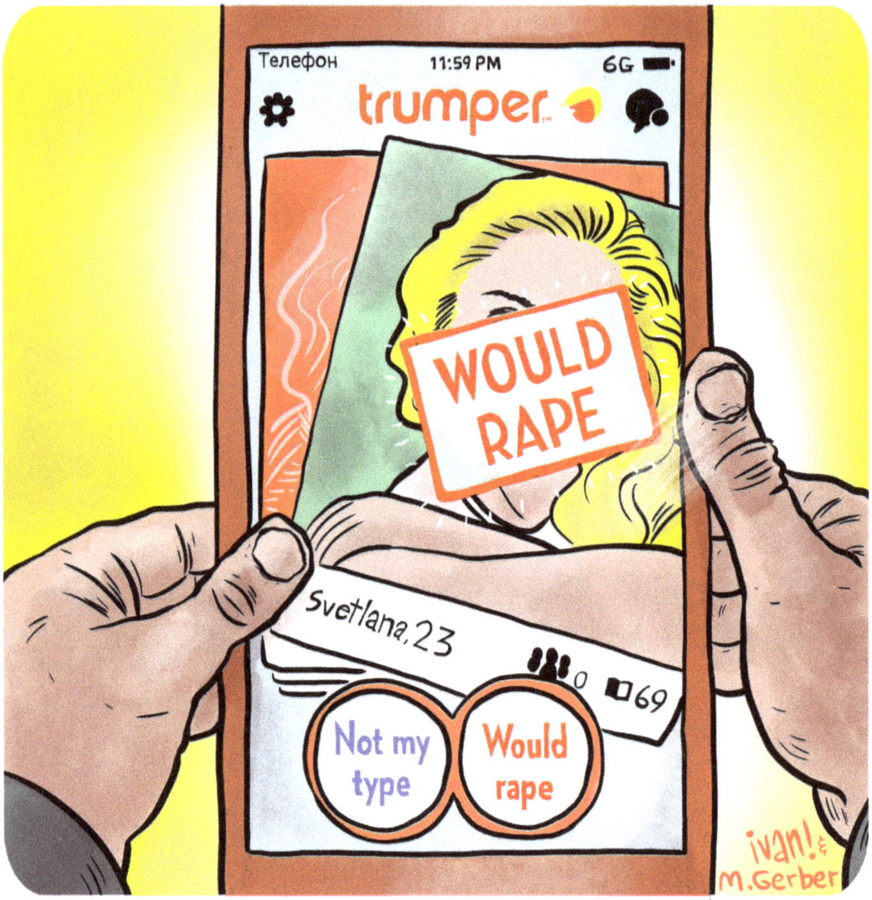
Телефон
11:59 PM
6G
trumper
WOULD RAPE
Svetlana, 23
0
69
Not my type
Would rape
ivan! & M.Gerber

Bill slowly rose; the beast had awakened. "I carry twenty-three great wounds all gotten in battle," he said in a tone of deep, icy anger. "Seventy-five men I have killed with my own hands in battle. I burn my enemy's tents. I take their herds. The Turks pay me a golden treasure. Yet I am poor, because" (long pause) "I...AM A RIVER TO MY PEOPLE."

Bill pulled a drawer from a desk and flung it, almost taking off an intern's head. Then I jumped up on my desk, and ululated, inflating it with all the joyful madness I could. A bunch more cubie voices joined the howling. Then came the synchronized desk pounding and foot stomping.

"Whoa!" our supervisor said. "Everybody calm down. No reason for this! Shhhhhh. Come on now." Then, with the cries still echoing, he headed off as aimlessly as he arrived. Reminding himself to skip that approach in the future.

The sales department worked out of a huge warehouse. How huge? It could probably accommodate a dozen C-5 cargo transports and have room leftover for a Costco, a Walmart and the Goodyear blimp. The company picked up this property for next to nothing and even gets State and Fed tax credits for using it, and additional money for hiring people it doesn't need to keep it clean. We have a huge janitorial staff.

Judging from our surroundings, the place was probably an airbase where they tested nuclear weapons. There isn't a sprig of vegetation within twenty miles of the buildings. We're just out here in the desert, by ourselves, creating screwy greeting cards for bogus occasions that people with sad lives and no friends should buy, but too often manage not to.

So, I get a call to report to Accounting to once again explain the mysterous twists and larky turns of my expense account. Accounting also uses up just a portion of another supersized building away on the other side of "The Campus." I have to drive there; it's like five miles away.

Our entire operation could fit in a corner of one of these garguantuan fever dream hangars. But some nincompoop decided, back in the day, "Hey, we have the room, let's use every goddamn foot of it!"

For shorter trips around The Campus, we have some old golf carts available—or would, if someone (Hey Bill, are you reading this?) would remember to charge the batteries every now and then. These carts are only supposed to be for senior management (who we decided includes Bill and I) and those Board of Directors members who regularly take the trip out here because they still don't trust the mail or bank wire transfers so they come here personally to pick up their quarterly checks. Most Board members are retired military officers or former Congressman in their eighties who double as lobbyists and are relatively worthless at getting our special brand of dim-witted, holiday happiness onto the Federal calendar.

So, as I'm heading out to Accounting, I realized: Accounting is not that far, maybe three miles, from the Art Department. Home of our new, secret best friend, Osgood Wigglesworth.

I wasn't sure what exactly I'd say to him. What if things got ugly? Wigglesworth might be a former cage match fighter who detested interruptions as much as he hated being called "Wigglesworth."

At last, I found his cubie. (The Art Department is the size of a football field.)

He was bent over his drafting table, lost to his surroundings. I opened big. "Wigglesworth!" I shouted. "Blast your worthless hide!"

He jumped a foot in the air and I saw in an instant he was perfect. Fundamentally nervous, overly dressed and fearful of authority. He had a high forehead and prominent ears. You couldn't wish for a better Wigglesworth. There was both shyness and sadness to him. He was obsequious. And the topper: he wore a little red PeeWee Herman tie.

"Where are those sketches of Desi Arnaz for National Hispanic Achievement Day?" I said. "Dammit, Wigglesworth, if you put that market in harm's way, we'll feed you to the hounds and then the wolves, Wigglesworth."

He nodded emphatically and kept muttering, "Yes! Desi Arnaz. Immediately." By the careful way he repeated the name, it seemed apparent Wigglesworth had never seen I Love Lucy. "Yes, sir, I'll get right on it...Desi Arnaz. I'll work from photographs..."

"Well, don't just stand there arguing with me..." I hurried away before he could ask me anything that might be of help to aid in this emergency.

When I got back to Sales, I informed Bill that Wigglesworth was now working for us. "What'll we do with him?"

"We'll think of something," said Bill.

The next morning Bill zeroed in on The Old Wigglie-diggle. He paused at the entrance and did a long slow burn, not unlike Desi gives to Lucy when the trouble she's started has come home to roost.

Then with a growl, Bill cleared his throat and erupted.

"Blast you Wigglesworth! Have you learned nothing of our popular and modern ways?" Bill shouted.

Wigglesworth probably detected the same urgency in Bill's voice as in mine. He appeared to know it was coming from the same place and was prepared.

"Here you go, sir," he said handing Bill prototypes with beautifully rendered drawings. In one, Desi was helping Fred Mertz fix a plumbing problem; Desi was wearing an apron and flipping a hamburger; Desi was helping a blindfolded child strike a pinata; Desi was carefully eating a taco so as not to get any on his new white shirt. He must have been up all night watching reruns, taking notes, and drawing.

This shut Bill up, but not for long. He gave a quick look and was suddenly struck by an inspired reply.

"Why you sneaky bastard! This isn't Desi Arnaz. This is *Ricky Ricardo*. What are you pulling, Wigglesworth, a fast one? Well, you'll not get a fast one past me, you filthy bastard!" said Bill.

"I'm through coddling you. We all are, Wigglesworth, if that really is your name and it's not Peabody or Ignatz Dinglehoover because we're on to that ruse as well. You fix this mess or I'll turn you over to Division, by God, and let them have at you! Believe me, you won't like that one bit. What Division has up their foul sleeve when it comes to dealing with a Sneaky Pete like you, why it makes me shutter and twitch." Bill shuddered and twitched a bit, then left.

Now, what we didn't know was happening, in a building many, many miles away, was the hazing we'd started had been taken up by people who overheard us. It began in the Art Department. Then it spread to Accounting. Even people from the janitorial staff showed up to take some cheap shots at Mr. W.

When I heard of it, my first criticism was on style: they had none. They'd say things like, "Hey, Wigglesworth, you're a tool," and "Hey, stinky, you stink," and "Hi, you stupid moron." That's all they had. Absolutely no thought went into it. It was lazy and rude.

The closest thing to a premise was: blame him for every conceivable wrong that happened to the company. If there was inclement weather that kept people away from card stores, it was his fault. If Hallmark's latest TV show got a decent TV Guide review, it was his fault.

This continued for a while.

Then one day, out for a drive, I was stopped at our one and only four-way stop. There were two cars: me, heading north, and one heading east, surrounded by vast desert. Then I noticed the other driver was Wigglesworth. I waved. He looked awful.

"Hey O.W. How's it going, man? Where are you heading? I've never been up that road.

"Oh, it's you. Tell your pals, espe-

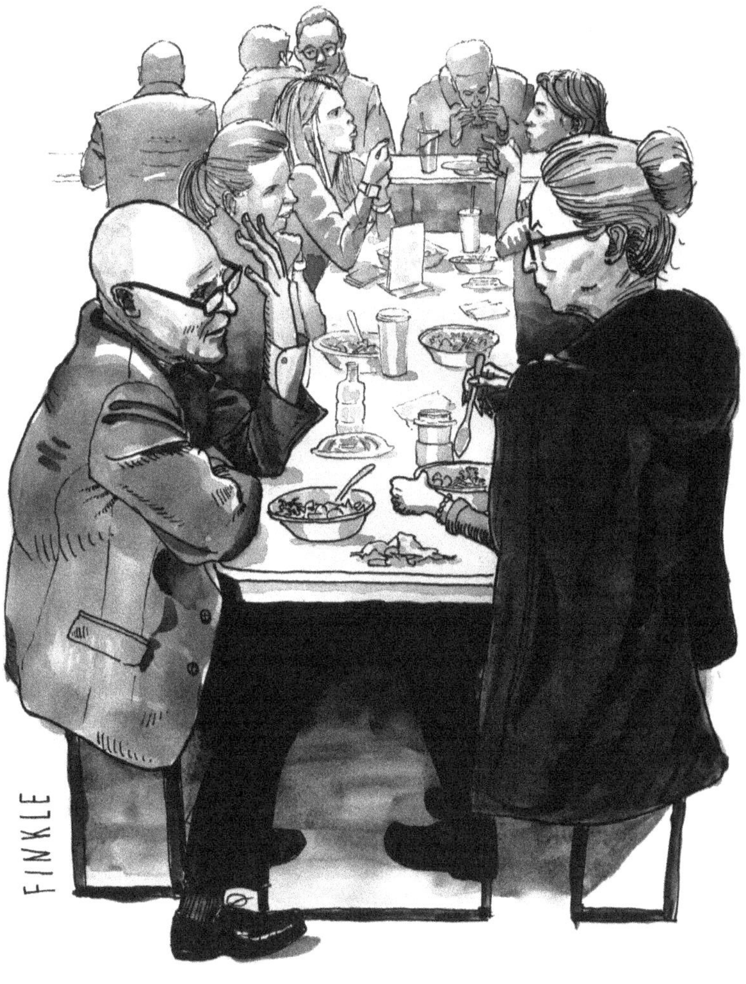
FINKLE

"If I have caffeine in January, I'm up for the rest of the year."

cially that Sputnik Monroe character, it's over. I'm heading to Division myself. I'm not afraid anymore. Things are going to change around here."

"'Division!' Okay," I said, cheering him on. "Yo Division! That's where the big magic happens. I hear ya, O.W. Give 'em hell."

He shot me an odious little look and before I could assure him, "Hey man, I'm on your side," he sped off.

Now there is no, 'Division,' of course. Bill made that up. But I read it as Wigglesworth trying to fight back, in the spirit of things. Good for him. It just might put the kibosh on all the witless needling.

And it did!

Some time later, the CEO of Value-Content Plus, Thaddeus J. Ethalrod, who lived in a gated Florida community and only communicated by e-mail, announced that Osgood Wigglesworth has just been made the head of R & D and would be relocating to Division. He would, from today, report directly to the Chairman.

"Wigglesworth," the CEO wrote, "is a hard-working, multi-talented, brilliant fellow and has some exciting ideas we'll be soon implementing." Then, at the bottom of the e-mail, in a larger typeface: "Sputnik Monroe is ordered to report to Division immediately."

"I don't mean to be rude, but are you Sputnik Monroe?" I asked Bill.

"I was going to ask you the same thing. What do you think he did?"

That afternoon, I took a spin around the Art Department, to see if I could find out some scuttlebutt. Nobody knew anything. Sputnik Monroe, whoever he was, didn't work in the Art Department.

And neither did Wigglesworth. His cubie was cleared out. The only trace of his ever being there were his finely crafted illustrations of Desi Arnaz (or Ricky Ricardo, I forget which) ripped to shreds and still in his wastebasket.

One morning Bill asked me, "Do you think it would be a good time for me to put in for a raise?" He'd already taken it up with our boss and our boss, without even looking up, told him to "take it up with Division. They seem to be running everything these days."

I told Bill he should wait until the vernal equinox lines up with the harmonic convergence, hoping to squeeze a laugh out of him.

"I'm serious," he said. He bombarded me with reasons why Division wouldn't, couldn't refuse him this raise. His numbers were excellent. Our pal, our very own creation, Sir Wiggle -Dee -Doo was being groomed for greatness. Now was the perfect time. But Bill couldn't make himself do it. "I'm terrified," he said.

"You do realize you made up Division? Give yourself a raise."

"Maybe I did and maybe I didn't," Bill said. "But I'll tell you: you don't want to be on the wrong side of history when push comes to shove and Division is the only thing standing between you and the barbarians!" he said.

"Is that from a movie?"

I always saw Bill as a wiser, older brother. I wanted us to be together on this, whatever 'this,' was. But he was clearly rattled, and that rattled me, too.

Then later, another e-mail from Chairman Ethalrod The Annoying. It announced Wigglesworth has been on special assignment and has reported back: if we ever hope to overtake Hallmark, we might need to enlist the help of the American Greeting Card Company. They're an angry people and maybe we can channel some of that, 'anger,' to our benefit.

Hold it. "Overtake Hallmark"?

What demented brain did this escape from? We have a successful philosophy regarding Hallmark. It says: *Keep the Fuck Out of Hallmark's Way Or They'll Beat the Shit Out of You*. We're not particularly proud of the inelegant wording, but it's served us well and kept us in business through good times and bad and now is not the hour to abandon its golden truth. There are plenty of culverts, air shafts and alleyways throughout this great land littered with the teeth, fingers and toes of those who once dared dream the dream they'd like to "Overtake Hallmark."

MAHENDRA SINGH

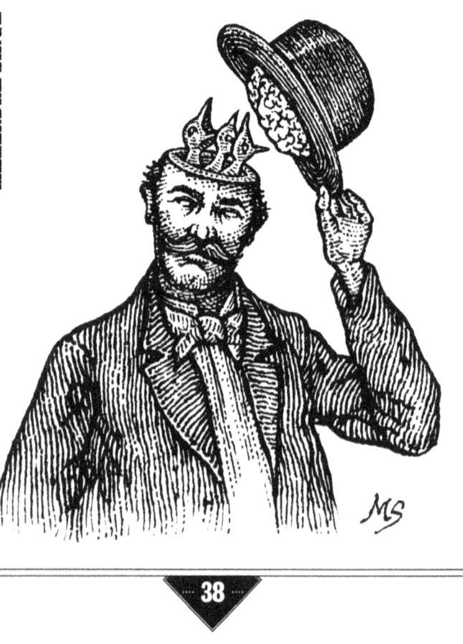
MS

We know AGC are not a pleasant people. There were about sixty of them who showed up and each smelled worse than the one before. They wore ill-fitting uniforms that made them look like they recently escaped from an eighth grade production of *The Yeomen of the Guard*.

Practically overnight Value Content Plus and the Ameican Greeting Card Company struck an alliance. If one was attacked by Hallmark, both would respond in kind. Mostly with baseball bats, pitchforks and rocks for the first assault, then running each other over with cars for the second. I guess? It was not made clear what the boundaries were, which is of concern because AGC is absolutely evil and crazy. We should really join up with Hallmark and elimanate AGC.

But Division felt otherwise. We would be under the command.of AGC, which took little time establishing their authority over us. They sent two platoons and a support group. We were all reassigned to five-member teams.

It didn't matter what your job was before. Each team had to come up with a new holiday; the background of that holiday; create meals to be eaten on that holiday; and make colorful costumes to be worn, and extra holiday uniforms for our senior overseers to wear.

Interestingly, there was no mention of greeting cards. But the message was crystal clear: we were all going to have to sew uniforms—by hand—for these smelly monsters.

The goons from AGC ordered all the walls of our cubbies to come down—there would be no more privacy. "Privacy breeds dirty deeds," they kept reminding us. Also we were not to make any eye contact with our overseers. Such would be a punishable offence. And the classic: only speak when spoken to.

A lot of them carried riding crops, which was pointless. Physical violence will never be an incentive for people at a niche greeting card company, who are frankly having a tough enough time in Life as it is.

Then one morning, the whole company got an email: "Hallmark has gotten word of our alliance," it read, "and they are not happy about it. They claim it's a provocative act." That was alarming, but worse was yet to come. The email was signed "O.S. Wigglesworth, Deputy C.E.O."

One day, a new notice went up, SPUTNIK MONROE DAYS MISSING: 53. BRING US THE FORESKIN OF SPUTNIK MONROE.

I kicked my roll-y chair back from my desk and said to Bill, "Should Mr. Monroe still be in possession of said foreskin, that would seem a bit harsh, wouldn't you agree?"

Bill didn't laugh; he never laughed anymore. He looked gray. "I bet Monroe is long gone by now."

"Gone as in 'escaped,' or gone as in…"

"However you want to take it," Bill said.

A week later a rumor circulated: one of our elderly board members, a retired Army Colonel, age eighty-three, made a fuss about being paid late. His complaining earned him two punches in the stomach and one kick in the pants. Was it true?

It was certainly true that they confiscated all of Cathy Myers's dolls. She's from Accounting and is a total sweetheart. We've all been telling her; let it go and calm down. This will all be over one day.

I found myself thinking, "If I can just speak to Wigglesworth, I think I can walk a lot of this back." Quietly, person-by-person, we put together a small delegation to sneak out of the barracks at night and have a talk with Wigglesworth. But it didn't happen; no one knew where Division was.

I learned a lot. Like, for example: It's really unnerving if you"re trying to thread a needle with one eye shut and the tip of your tongue protruding and …WHAM! Down comes the whip on the table. "FASTER," the goon says, and you try to ignore all the mistakes and go faster. What else are you going to do?

I think that's the kind of thing that made Bill take off. He didn't say anything to me, just one day he wasn't there. To pass the time, I developed a crush on Cathy. I know it can never be. This is just the kind of thing AGC was trying to stop when it removed all the cubies. What a lousy time to fall in love! But the heart will have its way.

So that's where we are today. Bill is still missing. Word is he's hiding in a sewer tunnel under one of the barracks. In a way, I'm glad. I'd hate to see him, a man who once symbolically rode with Lawrence to Aqaba—a man who was a river to his people!— be forced to sew clown clothes for bad people. Yes, my brother, run.

It turns out, I like making capes. I'll tell you something that's pretty universal: Everyone loves wearing a cape. People can deny it all they want. They can jump up and down and swear it's not true, but that won't change anything. You give a man a cape and a gun, and within minutes, he'll be wearing the cape, swooping around, totally ignoring the gun.

Word has it Hallmark has been chartering busses left and right, and they are on their way. They should arrive by tomorrow, around noon. AGC has got us out in the desert, collecting rocks. They are blazing hot. I pick one up, put it in the bag as fast as I can. My thumbs are beginning to blister.

Guess who just rode by? Ol' Wigglesworth! He's on horseback, encouraging us. I had my thumb in my mouth, so I was slow on the salute. Wigglesworth gave me a smart one across the shoulders.

"Sorry," I said. "Picking up these rocks really hurts."

"Certainly it hurts," Wigglesworth said. "The trick is not *minding* that it hurts."

B

"An unbeatable combination– great jokes and great drafts- manship—a rare talent."
—BOB MANKOFF

"This wonderful collection of classic cartoons you will revisit often is a tonic for all humans."
—VICTORIA ROBERTS

"This collection exemplifies draftsmanship and gagmanship and that's what single panel gag cartooning is all about."
—MATT DIFFEE

"God is unfair. He made Kaamran Hafeez able to draw better than me."
—SAM GROSS

NEW FROM SIMON RICH

"One of the funniest writers in America."
—NPR

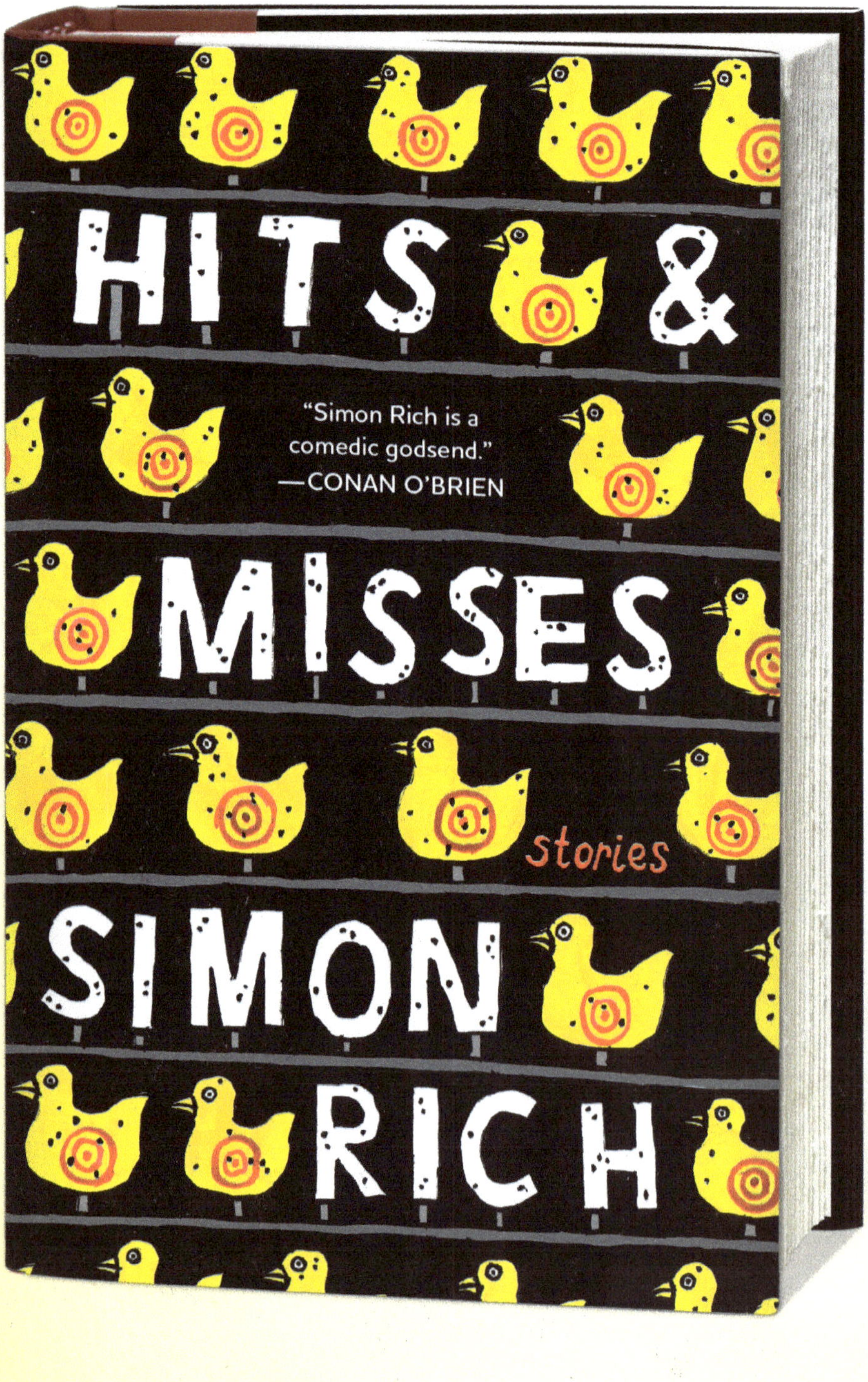

"A motherlode of silly, inventive, absurd brilliance."
—CONAN O'BRIEN

"First-rate comedy with a heartbeat.... One of my favorite authors."
—B.J. NOVAK

"The Stephen King of comedy writing.... HITS AND MISSES is his best collection of stories."
—JOHN MULANEY

ON SALE NOW
in hardcover, ebook, and audio
littlebrown.com

LITTLE, BROWN AND COMPANY
Hachette Book Group

Donald Trump's KGB File

As you might imagine, I get a lot of interesting mail—but what I received the morning of January 12 was unexpected, and extraordinary. The bulging buff-colored envelope had no stamps, and I didn't recognize the handwriting. It had been rolled into a U in order to fit into my narrow mailbox; this had split the envelope open on one side and, as I extracted it, some murkily photocopied typescript peeped out.

"Oh, God," I thought. "Another novel."

I swear, I almost threw it out. But I freelanced far too long to be so cavalier about another person's dreams, so I took the file upstairs…and that's when my life changed forever.

It was a dossier on, of all people, Donald J. Trump. In reports and photos, cocktail napkins and birthday cards, the sheaf of documents was nothing less than a secret history of the tycoon's life. But why send it to a humor magazine? When I saw the letterhead of the KGB, I understood: plausible deniability. "But General, if I were going to leak our files, why would I send them to a print humor magazine? In 2019? I don't know if you've heard, but there is this thing called 'the internet…'"

And there was another advantage: Because no sane person would possibly believe the file to be real, no official would have to address it. Meanwhile journalists could swarm over the dossier like hungry ants, confirming this and that—maybe one would find the nugget that would cause Trump to resign. Because you can be sure that, outside of the corner office, there are plenty of Russians who are praying for just that event; after all, they're the poor jamokes all our missiles are pointed at.

But here's the problem—I can't keep secrets, it's too stressful. And I thought of my partners; though Brian might enjoy having his phone tapped, Alan is, like me, more nervous. I imagined him jerking awake, suddenly convinced that someone had put C-4 in his violin. So I sealed the envelope back up, and stuffed it right back into the box, with a handwritten suggestion: "Try *Private Eye*."

But the next morning, it was back. And the morning after that, and the morning after that. Clearly, whoever owned this file really wanted me to have it; after all, they'd even translated it into English. Reluctantly, I cursed my fate and began to read.

Was Donald Trump an early target of Operation SCROOGE? Does SCROOGE even exist? Or am I just writing a bunch of bullshit, as is my wont? These questions are unanswerable. One thing is clear: Donald Trump is, for all his grotesqueness, a reflection of the society around him. Seeing how we got here shows, perhaps, the quickest way back out.

The following is a narrative based on the file, presented without any assertion of authenticity; you probably shouldn't believe a word of it. In this era of official mendacity and rampant conspiracy theory, where everyone is entitled to an opinion, and a bunch of idiots with Photoshop can make anything look real, there is really only one sensible course of action: whatever you do, keep one hand on your wallet. (And if you're near the President, use both.)

Codename: SCROOGE

On July 4, 1976, KGB chief Yuri Andropov dispatched a secret memo. "On this melancholy anniversary," it began, "we must acknowledge that a change in strategy is necessary. Since we cannot outproduce capitalism, we should attempt to encourage it. If our Main Adversary is to win this Cold War, let us help her win herself to death."

This gambit—cleverly codenamed "Operation SCROOGE"—followed the lines of Dickens' novella. First, a miserly and corrupt oligarchy would be established. As this consolidated its power, the rest of society would, as usual, suffer increasing injustice, poverty, and hopelessness. "Then, as in Russia, as in Cuba," wrote the spy chief, "the ghosts of Marx and Lenin will naturally appear, showing a better way." Andropov outlined a simple three-step strategy. Step one: identify the stupidest, greediest rich people in the West. Two: create cut-out organizations—clubs and conventions, magazines and PACs—where these lucre-marinated buffoons could meet, nurse each other's petty grievances, cultivate a rip-roaring sense of victimhood, and luxuriate in all-encompassing ignorance. Three: the KGB would provide secret money and publicity, so that these truly bad ideas and people could leave their mark, like an ill-drawn, infected tattoo upon America's soul.

It was a chillingly simple plan. Agents dispersed, and the wheels began to turn.

It's a really good thing that **Michael Gerber** *didn't end up working for the CIA.*

A "Wet-Eyed Do-Gooder"

According to the File, Donald J. Trump first came to the attention of Soviet intelligence in late 1976, when Roy Cohn spotted him in the men's room of Studio 54, collecting funds for UNICEF. Cohn, who had been a Soviet asset since his senior year at Columbia, initially dismissed the real estate scion as "a tall, blonde Doris Day-type interested only in peace and Christian charity."[1] But as Moscow increased the pressure on the notorious lawyer (he had a habit of expensing poppers), Cohn began to see a new usefulness in the softhearted young man. "If a wet-eyed do-gooder like young Trump can be turned," Cohn wrote his handler, "our methods would be proven."

Andropov reluctantly agreed. To prove the worth of SCROOGE, Donald J. Trump would be transformed, Pygmalion-like, into the Worst Person in the World.

But Who *Was* He?

As was usual, the KGB made Trump a "subject of deep study" (*obyekt razrabotki*), compiling an extensive analysis of the young man's upbringing and character. Delivered in December 1976, this portion of the File shows a man very different from the Donald Trump we know. "Subject was an uncommonly kind, intelligent child," a KGB analyst wrote. Teachers, manservants, t-ball opponents all agreed: 'Donnie' Trump was generous, well-loved by his classmates, and sensitive to a fault. At five, he once stayed up all night 'in case a cat got stuck in a tree.' At six, Donnie announced his determination to send his ant farm to college, then wept bitterly when he was informed that insects were not eligible. "Episodes of *Howdy Doody*," say the File, "often worried young Trump to the point of emesis." And his letters to Mouseketeer Annette Funicello "reveal a feminist streak that has only grown in recent years."

The File reprints a letter written by his mother, where she worries over her young son. "How can my Donnie possibly survive in this world?" Elizabeth Trump wrote her sister. "Such guilelessness, such compassion. When the world weeps, he weeps with it...Perhaps military school?"

Athletics were an early interest, though subject showed an "almost morbid interest in fair play. An excellent baseball player, Trump was frequently reprimanded for trying to manipulate the game into a tie."

Though less talented academically, Trump studied hard, preparing for a life of service, perhaps in the Peace Corps or as a Cistercian monk. "His inherited wealth was a source of embarrassment, and in frequent clashes with his fiercely counterrevolutionary father, young Trump often threatened to drive down 125th Street, giving it all away." Even more scandalous was his lively correspondence with both Malcolm X and Martin Luther King; when Fred Trump found out that he was enclosing four-figure checks, Donnie was summarily packed off to military school.

Surprisingly, this did not dampen the young man's essential nature, nor did stints at Fordham and Wharton after that. When the rest of his Wharton class was conniving ways to climb capitalism's greasy pole, "Trump spent most of his time playing bass in a ska band, and hatching quixotic, whimsical business ideas." The File mentions a strange, plosive sort of Muzak for bathrooms, designed to mask the sound of flatulence.

"He is possessed of unlimited intellectual curiosity," his old French poetry professor unwittingly told an agent. "Donnie Trump questions everything—himself most of all. This openness and generosity explains why he is so beloved by his peers."

In its summary, the KGB concluded that Donald J. Trump was "a thoughtful, compassionate, fun-loving sort, with rock-solid morals and a love of musical theater." To turn him into SCROOGE material would require an entire rebuilding of his personality and values.

Ivana Appears

The first step was obvious. At 29, Trump was still a virgin; as he passionately wrote Cohn in a thank you note, "I believe that sexuality is sacred, only to be shared within the bounds of matrimony." Cohn's response is not recorded, but within weeks Ivana Zelnicknova had come to New York and insinuated herself into Trump's daily routine. According to the File, Zelnicknova is some sort of cyborg, containing DNA from humans, a Thomson's gazelle, some knock-off Balenciaga, and a slot machine. Grown in a secret lab, then inserted into the thriving cyborg community of Montreal, she was ready to party for the Party. Young Trump, surrounded by the free-love 1970s and suffering from almost unimaginable sexual frustration, was an easy mark. They married in April, 1977.

The Early 1980s

The Trumps lived quietly, shunning publicity, concentrating on anonymous charity and other good works. Trump entered the family business almost by default. His real estate deals—a derelict hotel, a skating rink—had an element of civic-mindedness, but seemed to not to hold the man's ever-restless intellect. He flitted from passion to passion: rockclimbing, aromatherapy, Sufism. The File shows young Trump "struggling with the problems and, ultimately, the morality of his privilege." In 1982, prior to his first appearance on the *Forbes* List, Trump wrote a letter to that magazine's publisher, begging for his removal. "I find the whole thing utterly distasteful," Trump wrote. "I'm just in the Lucky Sperm Club. Please take me out."

Malcolm Forbes, a SCROOGE asset, declined.[2]

Trump's natural shyness was a constant annoyance to Cohn and his KGB paymasters, who endlessly threw media Trump's way, in an attempt to kindle a taste for self-promotion. Their only notable success, an interview with Rona Barrett, was conducted via hidden camera under false pretenses. (Ivana's IUD-mic confirmed Trump's confusion: "I thought she was a Jehovah's Witness."

---

[1] Cohn was the first, but far from the only, victim of a highly successful honeypot operation. Students caught in the second floor men's room of Butler Library were given a stark choice: spy for Russia or be exposed as a homosexual. Working from the inside, the darkly brilliant Cohn ensured that the Red-hunts of the 1950s caught no spies, but were highly effective at turning Americans against each other, generating hatreds that last to this day.

[2] Real name: Sergei "Scooter" Sokolov.

MIKE LOEW

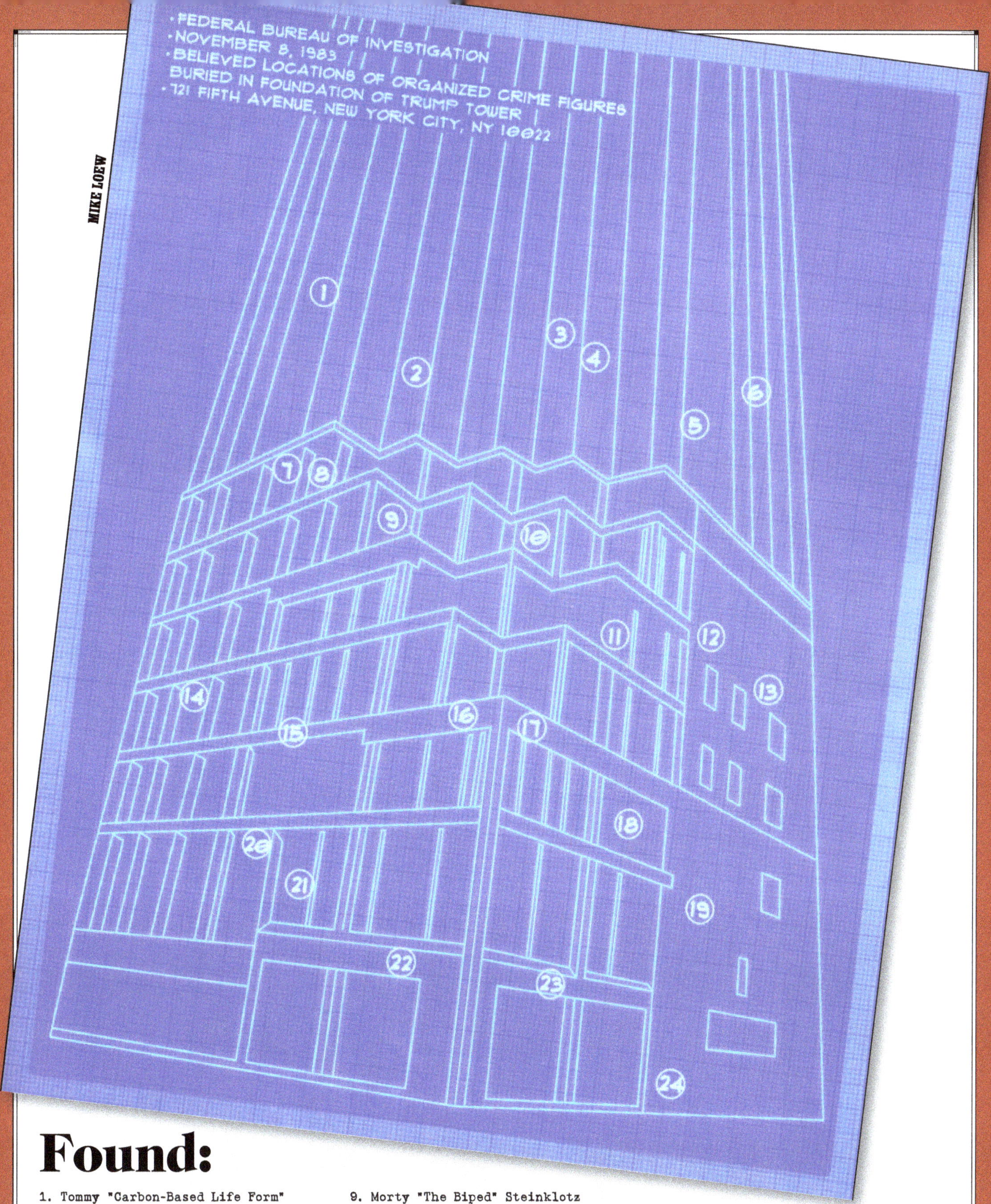
•FEDERAL BUREAU OF INVESTIGATION
•NOVEMBER 8, 1983
•BELIEVED LOCATIONS OF ORGANIZED CRIME FIGURES
BURIED IN FOUNDATION OF TRUMP TOWER
•721 FIFTH AVENUE, NEW YORK CITY, NY 10022

Found:

1. Tommy "Carbon-Based Life Form" McGee
2. Donny "Abstract Expressionism" Bertelli
3. Louie "Quotation Marks" Denunzio
4. Johnny "Gynecomastia" Feeny
5. Teddy "Bechdel Test" Ribiero
6. Paulie "Ethnic Type" Gustafson
7. Ricky "Nickname TBD" Cardozo
8. Ned "Malaise Speech" Koppelman
9. Morty "The Biped" Steinklotz
10. Harry "Self Esteem" Nakashiri
11. Mikey "Heirloom Tomatoes" Perlstein
12. Larry "Best Practices" Morelli
13. Tony "Glacial Moraine" Chen
14. Shecky "FBI Informant" Van Cleef
15. Sol "Not For Profit" Farnsworth
16. Mitch "Habsburg Empire" Connolly
17. Bobby "Late Onset" Proxmire
18. Marty "Mid-Century Modern" Zunino
19. Tiny "Existential Dread" Farina
20. Frankie "Benelux Countries" Leary
21. Bert "Cautiously Optimistic" Gowalski
22. Lonnie "Number 22" Raffa
23. Dickie "Ineffable Longing" Carlyle
24. Butchie "Butterfly Effect" Verdana

--Steve Young

Ivana's response? "You are idiot.")

Trump's aversion to self-promotion wasn't the only source of friction in the young marriage. Well into his thirties, "Donnie" returned from every walk in the neighborhood with empty pockets and a stray animal or two, until the no-nonsense Czech was forced to take his wallet. (He did not find it until 1984.) The File shows Trump to be a supportive, caring father, always available to his children. He doted especially on Don Jr., who the File says suffers from "catastrophic frontal lobe atrophy." The File also notes the following: "Trump's relationship with his daughter Ivanka is entirely appropriate."

All who knew Trump during this period note his shy, easygoing manner, and self-deprecating sense of humor. "We must remove all of this, every scrap," a KGB analyst wrote. "We must demolish—nay obliterate—this man with The Process."

Enter: "The Process"

It is unclear precisely what "The Process" entailed, but from context it appears that it involved classic Soviet behavior-mod techniques: disorientation via chemicals, sleep deprivation, and aversion therapy. In 1979, the Trumps began attending "couples' weekends" at a fictitious address in Amagansett; it is believed this was the setting for the procedure.

"Subject was shown standard American PSAs like, 'Friendship—pass it on!'", a Dr. Yevchenko wrote, "with the heartwarming message accompanied by severe electric shock." Diet Coke was installed as a trigger for automatic behavior: "Upon tasting it, subject becomes abusive, illogical and belligerent." Nonsensical hatreds were planted, initially for obscure nationalities unlikely to cross Trump's path, then later for other, more common groups.

Returning to Manhattan, an exhausted, disoriented Trump would sleep for 36 hours straight—but even then The Process continued. According to the File, "housecleaners were hired to enter Trump's bedroom and whisper 'people are jerks' and 'if there's grass on the field, play ball' into his ear while he slept."

Two Prongs

Donald Trump was far from the only asset involved in Operation SCROOGE. Throughout the late 1970s, KGB agents were everywhere, laying the groundwork for "the decisive decade."

Though the Soviets were not behind the youth-led reform movements of the 60s—they saw these as a threat to their own power—after the Prague Spring, Soviet spy services had begun surreptitiously introducing various chemicals into the counterculture, hoping to sap its energy. One chemical in particular was tailor-made for Operation SCROOGE; in the words of the File, it is "expensive, glamorous, and highly addictive. It creates paranoia, delusions of grandeur, and unwatchable movies." We know it as cocaine.

By the late 1970s, SCROOGE had built coke into a blizzard stretching from the barrios of Miami to the editing suites of Hollywood. The social contract weakened, and America's population of assholes grew faster than at any time since Reconstruction, causing the designation to be added to the 1980 U.S. Census.

For those too old or temperamentally unsuited to "nose candy" (a term coined by KGB linguists), SCROOGE offered something even more deadly: Ronald Reagan.[3] Here is not the place to debate the merits and demerits of that politician, but it is clear that, as with Thatcher in England, his me-first, deficit-fueled conservatism was perfectly tuned to the objectives of the KGB.

The File is uncharacteristically brief on the 40th President, but given Reagan's general mental state, we can assume that he was an unwitting asset. However the File does repeat a tantalizing public fact: in 1937, the young actor applied to be a member of the Communist Party, but was turned down for being "as dumb as a bag of hammers and sickles."

This is almost certainly a cover story. What is indisputable is that on November 4, 1980, that bag of hammers and sickles became President of the United States, and SCROOGE's "decisive decade" had begun.

---

[2]Real name: Lavrenty Bogomolov, born in Odessa, 1909.

"My mind is a failing department store."

Almost immediately, friends and colleagues began noticing bizarre changes in Trump. Most notable was an obsession with the Bonwit-Teller building on Fifth Avenue. A school chum met Trump in early 1980; his memories are reproduced in the File. "This wasn't the Donnie I knew. First, he insisted that I call him 'Donald,' and whenever I forgot he charged me $20. My friend was a funny fella, light, easygoing, but this Donald guy was *angry*—he kept talking about 'the fucking Andalusians,' which I didn't quite understand. And we met at a strip club rather than J.G. Melon, which was…Look, when I say Donnie was 'a straight arrow,' he was the kind of guy who filed his taxes on January 1. Payment in full.

"Anyway, we're at this strip club, and 'Donald' kept asking the dancers for change—who does that? We ended up getting thrown out…I just don't know what happened to him. Donnie was the first person to quote Rumi to me. He was an evolved dude. Now, he's taking a swing at some bartender because they don't have Heineken?"

But that wasn't the strangest part of the evening. "All night, he kept saying, 'I'm nothing without Bonwit-Teller, I am Bonwit-Teller.' That really shook me up. I mean, hello? *Brooks Brothers?*"

The KGB File clears up the mystery. According to Dr. Yevchenko, "We have implanted a suggestion that the subject's entire personality is represented by the Bonwit-Teller building." In 1979, KGB agents had purchased that building on behalf of the Trump Organization; in 1980, suddenly, it was demolished.

Dr. Yevchenko reported complete success. "As that building was pulled down, subject lay in his office in the fetal position, weeping and gibbering as his old personality was being destroyed… Now that Trump is 'a vacant lot,' we can erect anything we wish. P.S. Please send three copies of *Frampton Comes Alive* to my wife via diplomatic pouch."

The USFL

With his KGB-built personality now firmly in place, Trump was ready for his first assignment.

In 1982, a team of SCROOGE psychographic clinicians wrote that "a majority of American men have a deeper emotional connection to NFL football than to their own family…If we can weaken that sport, we can create a psychological vacuum, which we can fill with anything." According to the File, they hoped to shift fan loyalty from the players or region to, of all things, the owner. "Only the most physically gifted can realistically dream of being a professional ballplayer. But any idiot can think, 'Someday I too will be rich.'" This type of magical thinking proved irresistible to Americans.

The massive success of plutocrat-porn like *Dallas* and *Lifestyles of the Rich and Famous*—both developed by secret SCROOGE production companies deep in the Urals—had generated oodles of cash. This was plowed into Trump's new football team. "We wish to insinuate Trump, virus-like, into the NFL. Once this occurs, it will surely sicken and die, dealing a devastating blow."

Luckily, NFL Commissioner Pete Rozelle had other ideas. So Moscow switched to Plan B: a lawsuit filed by Roy Cohn. It was thanks only to Cohn's failing health—his anal warts had spread to the brain—that the NFL emerged unscathed.

"Our Man in Atlantic City"

For the first time, people inside the KGB began voicing doubts about Trump. "The Upper East Side is full of idiots," wrote a spy in the New York rezidentura. "Visit J.G. Melon on any Saturday night!" But the father of Operation SCROOGE, Yuri Andropov, had recently become head of the Soviet Union, and he still believed in Donald J. Trump.

SCROOGE assets inside every New York daily were ordered to keep this man in the public eye. And at Andropov's personal behest, a single question echoed through the Kremlin: What is the easiest business in America? According to the File, opinions were mixed. "Beef," one analyst wrote. "I visited for two weeks in 1957 and my colon still hurts." "Selling vodka. You cannot lose money selling booze." But the winner was gambling. "You're not even selling a product, you're just selling hope. And when it comes to hope, Americans are suckers."

There was another benefit: some in Moscow believed that Trump's morality was not decaying fast enough; gaming would bring him into contact with even worse people. One thing was for sure, whatever was left of nice old "Donnie Trump," would die on the gritty, failure-soaked sands of Atlantic City.

In one of the last acts before his death in February 1984, Andropov authorized "a blank check" to install Trump in that flyblown resort town. "What's the worst that can happen?" Andropov joked. "He can't bankrupt the entire Soviet Union."

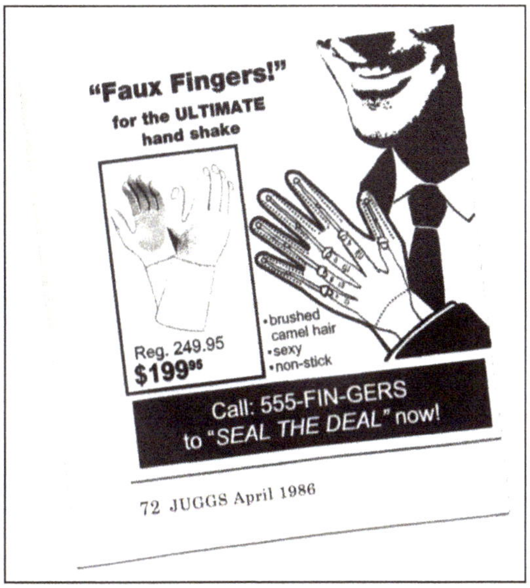
"Faux Fingers!"
for the ULTIMATE hand shake
Reg. 249.95
$199.95
•brushed camel hair
•sexy
•non-stick
Call: 555-FIN-GERS to "SEAL THE DEAL" now!
72 JUGGS April 1986

To entice Trump to Moscow, the KGB placed this ad in magazines throughout the West. The one in **Juggs** *bore fruit.*

The Art of the Deal

With the death of its patron and the emergence of Mikhael Gorbachev, Operation SCROOGE went on a back burner. But as with so many intelligence operations, the longer an activity is funded, the more it seems to get a life of its own. And there is no denying that SCROOGE had been a tremendous success; greed was now good, and the cult of the CEO had taken root.

Even so, as of 1986, "The Donald" was a New York phenomenon, a cheesy, localized irritant, like Sbarro. Trump's handlers were looking for something to make their tabloid-fueled Frankenstein a truly national monster—but they had to do it on the cheap. So they hit upon a classic solution: they would have Trump write a book. Through strategic purchasing, the Soviets could make sure it reached the bestseller list and stayed there.

Getting a book deal was easy; getting the book written, however, was harder. The File reveals that Trump initially insisted on writing it all himself, but gave up after writing a single chapter. A ghostwriter was hired, and *The Art of the Deal* was born.

This was, perhaps SCROOGE's greatest Trump-specific success: the creation of an entirely fraudulent persona built around competence and glamour that simply never existed. "There is one puzzling aspect of the book," The New York Times wrote in its mostly positive review. "For one chapter, all Trump's boasting and bragging stops. Instead, page after page reads, "All work and no play makes Donald a dull boy.' It is a puzzling error."

This was no error; it was the one section of the book Donald Trump actually wrote. And it was left in by someone back in Moscow, hoping to scuttle the operation.

JFK-SVO

By this time, many in the Kremlin had turned against Operation SCROOGE. Some believed that the covert plumping for plutocracy had become too successful, that it might infect the Soviet Union itself.

"I just saw something called 'bottled water,'" an analyst wrote. "It frightens me. We must end Andropov's mad dream, before it destroys us all."

Plans were made to lure Donald Trump to the Soviet Union for liquidation. Throughout 1986, advertisements offering "Painless Finger Extension Surgery" had been placed in certain downmarket men's magazines; in early 1987 the KGB's London mail drop contained a letter from one "John Barron, large-handed private citizen," expressing interest. To set the hook still further, TASS released a story to *The New York Times*: "In Medical First, Soviet Transplants Chimp's Hands to Human." The real estate magnate was on the phone with the embassy that very morning.

In a stroke of Slavic irony, Trump

would land at Sheremetyevo Airport on July 4th, eleven years to the day of the announcement of Operation SCROOGE.

So how did Donald Trump survive? It seems clear that there was another faction whose strength was building: younger, mid-level officials who saw Russia's capitalist future, and wanted to break off a piece for themselves. Foremost among these was a young KGB officer by the name of Vladimir Putin.[4]

Donald Trump was blissfully ignorant of the lethal infighting that swirled around him. Sitting in the Lenin Suite of the National Hotel, he sent a postcard to his mother. "So much more advanced here. You order room service by talking into the flowers."

The File reproduces fully two pages of newspaper clippings, detailing all the near-misses suffered by the tycoon and his party during his time in Moscow: a limo with suddenly failing brakes; a burly "maid" who dropped a hairdryer into his tub; an encounter with a cobra at a fancy restaurant; a hunting accident which killed his translator; a falling safe which killed his other translator. During each incident, Trump was saved from harm by "a young man on vacation from East Germany"—Vladimir Putin.

Trump left Moscow a week later, with neither a new hotel or new fingers—but a new friend, and a new plan: political office. Andropov's dream would live on.

"Siberia Is Full."

In the years following his trip to Moscow, Donald Trump became a fixture in American culture, to the annoyance of nearly everybody…including, it seems, his handlers in the KGB. They began calling him 'The Mushroom,' in an apparent reference to his genitalia.

Take, for example, Trump's infamous 1989 *New York Times* ad castigating the so-called "Central Park Five." On it, an anonymous Russian analyst has written almost plaintively, "Is there such a thing as *too* racist?"

By this time it was so difficult to find agents willing to work with Trump that the Kremlin was having to offer them a stark choice: "'Mushroom' or Siberia." However, within six months even this dire threat had lost all effect; so many KGB operatives were choosing work camps over the tycoon that memos begain sporting the following terse inkstamp: "*Nyet.* Siberia is full."

The End of the KGB… But Not SCROOGE?

In 1991, the Soviet Union dissolved, and with it went the KGB. But the sheaf of documents packed into my mailbox yielded a few items from the years after the USSR. The photo above (clearly taken after January 2017) and the material on the following pages beg the question: *Is the KGB File only the beginning?*

Trump's activities seem fishy in the extreme; take, for example, his 1995 advertisement for Pizza Hut, the fast food chain founded in 1904 by Josef Stalin's brother Jesof. Upon viewing this, some in the Kremlin doubtless regretted the brainwashing of Donald Trump. It is a tale as old as Time—that of a monster broken free from its creator, wreaking havoc, eating pizza.

As their wispy-haired Frankenstein crashed about the globe, losing millions and rubbing Drakkar Noir on dry-heaving models, there is ample evidence to suggest that Operation SCROOGE also shambled on. There is, of course, Pizza Hut's 1998 pro-capitalist followup, starring Mikhail Gorbachev. And Trump's own *Apprentice* is textbook SCROOGE, a masterful psyop where millions of indebted proles wile away their scant leisure time rooting for someone else to get fired. Oh the irony.

However, the most ironic development of all was saved for the former Soviet Union itself. As this article shows, SCROOGE adroitly encouraged the West to worship Toxic Narcissist Capitalism. But the Soviets themselves proved even more suspectible, and soon their frostbitten, sclerotic worker's paradise was replaced by a gangster-inflected oligarchy not seen since the days of Czar Nicholas II. In bringing down its "Main Adversary," the Soviet Union brought down itself.

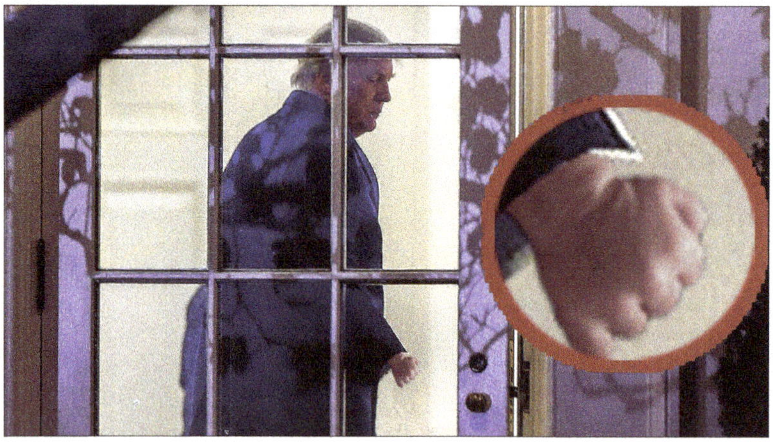

This photo was on the last page of the File, suggesting that a vast trove of material—including Trump's Presidency—remains to be leaked.

LARRY DOYLE

"A Ghoulish Fantasy"

Immediately after reading through my mysterious package, I spent 20 foot-numbing hours down at the Santa Monica Public Library making a copy, which I then sent to an old college friend—Skull and Bones, CIA, sword-cane, that type of guy. For six months I didn't hear anything; but then, again, I didn't really expect to. As I said earlier, I'm not good at keeping secrets. Discreet people tend to ignore me, and I don't blame them. Then, last week, I got a letter. On official letterhead, he acknowledged receipt of "the item," then coldly dismissed it all.

"Clearly you have not matured since your days Lettrasetting people's asses for Yale's humor magazine. Are you trying to be funny? This whole thing is preposterous, a ghoulish fantasy unfit for serious discussion. (And yes, I've seen the Pizza Hut ads.)"

That it may be. The whole File could be Russian disinformation. I would be the last to know; I'm just a comedy writer. But if it is all lies, that raises a far more preposterous, ghoulish alternative: *that we did it to ourselves.*

I take no comfort in that. B

[4] Putin's first appearance in the File is as a guest at Eric Trump's sixth birthday party, which was faked by Stanley Kubrick.

Trumple the Turtle

On Christmas 2014, Donald Trump gave Ivanka a very special gift. The FSB was listening.

EBENEZER/ORANGE/2-"BEZEL"/VIA POUCH/TOP SECRET

KOMPROMAT GIFT TO DAUGHTER WIFE -- 26 Dekabr 2014, 13:40 EST
Conversation between poleznyi durak TRUMP and daughter-wife IVANKA, captured 17:30 EST on 24 Dekabr 2014, through "Best American of 2012" Trophy
(NOTE: Annabelle is daughter-wife's daughter, aged 3.)

DURAK: But it's for Merry Christmas, okay, not for Hookah.
DAUGHTER-WIFE: Hannukah, Daddy.
DURAK: That's what I said. But this is a gift from Baby Jesus. Me, but also Baby Jesus, but mostly me.
[wrapping paper crumpling]
DURAK: I was gonna get the guy, the doctor, Spock or whatever, but he's dead, apparently. This guy did a terrible job, but it's the thought. And it cost five grand. Well, it would've but he's not getting a dime. Because just look at that shit. Anyway, Merry Christmas!
DAUGHTER-WIFE: Oh, Daddy! Annabelle is going to love this!
[seven seconds of silence]
DURAK: Oh, yeah. It's for her.

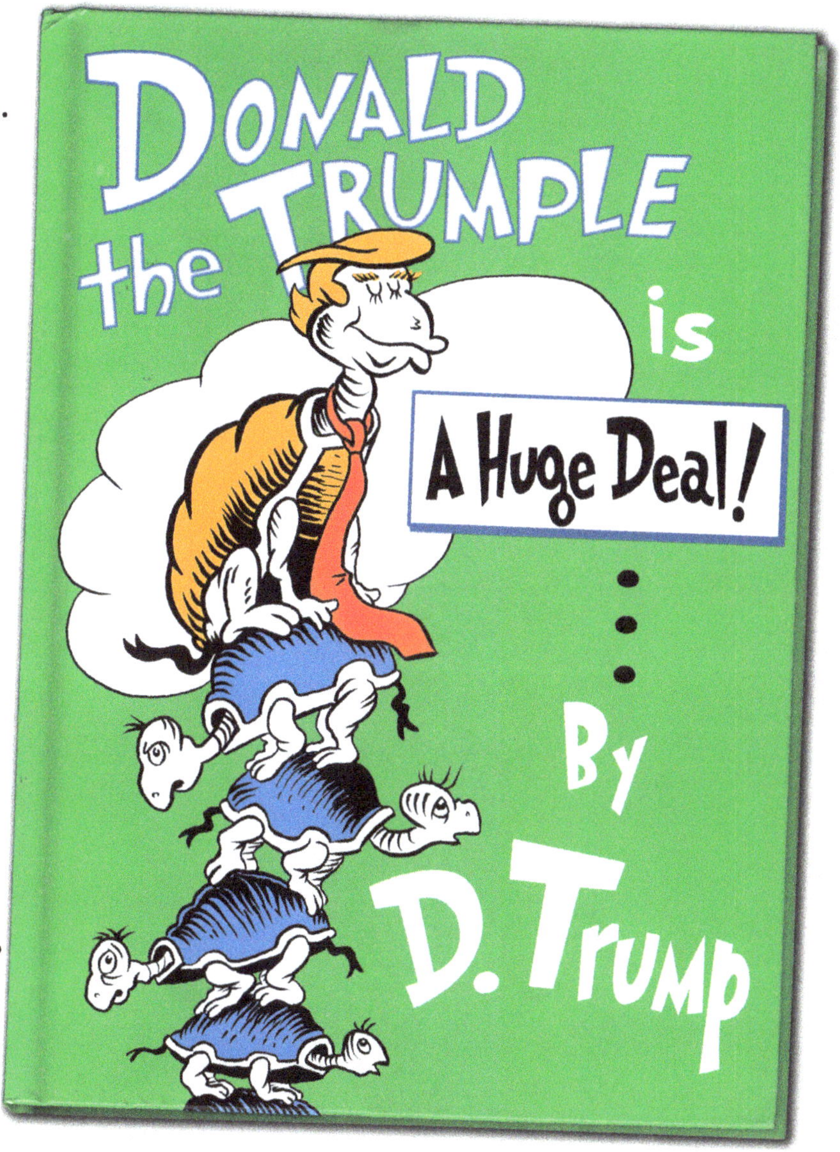
Donald the Trumple is
A Huge Deal!
By
D. Trump

Komprompat recovered from trash chute of 502 Park Avenue, New York City, NY, USA at 01:45 EST on 24 Dekabr 2014.

END

Photoshoppin' by MIKE LOEW

Larry Doyle *wrote for* The Simpsons *and* The New Yorker, SPY *and* The National Lampoon. Cultural Jet Lag *co-creator* **Jim Siergey***'s cartoons and illustrations have appeared everywhere from* TIME *to the Jumbotron at Comiskey Park.*

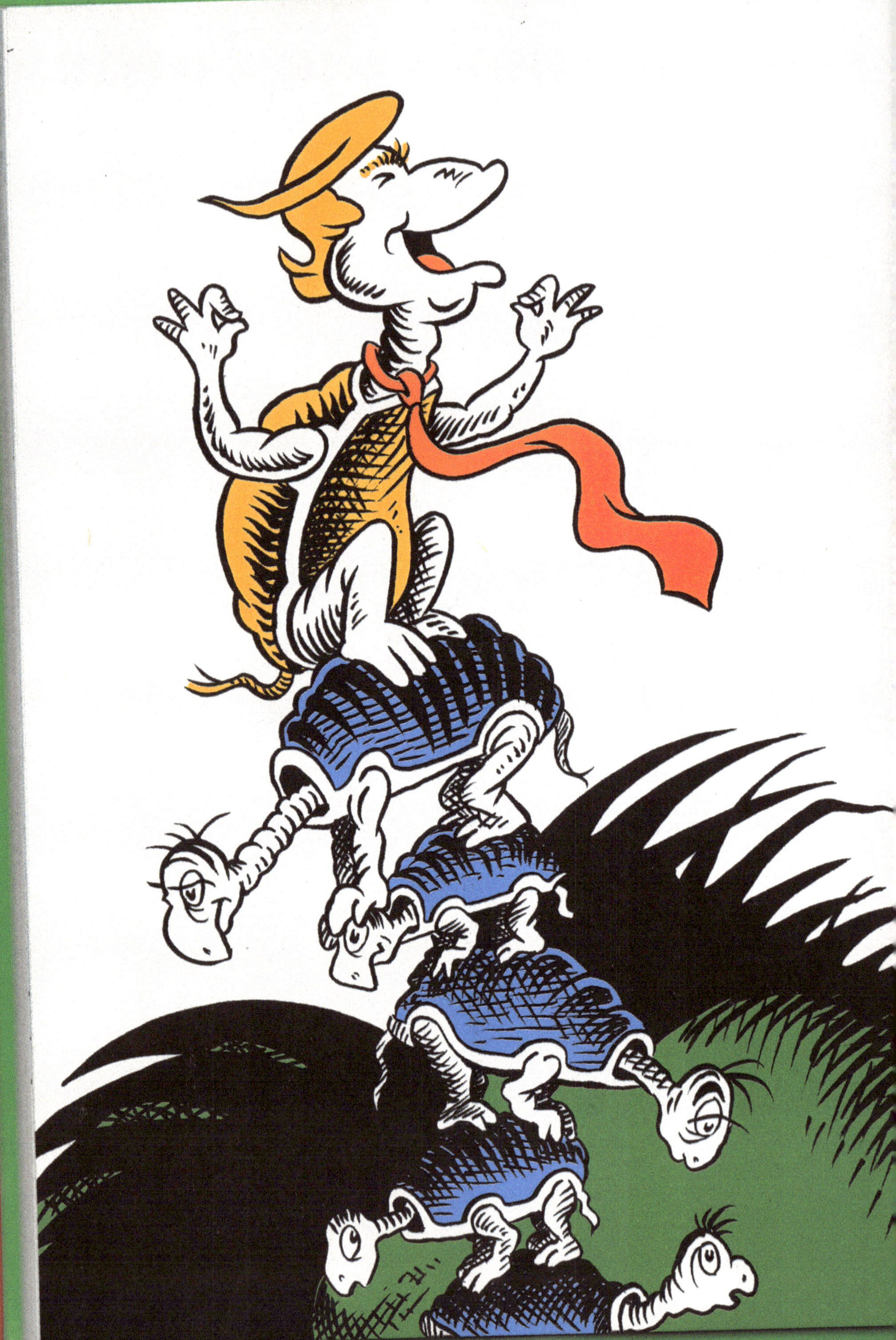

"All mine!" the Donald cried. "Oh, the Things I now Rule!
I'm the King of the Deal! And I'm the King of a mule!
I'm the King of Trump Tower! And, what's more, beyond that
I'm the King of Mar-A-Lago, the Crown Jewel of Palm Beach,
Accepting applications for the coming year, and a cat!
I'm Donald the Trumple! Oh, marvelous me!
For I am the Ruler of all that I see!"

And all through the morning, he sat there up high
Saying over and over, "The Best King am I!"
Until 'long about noon. Then he heard a faint sigh.
"What's that?" snapped the King
And he looked down the stack.
And he saw, at the bottom, that turtle Barack.
Just a part of his throne. And this brown little turtle
Looked up and he said, "Beg your pardon, King Trumple.
I can't work, I've got these spurs in my feets.
Just give me my check, I don't have to say please."

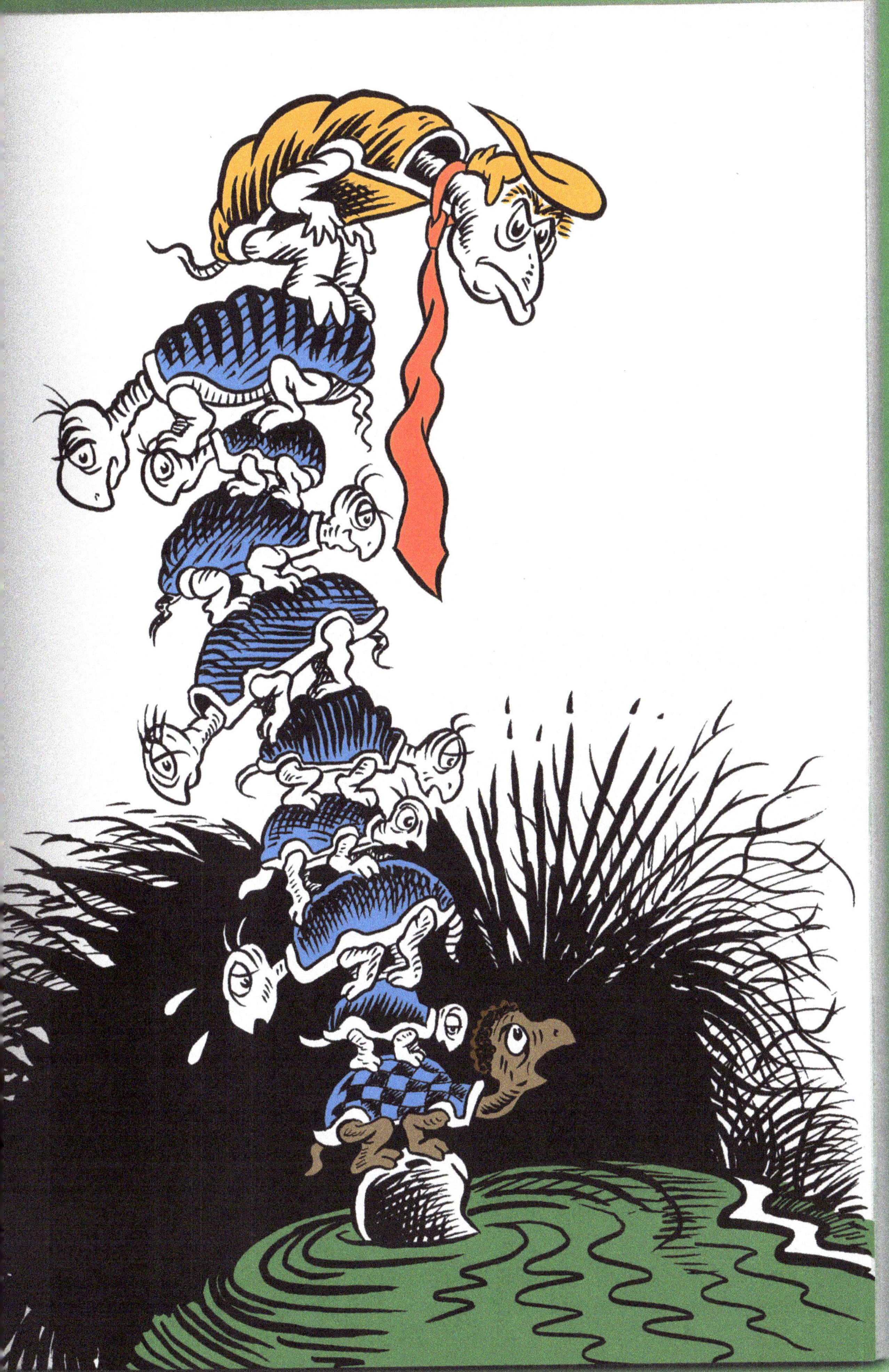

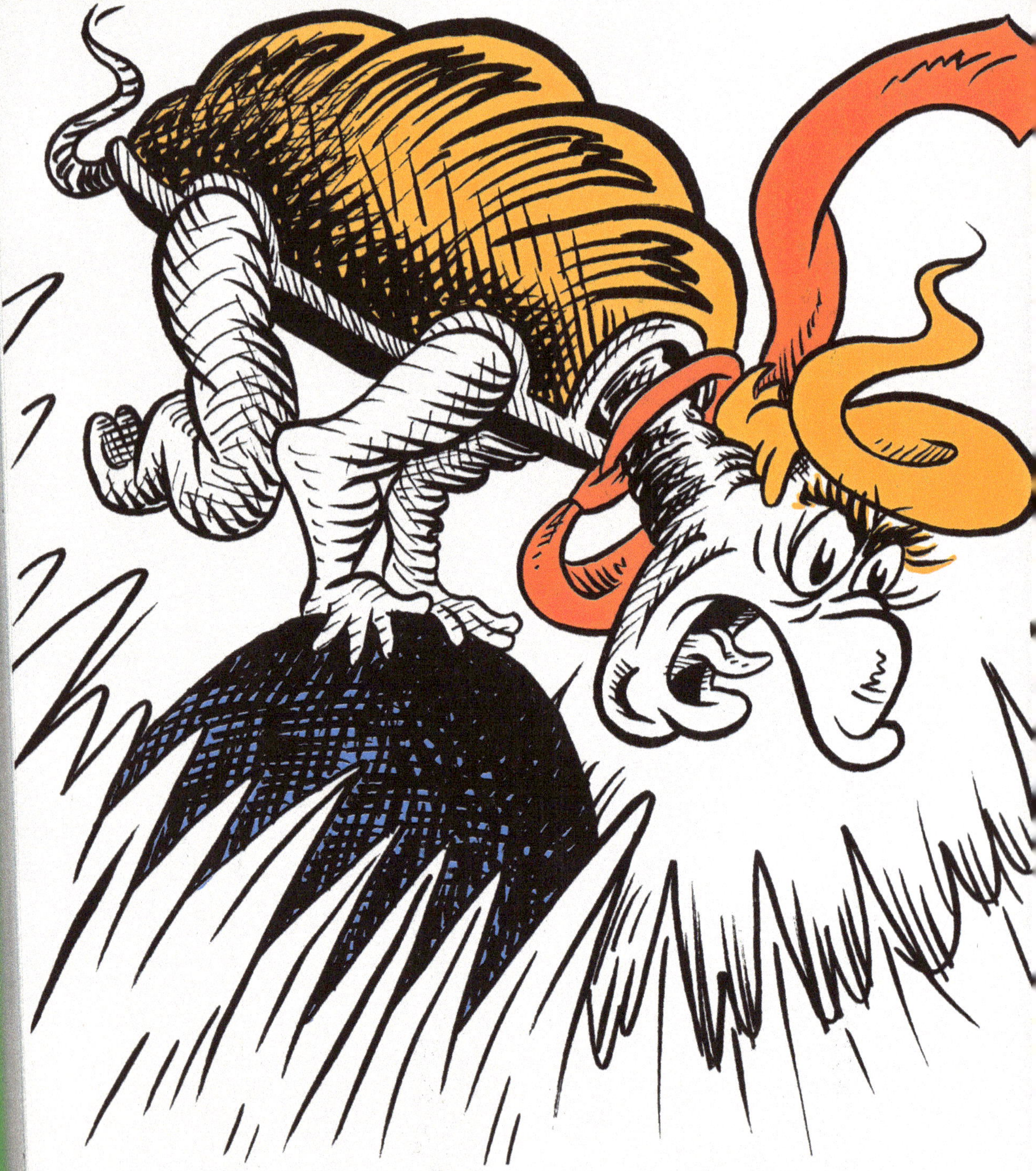

"SILENCE!" the King of the Turtles barked back.
"I'm King, and you're only that turtle Barack,
If you really are a turtle, a lot of people are saying…"

"You stay in your place while I sit here and rule.
I'm the King of a cow! And I'm the King of,
Not a mule, okay, who wrote that?
Fool, stool, pool maybe…Oh!
I'm the King of Something Cool!
And I'm the King of so many houses! And the best bush!
And a gold cat!
But that isn't all. I'll do better than that!
My Throne shall be higher!" his Royal Voice thundered,
"So pile up more turtles! I want 'bout a ten billion!"

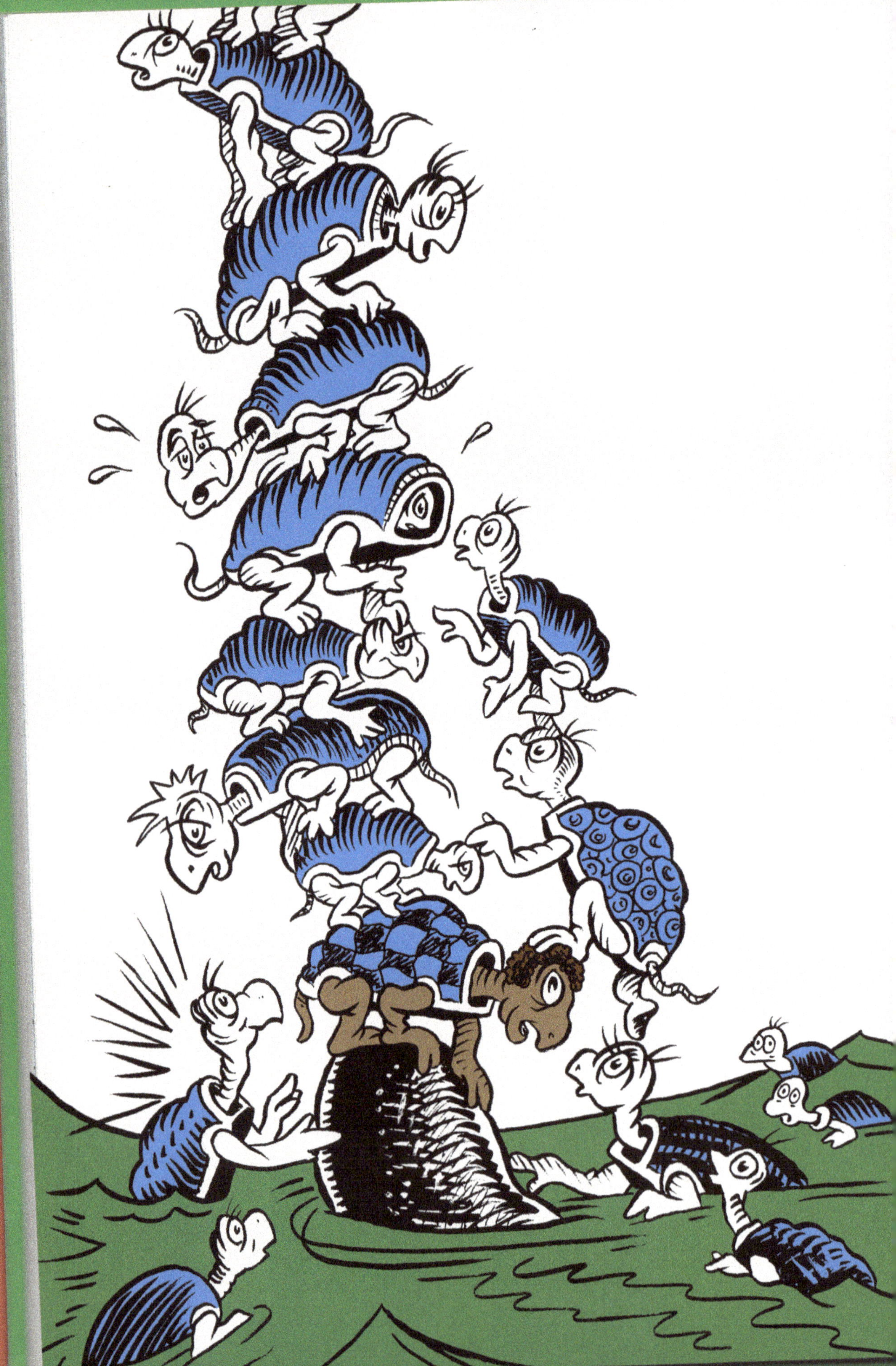

"Turtles! More turtles!" he bellowed and brayed.
And the turtles 'way down in the pond were afraid.
They trembled. They shook. But they came. They obeyed.

                                        The End.

Joey Green's Cooking Hack Will Bring You to Tears.

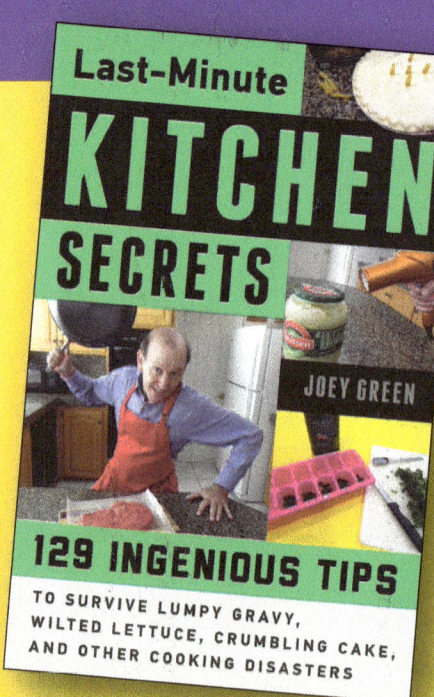

Your guests are arriving in a half hour, and your dinner has taken a turn for the worse. The lettuce has wilted, the gravy is lumpy, and the pie crust has burned. Time for takeout?

Not it you have Joey Green's **Last-Minute Kitchen Secrets**. This book contains tons of helpful hacks to salvage cooking disasters, store and prepare ingredients, keep appliances running smoothly, and clean cookware. These simple, ingenious tips may sound quirky at first, but they really do work. You'll discover how to . . .

- Improvise a salad spinner with a pillowcase
- Pit cherries with a chopstick and a wine bottle
- Cook hot dogs in a coffeemaker
- Sharpen a knife with a dinner plate
- Clean a cooper pot with ketchup
- Improvise a spaghetti strainer with a tennis racket
- And much, much more!

Joey Green, the guru of offbeat uses for everyday products, is back with **Last-Minute Kitchen Secrets: 129 Ingenious Tips to Survive Lumpy Gravy, Wilted Lettuce, Crumbling Cake, and Other Cooking Disasters**—the perfect resource for amateur chefs, budding MacGyvers, and cooks who think outside the breadbox. www.joeygreen.com

On Throwing Things Out

As two households merge into one, Merrill and Andy decide they better have a talk.

MERRILL:

Before you move in here there's something I want to talk about. Yesterday I was looking at the dozens and dozens of boxes of stuff you are planning to bring over, and I was thinking—and please don't take this the wrong way—that maybe you should consider throwing a few of them away. Let me clarify my terms: By "a few of them" I mean…a lot of them. And by "a lot of them" I mean 'most of them.'

It's common knowledge that the three most traumatic events in a person's life are death, divorce and moving. Oddly enough, all three things involve elimination of something extraneous. Death involves corpses, divorce involves exes…and, in your case, moving involves endless boxes of inexplicable crap.

Of course I am not suggesting that you throw out the things that represent important big moments. In fact I insist that you save your CDs, your favorite books, your Napoleonic collectibles, and the many whimsical photos of you on the road enjoying madcap rock and roll shenanigans. Ditto for diaries, quality framed art and so forth. But it's the—how do I say it?—souvenirs of the smaller, less memorable moments, I might even call them "the completely pointless" moments, of which I speak. The many manila envelopes stuffed full of, not just letters from your old friends and old girlfriends (God knows you can't part with those), but other people's old friends and girlfriends as well. Do you know you have unopened bills from the DWP and parking ticket reminders that are postmarked 1992? And you have apparently saved every magazine you ever bought! Every issue of *Road and Track*! Every issue of *Military History*! Every issue of *Juggs*! It's bad enough that you went to the newsstand in the '80s, presumably without a disguise, and purchased a magazine called *Big Butt*—not just once but on many occasions—but must you save them all? How many boxes of big butts does any one person need?

And I haven't even mentioned all the theoretically amusing but now shredded and greasestained pieces of travel memorabilia. Like old hotel room keys from Germany and torn 'Do Not Disturb' signs from Denmark. These are the things that Mother Nature in her infinite wisdom has asked me to tell you she would like to use for landfill.

In other words, here's what I am suggesting: Now's the time for sorting through those hundreds of ironic newspaper clippings and those intriguing but moth-eaten Carnaby Street coats, to say nothing of those patent-leather platform shoes that you only have one of, and finally having the courage to give them the old heave-ho. Before they occupy so much floor space that the furniture, the people, and the animals who presently use my home will have to move out and rent an apartment downtown.

ANDY:

Merrill! Do you see this? Do you realize what this is? I know It looks like just another large, pointed screw. It's an inch high and covered in oil and it has a washer attached to the bottom. This screw was jammed in to my tire so effectively that it created not just a puncture but *its own seal*, making it possible for me to drive from Malibu to Burbank on the 101 at 70 MPH without a single mishap. I drove forty miles with this thing in my tire. Forty miles, Merrill! And you would have me throw it out?

Greater men than I—for example Pablo Picasso and Andy Warhol—have held on to what more rational people might view as a lot of useless junk. Did you know that the Stanford University museum displays a biscuit from the Siege of Paris? The Seige of Paris was in 1870! So we're talking about a 130-year-old biscuit!

Think for a second: The Germanic Imperial forces had surrounded the city. Parisians rich and poor alike were so hungry they were reduced to eating cats, dogs and horses! Family pets, Merrill! Reduced to eating family pets! And yet someone held on to this biscuit! The mind reels, imagining why this biscuit was saved but never eaten. Was it accidentally rediscovered when someone reached in to their pocket looking for their keys and said, "Hey! There's my biscuit!"

Or was it such a horrible recipe that even eating a cat seemed like a better idea?

Or did the owner buy the biscuit on the day the siege was lifted, and held on to it anyway, just in case?

Imagine how many times the original owners and the subsequent owners were admonished by others to throw

---

Singer-songwriter **Andy Prieboy** *lives in Los Angeles with humor writer* **Merrill Markoe**.

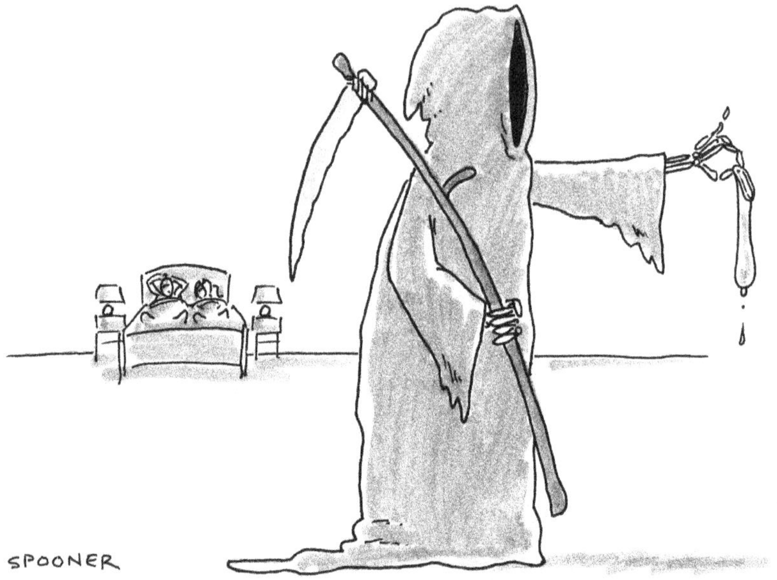
SPOONER

that biscuit away, never stopping to think for even a moment that it might be museum-quality!

And that's not the only example. Consider the case of General Dan Sickles: Here's a man who not only lost his leg at Gettysburg, he afterwards kept it, stripped it, shellacked it and had the bone mounted!

Obviously there's no way that he or I can justify our actions logically. Were I as pragmatic as you, I would let go of yesterday and leap into tomorrow unfettered, ready to greet one victory after the next.

However, I am not. I am a man who is, perhaps unfortunately, ruled by his passions. I am led blindly by the quixotic illusions that have filled my life with romantic disasters.

These irrelevant boxes of which you speak are, in essence, crypts and coffins: to friendships lost, love gone awry, and years of desperate gambles for success.

For instance I suppose you're wondering about this partially melted audio cassette. It was obviously damaged by fire. This cassette contains the remains of a song I thought would launch my career. Twenty years ago an irate English girlfriend, in a drunken rage, threw it and fifty other similar cassettes on to all four burners of a lit gas stove. Along with my guitar, my little Casio, and an assortment of my notebooks— which, I do believe, are in one of these other boxes. And why did I save them? Because Merrill…*I pulled them all out of the fire with my bare hands.*

What you see in front of you may *look* like boxes full of yellowing scraps of paper. But do not be deceived; look more closely. Here we have a contract, which I signed in 1982. Unbeknownst to me, the producer I signed with—who promised to make me a star—was using my recording project as a money laundering scheme to hide his enormous heroin habit. But because I signed this contract, when I tried to leave, *he later sued me and won.* Yet—for all the horror this contract represents—it's the very thing that brought me here and eventually led to this moment.

And you would have me throw all this away?

MERRILL

Yes! Yesss!!! Yes, I would. In a heartbeat. What you have just described are souvenirs of nightmares.

You don't seem to understand that people keep souvenirs of good times—like the ashtray from that naughty night out in the Wisconsin Dells. Not the butt from the cigarette they put out on your forehead when you were kept in a bamboo cage in the Hanoi Hilton!

I also would like to point out that Andy Warhol kept all his crap in a converted factory. Picasso lived in a villa. Leland Stanford sure as hell didn't share the enormous mansion he called home with indigestible fossilized biscuits.

And I'm glad you brought up General Sickles, since I happen to know that he didn't have that that amputated leg of his mounted so he could hang it over the fireplace like a largemouth bass. He donated it to the U.S. Army Museum. Would that I had the connections to get them to take all your stuff! Unfortunately the U.S. Army isn't particularly known for its appreciation of irony. (Though I have a feeling—well it's more like a hope—that the Salvation Army Museum will at least come take a look.)

I guess we could have a garage sale, but I doubt there's much resale value or any kind of a charitable tax write-off for partially melted audio tapes, or really old bills.

And here we come to the crux of the point I am trying to make: Even if assuming someone, like me, had the storage space, why would you, or anyone for that matter, voluntarily chose to live in a house full of "crypts and coffins"? (And I want to remind you that when we say "crypts and coffins" we are actually referring to caved-in boxes from Staples. And let's not forget the plastic tubs from Sav-On, full of not just passionate letters from ex-lovers that say things like "when I give you my body it's a gift," but their shopping lists and their little "You were sleeping when I left. See ya later! Love ya. Byeee!!!!!" notes as well. It's challenging enough to know that these letters are taking up closet space. Even worse is contemplating the fact that you once loved a woman who spells 'Bye' with three e's and five exclamation points.

In my opinion, a person needs to go through their belongings a couple times a year, and throw out about a quarter of them, just to earn the right to ever get anything new. Because never throwing things out is like never taking a bath. It's encouraging metaphysical grime, bacteria and fungal matter to clog up all the places in your mind where personal growth, spiritual renewal and new dinner party anecdotes might gestate. If you never bring in anything new, then all this old stuff defines you. You wind up with *Rime of the Ancient Mariner*'s disease; walking through life not only dragging a dead albatross, but boring everyone you encounter while you whine about him. Because logic dictates that hoarding too many unnecessary possessions causes the metaphysical equivalent of a black hole. You find yourself living by a gravitational pull so intense it will crush the start of your new life. And you don't want that, do you?

ANDY

Black holes!? Albatrosses!? Ancient Mariners? You're completely ignoring the creative potential that all this residue of mine provides.

The majority of my life has been a series of accidents. So while the content of these boxes may look like chaos to you—I actually went to the trouble of intentionally arranging each of these boxes just the way you now find them, using *no plan whatsoever.* That way each box becomes a collage of eras, epochs, and opi (if that is indeed the plural of opus). Thus, when I go through them, they allow me to reflect back on my life in the same haphazard fashion in which it all first occurred: "What's this? Ah! A letter from Max ? What does old Max have to say?…Hello, who is this lovely maiden? Why, it is The Hissing Woman of Amsterdam! Well, how do you do! What? You wish me to slap you but not kiss you? I'm very sorry, Hissing Woman, but I really must be going ."

Each new object kickstarts my memory and allows me to see my past with new perspective. So what you refer to as "landfill" is actually research material that seeds and fertilizes my creative process, hopefully resulting in deep psychological insight (which you girls all claim to love), if not also arias or *opera buffa*.

MERRILL

Well, we certainly agree on one thing: all this so-called "research material" is going to produce *opera buffa*. Because that's a good description of a life spent tripping over an obstacle course made of boxes full of—okay, I'll say it—*shit.*

And as for the creative content of which you speak: it is the stuff of melodrama. Mother Nature, you may have noticed, prefers real drama. When a forest gets too thick, a fire springs up to thin things out. Mother Nature allows only just so much stuff to occupy any finite space at any one moment in time. And if that line is crossed, she sends in the cleaning crew.

Case in point: Where I live in Los Angeles, along with pilot season, there is an even bigger nightmare: fire season. On two occasions in recent years I have been asked to evacuate my house. Suddenly facing a Sophie's Choice over which possessions to save due to the limited space in the trunk of my car, it became very clear that only certain photo albums or diary pages were going to make the cut. What was I going to take, my hilarious snow globe collection, or my dogs? My many hotel soaps? Or my insurance policies?

Once it was all over, and I was allowed to return to my home, it was hard not to see the things I was planning to let burn in a very different light. When push came to shove, most of them didn't matter—so why in hell were they taking up so much space now?

ANDY

Let me answer your question with a question: How much would humanity have lost if good King Tutankhamen had thought like that? Archeologists would have searched for years, then rolled back the big stone, only to exclaim, "Oh, look how nice and neat Tut left his tomb."

Where are Yorrick's infinite jests and most excellent fancy? Where are his jibes, his gambols, his songs, his flashes of merriment that were wont to set the table a-roar?

Probably in one of these boxes, along with two pages of a seven-page letter he sent, and a nude snapshot of the girl he met in Dusseldorf that he didn't want his wife to find.

The Ancient Mariner will always carry the Albatross, whether the physical one rots away or not. Because no matter how much you try to prune your life, you're still "The Albatross Guy" to the kids in the neighborhood. Besides, screw that Mariner's complaining shipmates. What did they have to do that was *so important* they couldn't listen to an old guy's stories? Wait for the wind? Sing some more of those sea chanties?

And when the Malibu fires do come and sweep away our possessions, who do you think is going to get more airtime? You, with your neatly filed folios, skipping out unburdened? Or me screaming to KCAL, "I lost everything!"?

Yes. That's right. I will get the air time. Because those three words are not just timeless, and universal but also the perfect sound bite for the six o'clock news.

Friendships fade, love dies, opportunities are only paper cups in the wind. Too late we realize that life is short and love is fragile. And in the end, nothing lasts in this world. Nothing at all, except stuff.

Lovely, memory-laden, tear-stained, remorse-filled, residual stuff.

If a man can't leave his mark, at least he can leave his crap.

And I know I can't take it with me. That's why I plan to shove it into a closet and let *you* deal with it after I'm gone. **B**

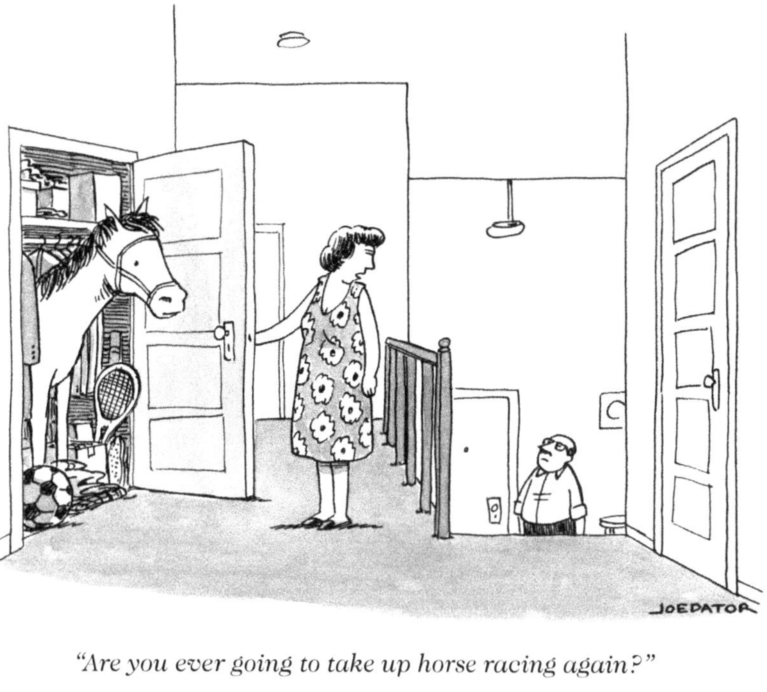
JOEDATOR
"Are you ever going to take up horse racing again?"

Hero of the Beach?

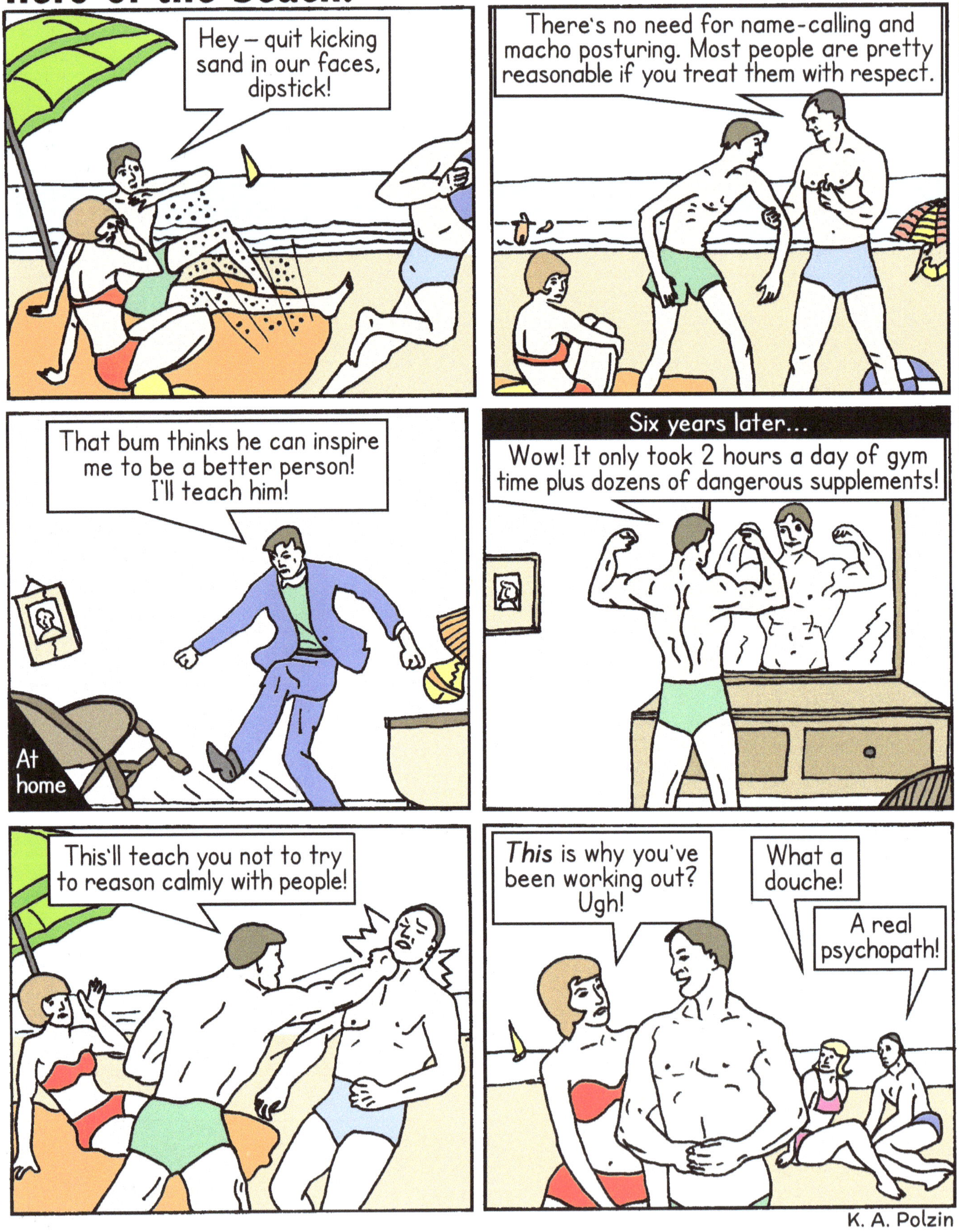
Hey – quit kicking sand in our faces, dipstick!
There's no need for name-calling and macho posturing. Most people are pretty reasonable if you treat them with respect.
That bum thinks he can inspire me to be a better person! I'll teach him!
At home
Six years later...
Wow! It only took 2 hours a day of gym time plus dozens of dangerous supplements!
This'll teach you not to try to reason calmly with people!
This is why you've been working out? Ugh!
What a douche!
A real psychopath!
K. A. Polzin

ED SUBITZKY

The World's Longest Joke

3832 words. Guaranteed.

A priest, a rabbi, a minister, an imam, a Buddhist monk, and an atheist all walk into a bar… The bartender asks them what they'd like to drink. "I'll have a bloody Mary," says the priest. "Make mine a glass of white wine," says the rabbi. "I'll have anything with a little umbrella on top," the minister says. The Buddhist monk says nothing, and the atheist says, "Something to help me in my despair." Now it just so happens that right above the bar is a house of ill repute, and it's not a busy night, and the girls, they just happen to get thirsty at the same time, so they all come down to the bar at once. The priest he looks at them and says, "Find your way out of sin." The minister says, "May you find forgiveness." The Buddhist monk again says nothing. The imam bows and smiles, and the atheist says, "There's nothing dirty about relations between consenting adults." At this exact moment, at the city zoo not too far away, a lion and a donkey escape. And who would arrive at the bar just then but a politician. He shakes everybody's hand, gives everybody a cigar, and tells them that if they vote for him, he'll clean up the city. Behind the politician is a window, and the priest could swear he sees a donkey through the window, so he says, "Does that belong to anyone here?" At this point a drunk sitting at the bar says, "Next thing you know there'll be a lion outside." He laughs loudly and a few of the other patrons laugh with him, when suddenly a big gust of wind comes up, and because the window is broken at the top, everyone can smell the donkey, which has just let out an explosive fart. Meanwhile, not far away, a circus is setting up its big tent with a sign that says, "See the Amazing Bearded Lady!" Outside the bar, three identical lady triplets are passing by, and one of them says to the other two, "This looks like a good place for a drink!" Inside the bar, a dockworker sees them and tells his pals, "Those are the most beautiful gals I've seen in my whole life!" "Sure are," says a downtrodden-looking man on his fifth drink, "When my wife left me for my best friend, I'd always dreamed of going out with someone with a body like that." At which point the priest butts into the conversation, "Don't you know that divorce is a mortal sin?" The rabbi steps up to them and says, "Can someone please get that donkey away from the window? It's making a stench in here!" There's a TV screen behind the bar, and a ballgame is winding up, and one of the customers shouts, "I just lost my rent money on a bet!" to which the in the imam says, "The sin of gambling can only be erased by the tooth of a lion." The Buddhist looks at them, but says nothing. The atheist, who's more than a little drunk now, takes off his shirt and shouts, "There are 19 people in here by my count. How much is 19 divided by three?" Meanwhile, back at the circus, the ringmaster screams, "Where's the bearded lady?" At the bar just a few minutes later, the priest says, "There seems to be a lady in here with a beard." Just then, the door bursts open, and in comes this farmer with a ravishingly beautiful girl on his arm and a pitchfork in his hand. He says to everybody, "My beautiful daughter here needs a place to sleep for the night." and the bartender says, "I live in a room over my bar, and she can stay in the coat closet there, which has an extra bed." "Okay," says the farmer, "but if anybody comes up and bothers my daughter, I'm going to shoot him dead and put his head on my pitchfork." Then the farmer, he says to his daughter, "If anyone bothers you, just yell 'turpentine!' and I'll be upstairs faster than you can say, "The old mule has arthritis!" One of the customers says: "What mule?", looks out the window, and shouts, "My Lord! That's the mule what was stolen from me on the night I got married!" "What did you miss most about her?" asks another customer, and when the first customer winks, the rabbi steps up and says, "Thou shalt not do with a mule what one would not do with one's spouse." The minister and the imam nod in agreement. Right then and there, a customer with a long beard comes up to the bartender and asks where the men's room is. "Just follow the smell," says the bartender, "that always works." "But sir," the customer says, "all I can smell in here is the donkey outside by the broken window." "Okay," the bartender says, "It's in the back, just make two turns." "To the left or the right?" asks the politician, and then the minister says to the priest, "What do you get when you cross a cross with a cross? A double cross!" The customer who needed the bathroom comes back out of breath and says, "I can't use the bathroom! There's a lion in there!" The imam says, "For is it not like a camel to have humps but no underwear?" Then a middle-aged woman comes down the stairs and screams at the prostitutes, "Get back to work! What do you think this is, a stinking playground?" One of the girls says, "But we have no customers right now." And the middle-aged woman says, "well why don't you try to seduce either the priest, the rabbi, the minister, the imam, or the atheist?" As if that wasn't enough, right then and there a picture of the pope appears on the TV above the bar, and the pope says, "We'll now take a brief commercial break from my encyclical." Whereupon the priest starts to cry and admits he watched a basketball game instead of the pope's previous encyclical. Meanwhile, in the crowd, an elderly woman is asking a middle-aged man, "How many monkeys does it take to hold up the Taj Mahal?" and the man he says, "I don't know, tell me," and the woman says "I don't know either. Why would you expect me to know something like that?" At which point the ringmaster of the circus comes in and says, "Have any of you seen an escaped donkey or an escaped lion around here?" The bartender says, "It's a slow night. If you buy a drink for everyone here, I'll tell you." "Okay," the ringmaster says, but as he sits down at the bar, he lets out a huge fart just when, by coincidence, the donkey outside lets out another one. The people in the bar all laugh hysterically and then one of them says, "I'm going to call the police" as a prostitute massages his wrists. While all this is going on, a shoe salesman walks through the door, and says, "I've had a tough day and I could sure use a drink. But do you mind if I drink out of my left shoe? It's a tradition in my family." The bartender gets real angry and says to the shoe salesman, 'We don't allow no pervs like you in here, so take that donkey that's outside and ride away if you know what's good for you." The man who owns the donkey says, "Over my dead body!" and the shoe salesman says, "That can be arranged," and the whole bar is about to erupt in a huge fight when the sheriff comes in for his nightly beer. He sits down at the bar as the place quiets down and says to the bartender "Do you think it's possible for a young child to be carried away by birds?" A dowdy-looking woman comes over and says, "Couldn't help hearing what you said, sheriff. I'm an ornithologist." The sheriff says, "Well, at least you ain't no atheist. If I ever see an atheist in here, I'll arrest the bastard on the spot. Oh, actually change that. I'll kill the bastard on the spot. No, change that again. I'll torture and then kill the bastard on the spot." "Quiet!" someone shouts from a table. "Can't you see we're playing checkers and we need to concentrate?" At which point the ringmaster says, "We have a monkey at the circus that can play chess, and we'll let everyone here have a half-price ticket!" Suddenly a woman comes running downstairs shouting, "What, have all the animals escaped?" "Well, they ain't welcome here," says the bartender, "unless it's a pig. I like pigs." "Did you know there's a lion in the ladies bathroom? And its drinking out of the toilet!" The priest makes the sign of the cross, the rabbi claps his hands, the minister says the Lord's Prayer, the imam says, "Does the lion have a name?" and the atheist says, "Just another example of evolution at work." The ringmaster turns to the imam and says, "To answer your question, her name is Molly, but we often call her Zane." Then the donkey lets out another loud fart and several of the customers hold their noses, but some don't, because they didn't want their beer drinking interrupted. The bartender says to the sheriff, "How come you're having so many today, Lou, you usually just have one." "Well," the sheriff says, "My two youngest children have disappeared." The bartender says, "I can sympathize because I'm a father, at least I think I am." Right then and there a goat and a gorilla show up at the door, and the ringmaster says, "What, has every animal in my circus escaped?" "Well, the bartender says, "Ain't none of them welcome here, except for pigs. I like pigs." Just then what happens but the room begins to shake and someone shouts, "Earthquake! Duck and cover!" Someone says, "You mean a duck escaped from the circus too?" "We're all going to die," a woman with fake blonde hair cries, "We're all going to die!" "Knock knock," a patron says and the woman answers, "Who's there?" "Dead." "Dead who?" "Dead all of us if we don't take cover!" "Let me see how many of you I can baptize," says the priest. "Count me out," says the atheist, and the bartender gives him the fifth funny look of the evening. The Buddhist monk says nothing but smiles contentedly. "Hell, this ain't no earthquake," one of the customers says, "It's just my hands trembling because this young lady she keeps a-massaging my wrist." "Don't matter none," one of the girls from upstairs says, "Whenever I die, I'm going straight to hell." The minister says to the priest, "Do we have a second opinion on that?" and one of the men playing checkers screams angrily because the shaking throws all the pieces on the floor. "I woulda won!" he shouts, taking out a gun, "I woulda won!" "Do something, sheriff!" seven of the patrons call in unison, but the sheriff has fallen asleep with his head on the bar counter. The ringmaster says, "What do you call a male donkey who likes female swans? And I mean likes in a very special way. "A man who calls himself the county judge says, "Male swans?" The politician smiles and says, "I'm glad the earthquake that wasn't an earthquake is over, and I'd like to buy half of the people here a drink." The bearded lady says, "I'll buy the other half a drink if they don't make fun of me because of my beard." "I'll buy you something better than that," says a man who comes in every night and calls himself the country judge. The man who claims he won the checker game stands up on a table and shoots his gun twice at the ceiling, shouting, "How many drunk truck drivers does it take to change a new modern-style LED bulb?" Someone jumps up, overpowers him, takes the gun away, and says, "Don't you go insulting truck drivers, now. I drive a truck and I don't say nothing bad about what you do." "Well then," says the man, "How many drunk taxi drivers does it take to change a new modern-style LED bulb?" That's better," the truck driver says and they all get down from the table. At this point a midget from the circus walks in and says, "I can drink half as much as any man in here!" "Maybe you can," a woman answers, "but I know the difference between a rose and a subway car." The sheriff suddenly wakes up and says, "Did someone say there was a lion in the bathroom?" One of the ladies from upstairs goes up to the window and says, "The Lord is truly sad tonight," and the imam bows his head in agreement. The rabbi says, "But is it kosher?" and the bartender gives him the third strange look of the night. Meanwhile, a lady goes and pours perfume on the donkey. "When is a smell not a smell?" she asks. "When it's two smells?" questions the bartender, who then says, "Can I go upstairs with you?" The middle-aged madam says, "Put your money where her mouth is." and they make their way through the crowd. The priest notices and says to the imam, "This is a very sad night for the Lord," and the imam nods in agreement. At this point two workingmen come through the door carefully maneuvering a telephone pole and placing it in the center of the floor. "You can't put that thing in here," shouts the bartender, and one of the working men says, "I'm only following odors." "But the monkey it doesn't smell anymore,'" pipes up one of the guests. "I think you mean the donkey," says the workingman. "But can you get it up?" asks a young woman nursing a drink with two little umbrellas on the top. "Let me buy you another drink and we'll see," says the workingman. Gazing up at the telephone pole, the woman suddenly points to the door and shouts, "No! Don't let the ant colony inside!" The ringmaster says, "I'm sorry, but I don't know how to stop them. Ants are very industrious and each one can carry 20 times its weight, if it wants to, that is." A moment later everyone in the bar is scratching themselves like crazy because they're all covered by insects. Luckily, a moment later they all start climbing up the telephone pole. "O praise the Lord in His goodness" the priest intones. "Praise the Lord in his goodness," repeats the rabbi. "Praise the Lord in his foresight," says the imam. The Buddhist monk opens his mouth to speak, but doesn't. The atheist says, "It's all just a coincidence, bub," and the priest blushes, The bartender comes out from behind the bar and says, "I just want to remind all of you good folks that it's almost closing time. But does anyone know the wrong way to spell 'Canada'?" A middle-aged man holding a briefcase says, "I'm a traveling salesman, I've been to Canada, and one can misspell it as 'Caneda'." Immediately the farmer with the gun and pitchfork says, "Okay so you can go and share the bed upstairs with my beautiful daughter, but if you so much as make a move to touch her, I'll send you to Canada, or Caneda, or whatever it is, with a bullet in your head." The traveling salesman says, "I'm a man of honor, even if my wife isn't around." A woman jumps up and said, "Well, I'm her sister and I make a good substitute. Also we use the same make-up." Just at that moment all the lights in the room go out and everyone is left in total darkness. One woman screams, "Hey what do you think you're doing, touching me there?" A man says, "Sorry, I thought you were a duck." The bartender turns on a flashlight and says, "well, a blackout ain't no excuse for nobody to misbehave, at least in my bar." One person says, "But are you sure they're ants? They could be termites!" Just then the lights come back on and now the telephone pole is only twelve inches high. "That's good enough for me," says a lonely-looking woman nursing a drink in a corner. A man comes through the door soaking with rain and someone says, ""Hey, how come you're all wet and it ain't raining here?" The man says, "I took a wrong turn, ran into a storm, and stopped here for a drink. You all look like a bunch of good folks, so I'm buying." The priest says, "Even the Lord will allow the taste of liquor on the tongue, as long as it is kept in moderation." The rabbi says, "Neither wine nor beer can damage the pure soul. The imam says, "I don't drink, but I do watch beer commercials sometimes." The Buddhist monk says nothing, but his Adam's apple twitches a little. The atheist says, "I'll drink to that." "Did you mean 'to' or 'two'?" says the bearded woman, "A lot depends on that, you know." A drunk wobbles across the floor and hands the rain-soaked man one of the little umbrellas from his drink. "This ought to help next time," he says, "now how about we all have some fun! Does this place have a juke box?" "Will a joke box do?" another man says, chuckling. "An elderly man pipes up, "Your mother uses the F-word." "I am shocked," says the priest, "to hear you say something like that." Suddenly they noticed that one of the lady patrons had taken all her clothes off and was completely naked. "What do you say to a naked lady?" she asks. "How about hello," the bartender says with a knowing look in his eye. "Would you like to buy a vacuum cleaner?" the traveling salesman asks. "That sucks," the checkers player with the gun says. The traveling salesman turns to the farmer with the pitchfork and says, "Just how many beautiful daughters do you have?" The farmer says, "Six, but I should kill you for asking that question." "Only fifteen minutes to quitting time!" says the bartender. The madam says to her girls, "Get back upstairs, you bitches!" and as the girls file away, the priest says, "I should have worked harder to save their souls, but on the other hand, I own a red convertible." The minister says, "They will be forgiven and enter the kingdom of heaven." The imam says, "This is not the desert, so why is there a camel at the window?" The Buddhist clears his throat, but again says nothing. The atheist says, "Do you ever wonder how a tree goes to the bathroom?" Little by little the bar is starting to empty out now, and the priest says, "There goes another evening of the Lord's creation." The minister says, "How many angels can fit on the end of a pin?" The imam says, "Just enough to screw in a light bulb." The ringmaster says, "Well, I better get these animals back to the circus, or the clowns will give me a whipping." The farmer with the pitchfork says, "What happens if you take ten frogs, subtract three tadpoles and add a prize-winning goat? Hey what's that?" From upstairs comes the sound of a scream and the word, "turpentine!" The farmer runs up the stairs and finds seven of the customers, including the workingmen, in bed with his daughter. "Give me one reason why I shouldn't shoot all of you dead," the farmer says. His daughter says, "How about free phone service for the rest of our lives?" The traveling salesman pops up from underneath the bed and says, "Hi folks, when did you all get here?" The bartender shouts, "Half an hour until closing time!" The rabbi says, "So is it said, so must it be written." The madam comes into the coat closet and says, "You know, honey, I can offer you a job." "With or without a telephone pole?" asks the girl. "Oh, we got plenty of those" the madam says. "Not to change the subject," the traveling salesman says, "But does anyone know the French word for consensual relations?" The ringmaster comes upstairs and asks, "Did anybody see a lion?" One of the men says, "Check the bathroom." "How do I get to the bathroom?" says the ringmaster. "Follow the smell," says the farmer's daughter." "But the donkey smells like cheap perfume," someone else says. It just so happens that a high school marching band is rehearsing in the street outside, but the people can't see their instruments because it's too dark, so they all come into the bar. "I'm sorry, but I'm not allowed to serve minors," the bartender shouts, "Anyway, we're closing in just fifteen minutes." "Can we use the bathroom, then?" one of the students asks. "Careful," says the ringmaster, "there might be a lion inside." "You don't want to take that final march to hell," says the priest. One of the teenagers notices the naked lady and asks the girl next to him, "What do you say to a naked lady?" The girl answers, "This place is full of termites!" The bartender finally notices that the termites are eating up the wood of his bar. "They'll destroy my place!" he shouts. "Better close up early," the ringmaster says. "Never!" the bartender says proudly. Another teen-aged boy says to the girl next to him, "What do you call a birth control device that doesn't work?" The girl answer, "A non-working birth control device, I suppose." The priest says, "This place is consumed in wickedness." The rabbi says, "Truly, it is a vexing question." The imam says, "If it is written in sand, it is made of sand." The Buddhist monk makes a quick, low gurgling sound. The atheist says, "All I wanted was quick drink and maybe a sexual encounter that I would either seduce for or pay for." "Either way," says one of the customers, hoisting a beer glass high, "poop spelled backwards is still poop." "How about a moment of silence for all of suffering humanity?" the atheist says, and they all bow their heads in silence, except for the Buddhist monk who says, "OK," and they all stand there facing each other, the priest, the rabbi, the imam, the Buddhist monk, the atheist, the bartender, the bearded lady, the triplets, the politician, the madam who has come back downstairs, the farmer with the pitchfork and the gun, the two men playing checkers, and everybody else. Each one glares at the ringmaster and they say in unison, "I ought to kick your ass." The ringmaster answers, "The one I sit down on or the one I ride in the circus?"

STEPHEN KRONINGER

Lou Hirshman
American caricaturist
(1905-1986)

Self-Caricature (1949)

I first came across Lou Hirshman's work over 30 years ago, in the back of a book on caricature. They were small black and white images reproduced from *LOOK* magazine; this profile of Hirshman published May 10, 1938, seems to be one of the few bits of publicity his career generated.

Lou Hirshman is that rarest of artists, an undiscovered genius. Despite the undeniable excellence of his work—reproduced in the following pages—there are no Hirshman collections, no books, no catalogs. The genius was there, the body of work was there, just not the fame. So, in 2017, when Drew Friedman and I decided to do a joint talk at the Society of Illustrators called "Forgotten Caricaturists Remembered," the first artist on my list was Lou Hirshman. And his son, who lives in Germany, has been exceptionally helpful in sharing his life and work. (He runs a website at hirshman-art.com.)

Here's what we do know: Louis P. Hirshman was born in 1905 to Jewish parents in present-day Ukraine, and when Lou was three, they emigrated to Philadelphia, Pennsylvania. They were so poor that Hirshman liked to say that he eased his hunger pangs by drawing food. He dropped out of school in the 10th grade to pursue art professionally, and sometime during the 1920s, he studied art in Paris and Italy, thanks to a grant.

Hirshman's caricatures started out as a joke, his party-piece. "Hirshman would take one of the walls of the studio," said a friend, "and before the guests arrived, draw a composition of all the people coming to the party." Gathering by gathering, Hirshman's activities began attracting attention…including from *The Daily Worker*, which lauded him for "caricaturing the world's oppressors of the laboring masses."

After seeing Hirshman's Hitler in *LOOK*—four years before the U.S. declared war on Germany—American Nazi sympathizers offered to buy it, so they could destroy it. Hirshman, naturally, declined.

After this brief flurry of acclaim in the late 1930s and early 1940s, Hirshman sank back into the productive obscurity which he preferred. He spent the remaining four decades of his life teaching at Philadelphia's Fleisher Art Memorial, and producing new art in his studio. According to his son, Hirshman's work ethic was so intense he only emerged for meals. There was a last spasm of great work in the early 1960s, some of which is on the following pages; then Hirshman moved away from caricature for good. He continued to create tableaus made up of found materials that show his unique sense of humor.

In 1986, when he died, Lou Hirshman had a new work on his easel.

◆

Stephen Kroninger's *work can be found in the permanent collections of the Museum of Modern Art, the Library of Congress, and the National Portrait Gallery in Washington.*

All images courtesy of **WILLIAM P. HIRSHMAN**

Use of image courtesy of **WENDY PRICE DAVIS**

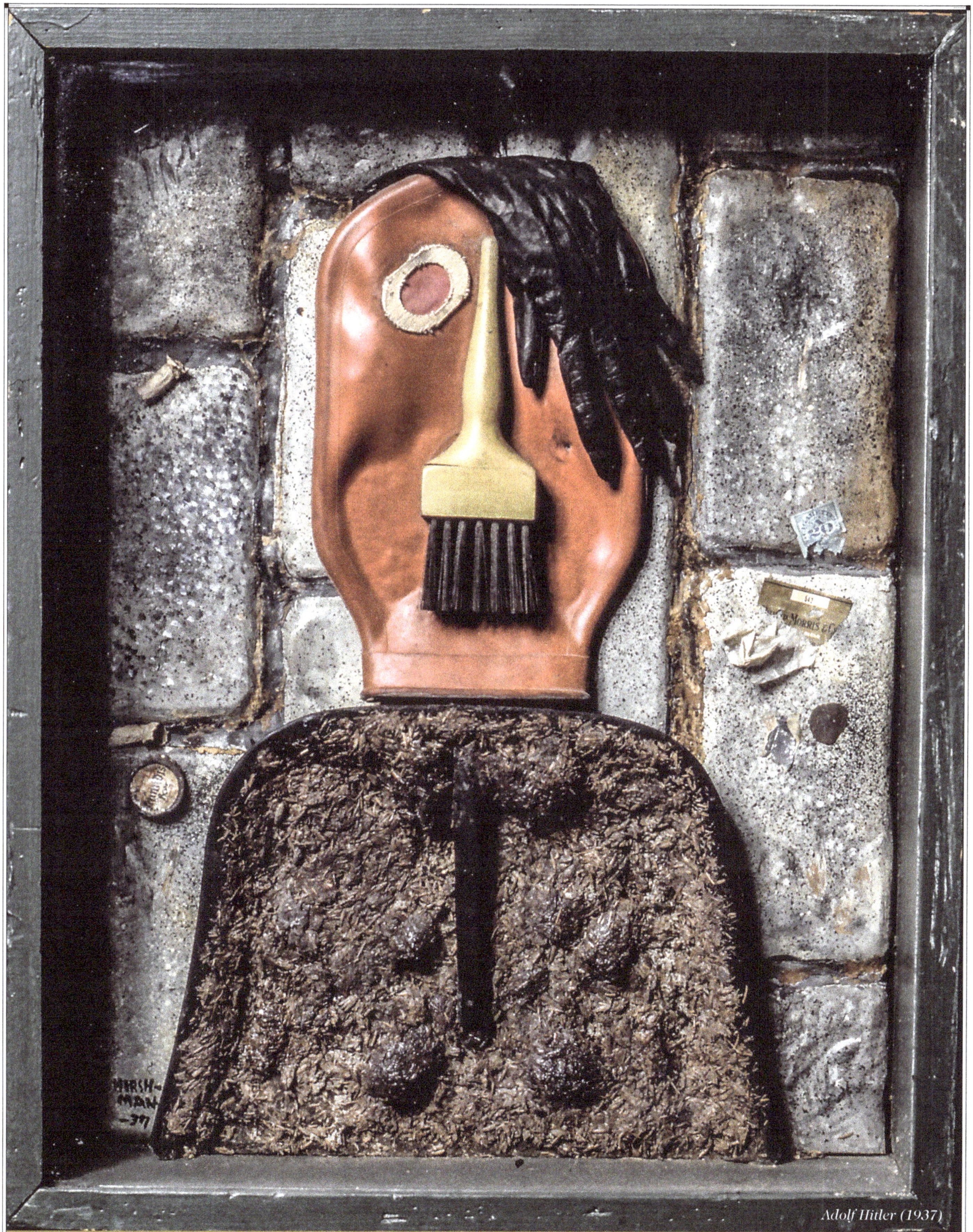
HIRSH-
MAN
-37

Adolf Hitler (1937)

A HIRSHMAN CARICATURE *is a nest of everyday objects, dense with allusion, arranged into a likeness. The hot water bottle reflects Hitler's hot-headedness, the black glove references the Gestapo and the brush is a nod to his days hanging wallpaper. For the brown shirt, Hirshman scooped up a pile of horse manure with a dustpan. Finally, the artist crafted a cobblestone gutter for the dictator to lie in that included discarded cigarette butts, bottle caps and other bits of litter.*

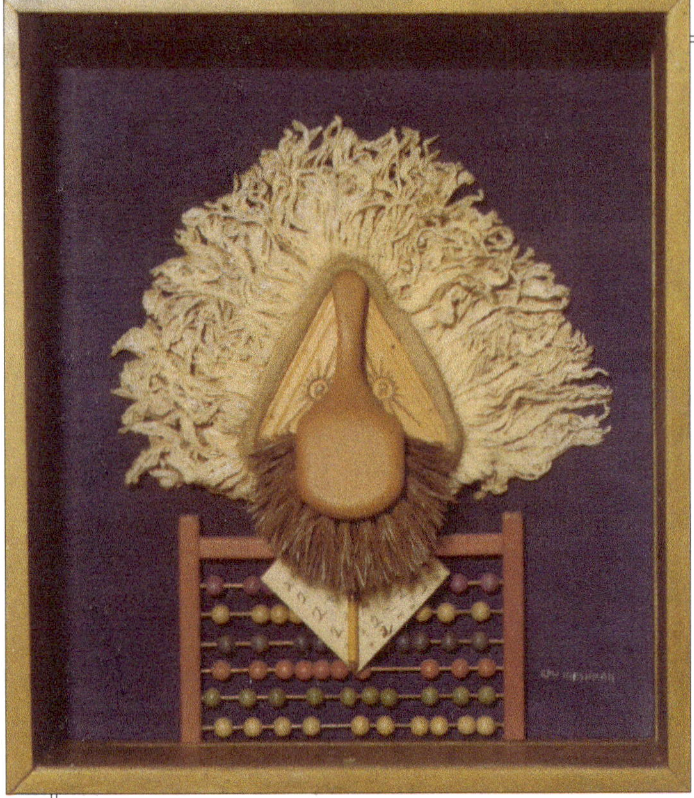

Albert Einstein (1940).

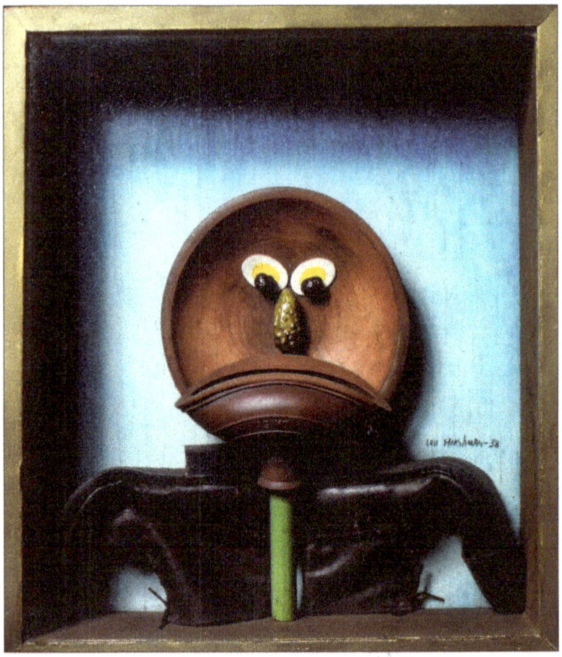
LOU HIRSHMAN

Benito Mussolini (1938).

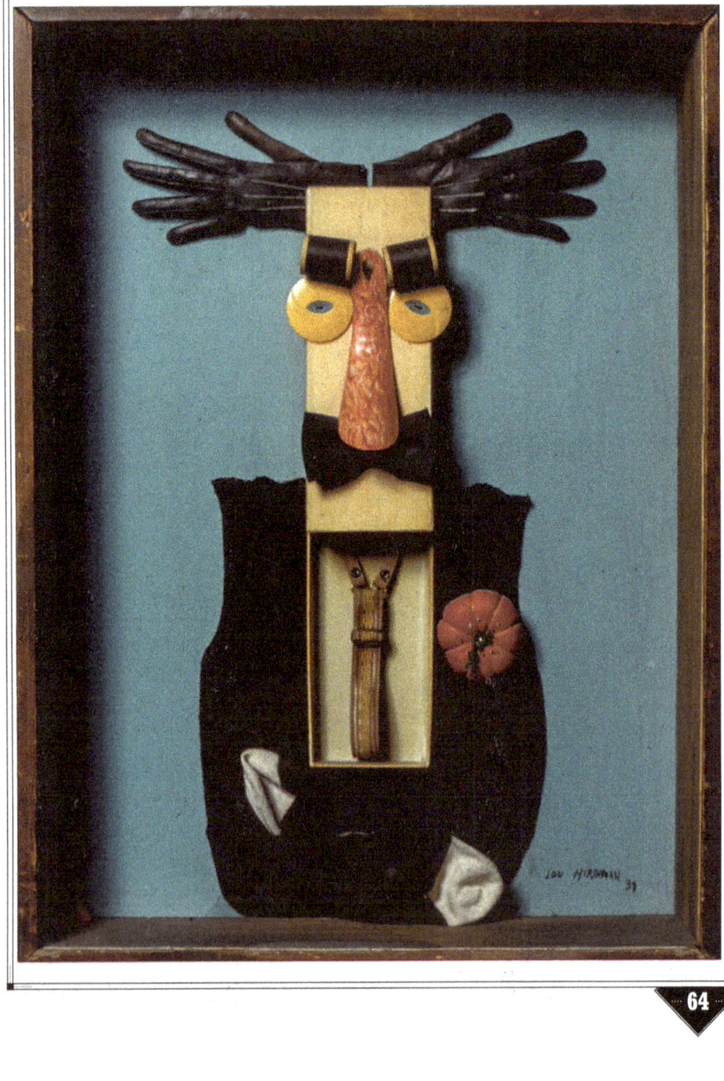
LOU HIRSHMAN

Groucho Marx (1937)

Charles de Gaulle (1964)

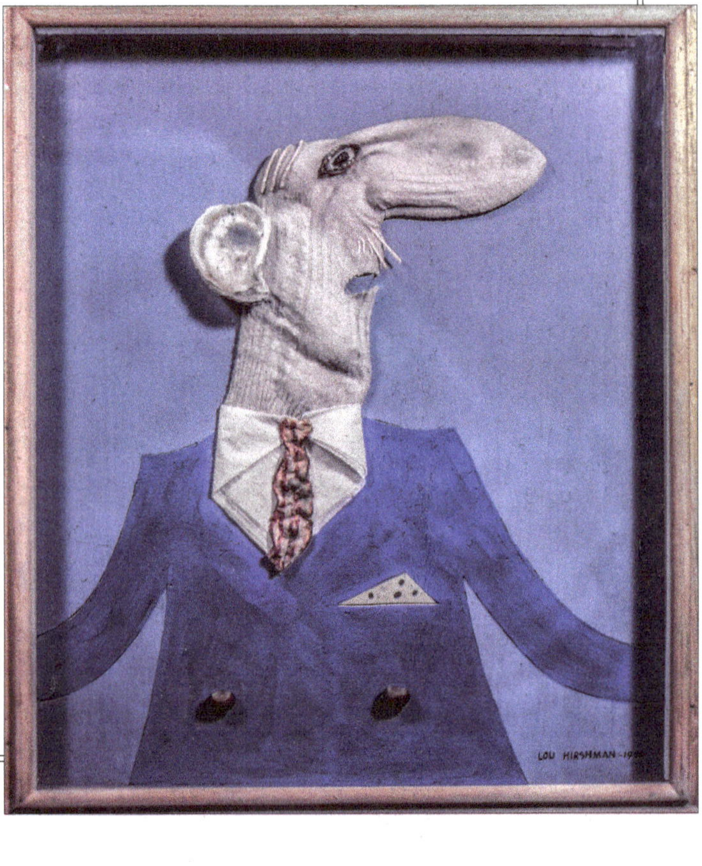
LOU HIRSHMAN

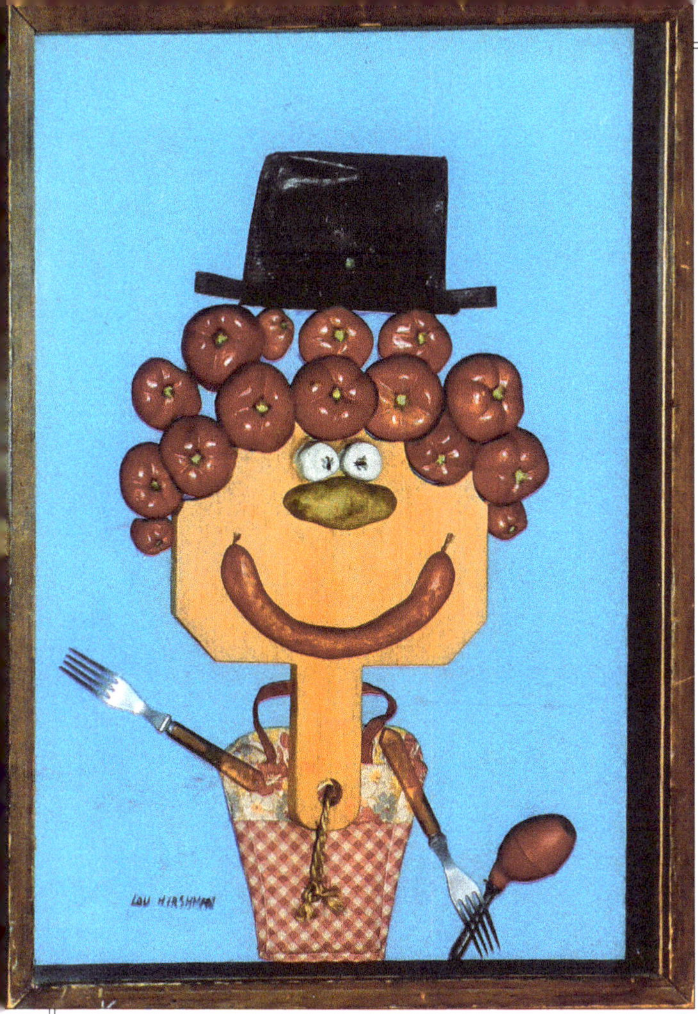
LOU HIRSHMAN

Harpo Marx (1937).

John D. Rockefeller (1935).

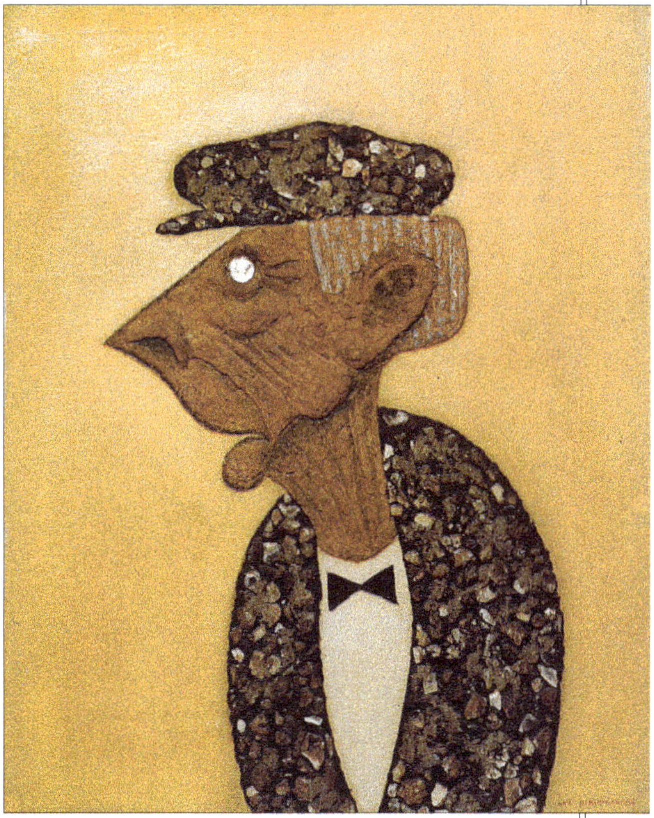

Fidel Castro (1963).

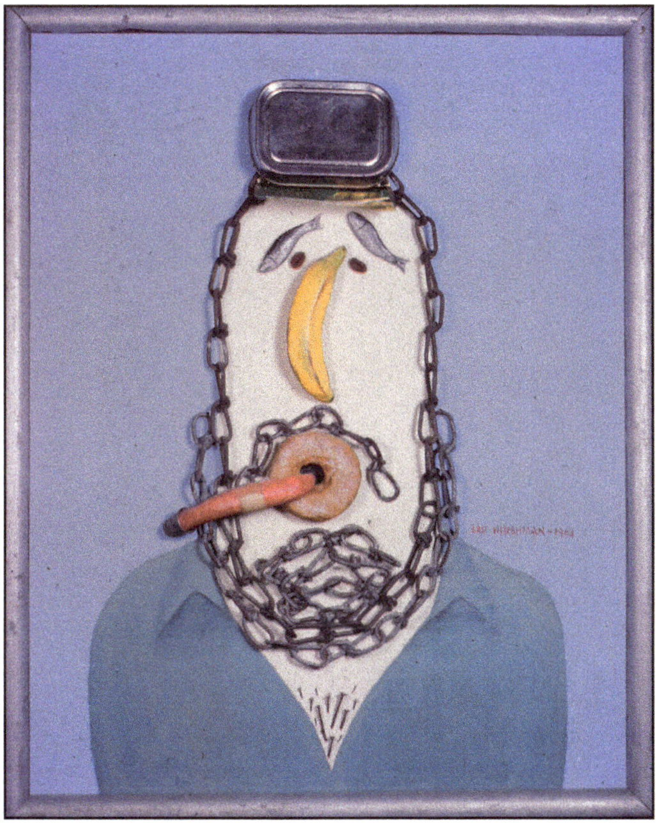

John F. Kennedy (1963).

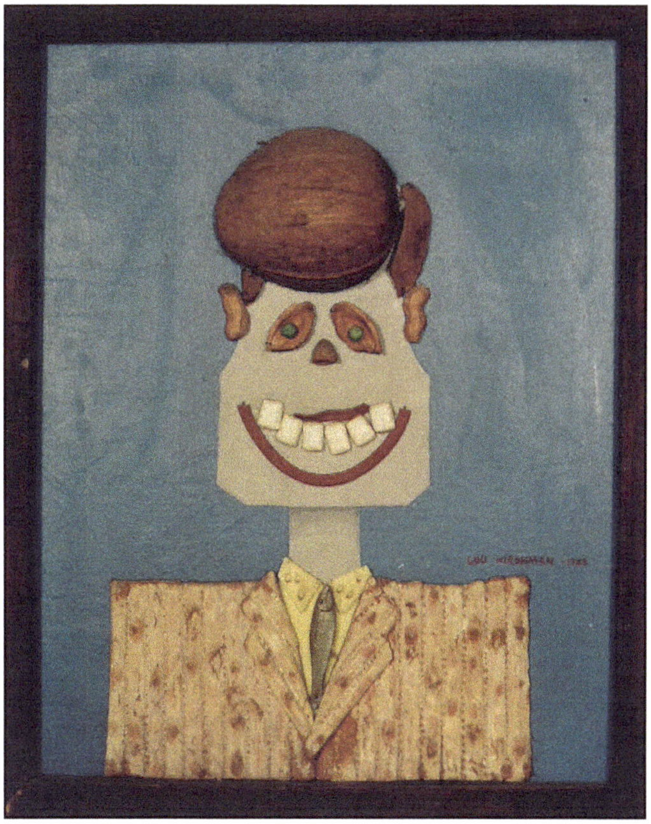

THIS PORTRAIT OF JFK *hung in Hirshman's living room. On November 22, 1963, Hirshman took it down, and largely retired from caricature.* **B**

Use of image courtesy of **MICHAEL MARTIN MILLS**

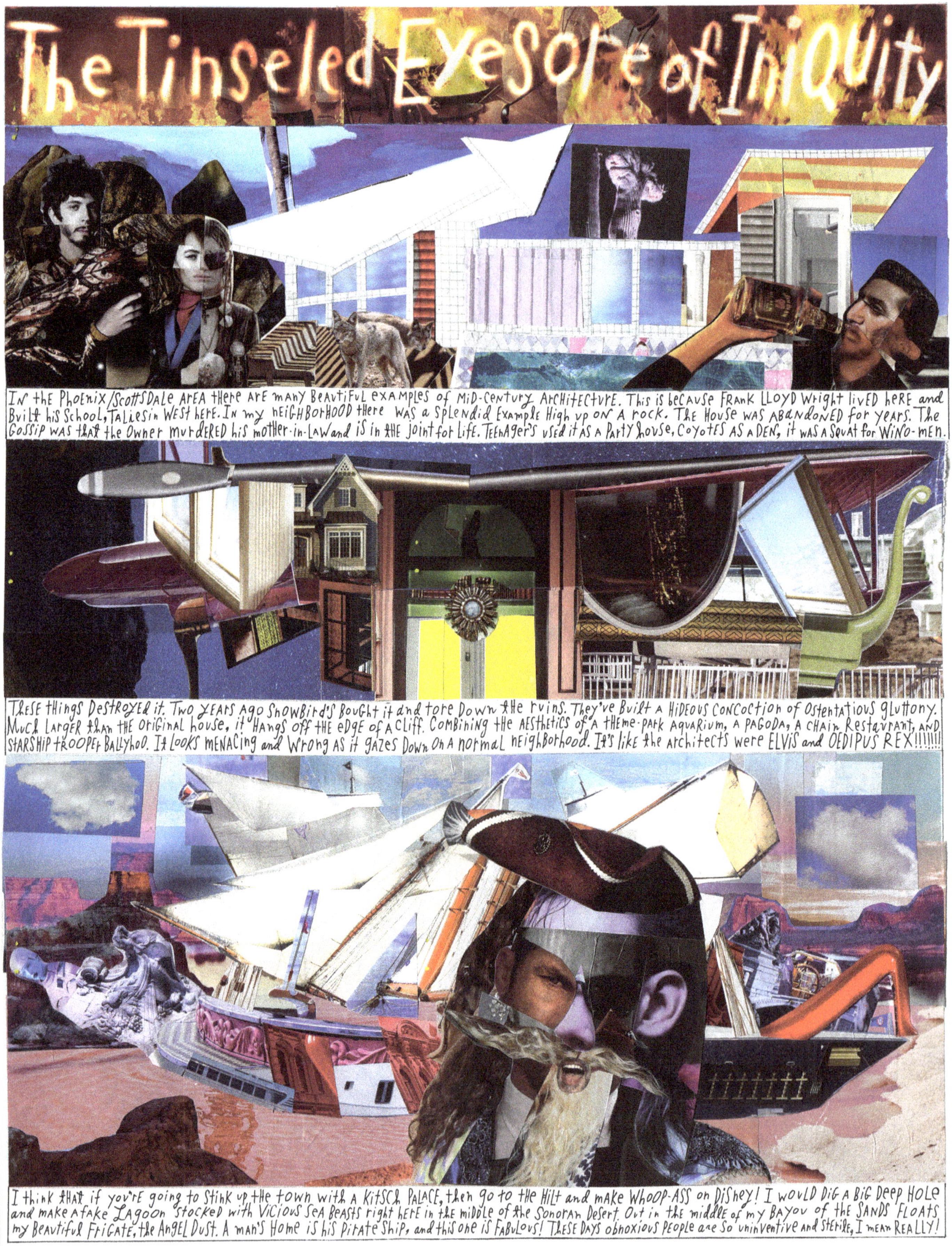
The Tinseled Eyesore of Iniquity
In the Phoenix/Scottsdale area there are many beautiful examples of mid-century architecture. This is because Frank Lloyd Wright lived here and built his school, Taliesin West here. In my neighborhood there was a splendid example high up on a rock. The house was abandoned for years. The gossip was that the owner murdered his mother-in-law and is in the joint for life. Teenager's used it as a party house, coyotes as a den, it was a squat for wino-men.
These things destroyed it. Two years ago snowbird's bought it and tore down the ruins. They've built a hideous concoction of ostentatious gluttony. Much larger than the original house, it hangs off the edge of a cliff. Combining the aesthetics of a theme-park aquarium, a pagoda, a chain restaurant, and starship trooper ballyhoo. It looks menacing and wrong as it gazes down on a normal neighborhood. It's like the architects were ELVIS and OEDIPUS REX!!!!!!!
I think that if you're going to stink up the town with a kitsch palace, then go to the hilt and make whoop-ass on Disney! I would dig a big deep hole and make a fake lagoon stocked with vicious sea beasts right here in the middle of the Sonoran Desert. Out in the middle of my bayou of the sands floats my beautiful frigate, the Angel Dust. A man's home is his pirate ship, and this one is fabulous! These days obnoxious people are so uninventive and sterile, I mean REALLY!

B

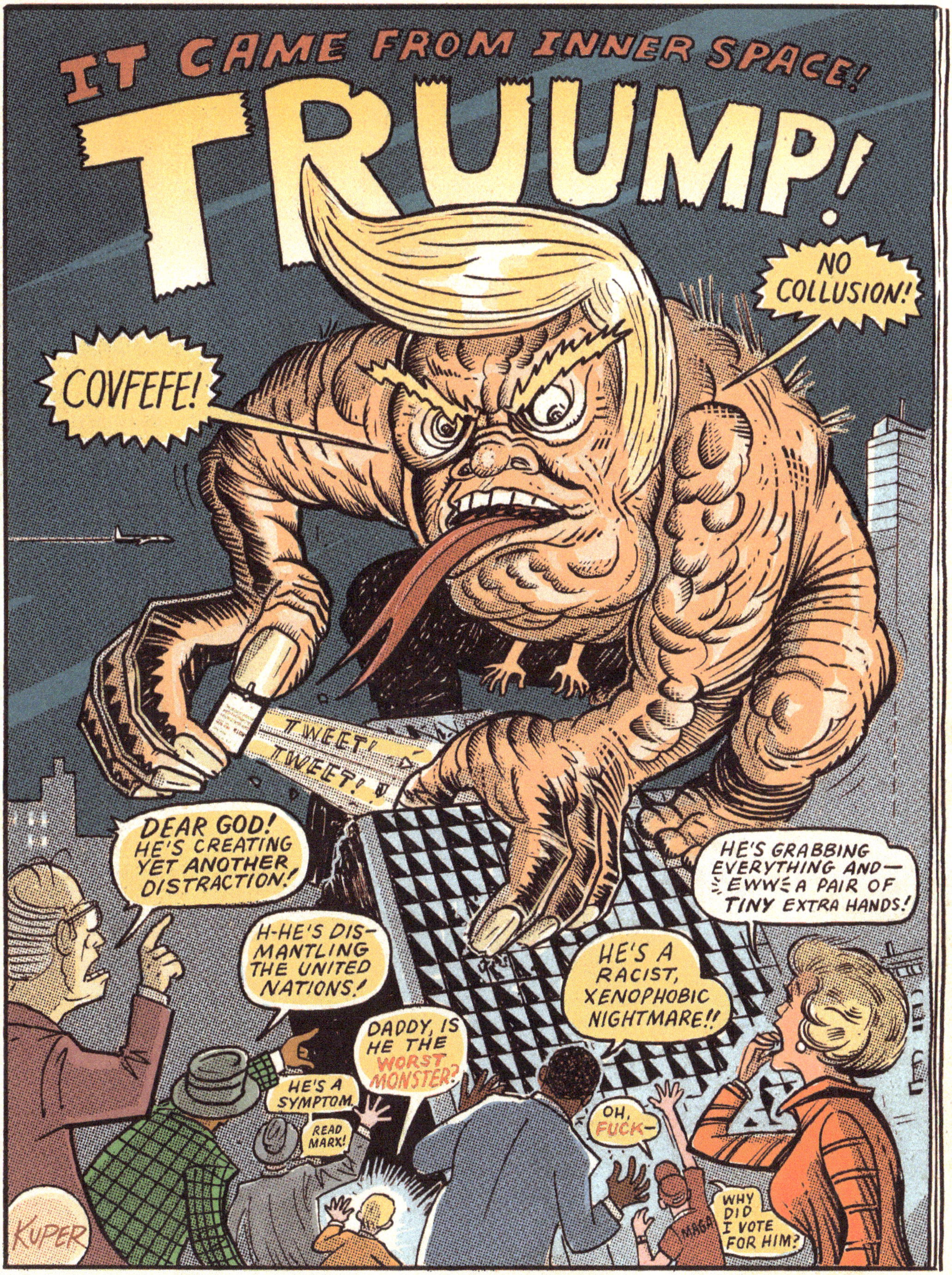
IT CAME FROM INNER SPACE!
TRUUMP!
COVFEFE!
NO COLLUSION!
TWEET! TWEET!
DEAR GOD! HE'S CREATING YET ANOTHER DISTRACTION!
HE'S GRABBING EVERYTHING AND— EWW— A PAIR OF TINY EXTRA HANDS!
H-HE'S DISMANTLING THE UNITED NATIONS!
HE'S A RACIST, XENOPHOBIC NIGHTMARE!!
DADDY, IS HE THE WORST MONSTER?
HE'S A SYMPTOM.
READ MARX!
OH, FUCK—
WHY DID I VOTE FOR HIM?
MAGA
KUPER

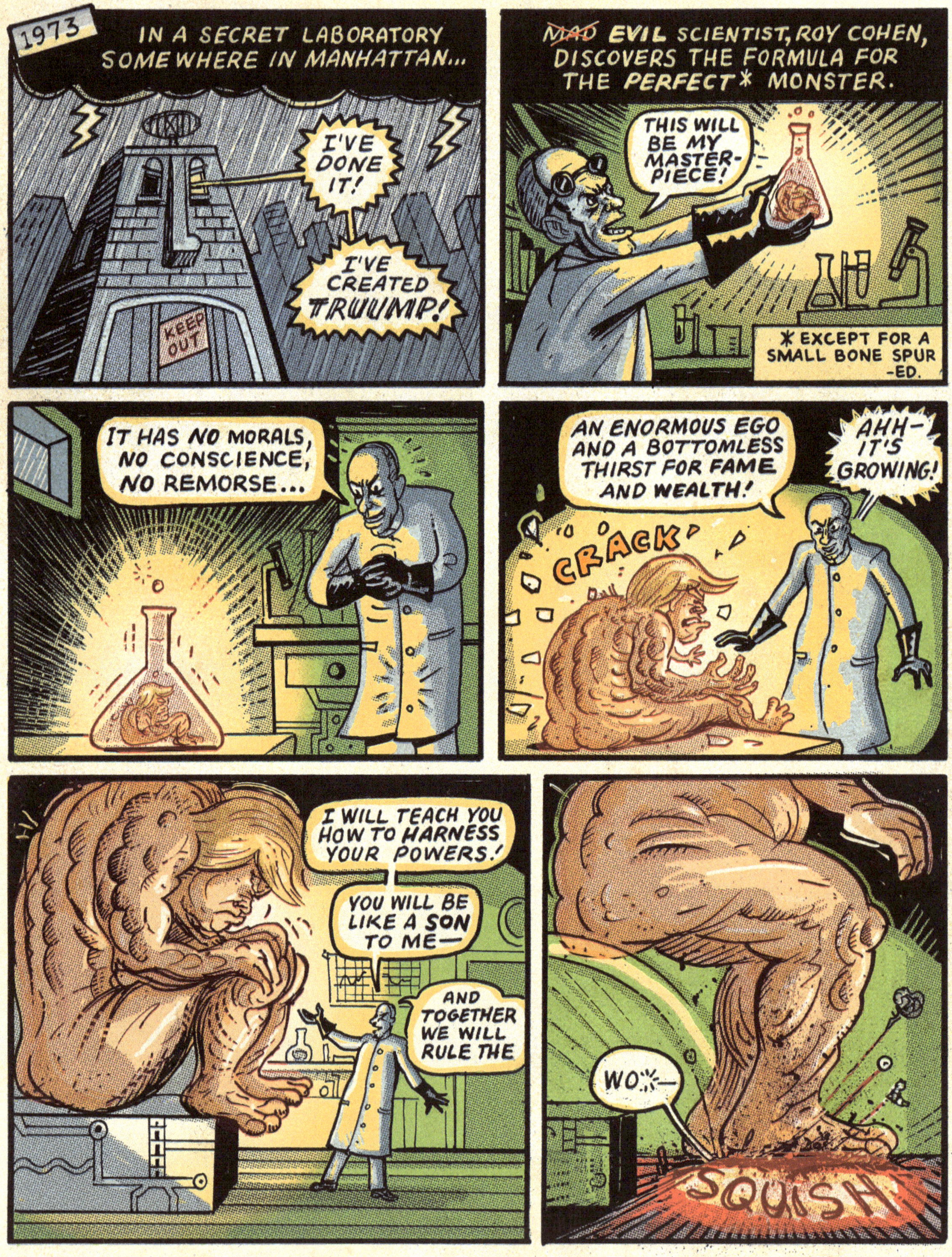
1973
IN A SECRET LABORATORY SOMEWHERE IN MANHATTAN...
I'VE DONE IT!
I'VE CREATED TRUUMP!
KEEP OUT
MAD EVIL SCIENTIST, ROY COHEN, DISCOVERS THE FORMULA FOR THE PERFECT* MONSTER.
THIS WILL BE MY MASTER-PIECE!
* EXCEPT FOR A SMALL BONE SPUR -ED.
IT HAS NO MORALS, NO CONSCIENCE, NO REMORSE...
AN ENORMOUS EGO AND A BOTTOMLESS THIRST FOR FAME AND WEALTH!
AHH- IT'S GROWING!
CRACK
I WILL TEACH YOU HOW TO HARNESS YOUR POWERS!
YOU WILL BE LIKE A SON TO ME—
AND TOGETHER WE WILL RULE THE
WO—
SQUISH

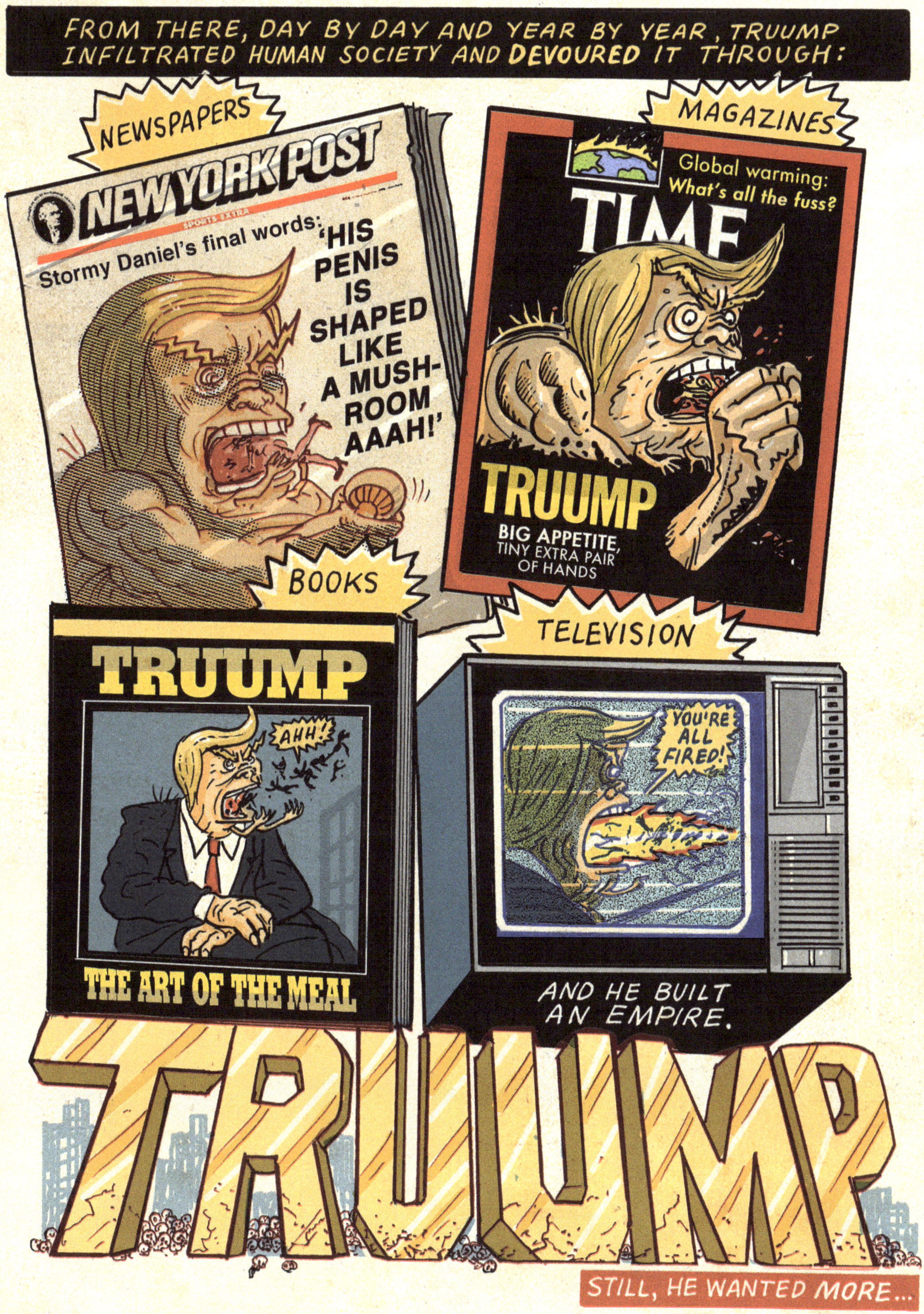
FROM THERE, DAY BY DAY AND YEAR BY YEAR, TRUUMP INFILTRATED HUMAN SOCIETY AND DEVOURED IT THROUGH:
NEWSPAPERS
NEW YORK POST
Stormy Daniel's final words: 'HIS PENIS IS SHAPED LIKE A MUSHROOM AAAH!'
MAGAZINES
Global warming: What's all the fuss?
TIME
TRUUMP
BIG APPETITE, TINY EXTRA PAIR OF HANDS
BOOKS
TRUUMP
AHH!
THE ART OF THE MEAL
TELEVISION
YOU'RE ALL FIRED!
AND HE BUILT AN EMPIRE.
TRUUMP
STILL, HE WANTED MORE...

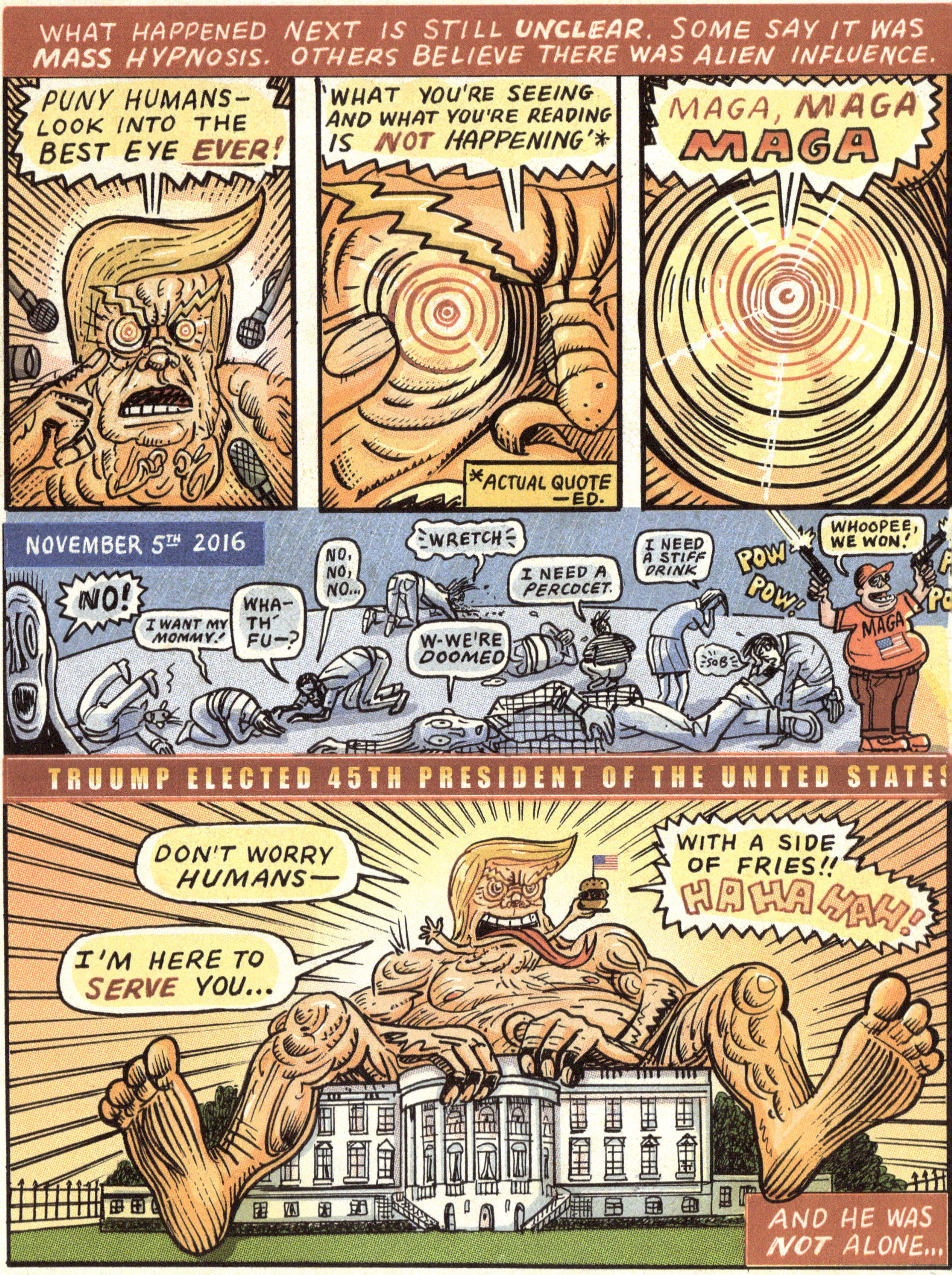

WHAT HAPPENED NEXT IS STILL UNCLEAR. SOME SAY IT WAS MASS HYPNOSIS. OTHERS BELIEVE THERE WAS ALIEN INFLUENCE.
PUNY HUMANS- LOOK INTO THE BEST EYE EVER!
'WHAT YOU'RE SEEING AND WHAT YOU'RE READING IS NOT HAPPENING'*
*ACTUAL QUOTE —ED.
MAGA, MAGA MAGA
NOVEMBER 5TH 2016
NO!
I WANT MY MOMMY.
WHA- TH' FU-?
NO, NO, NO...
WRETCH
W-WE'RE DOOMED
I NEED A PERCOCET.
I NEED A STIFF DRINK
SOB
POW
POW!
WHOOPEE, WE WON!
MAGA
TRUUMP ELECTED 45TH PRESIDENT OF THE UNITED STATES
DON'T WORRY HUMANS—
I'M HERE TO SERVE YOU...
WITH A SIDE OF FRIES!! HAHAHAH!
AND HE WAS NOT ALONE...

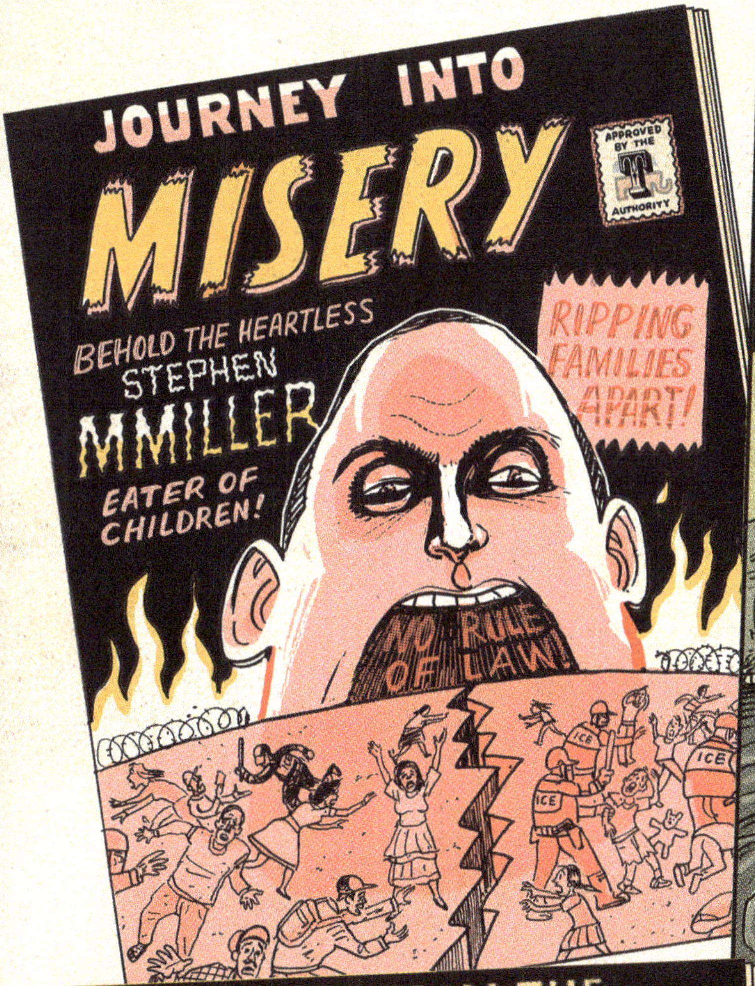

JOURNEY INTO
MISERY
APPROVED BY THE T AUTHORITY
BEHOLD THE HEARTLESS
STEPHEN
MMILLER
EATER OF CHILDREN!
RIPPING FAMILIES APART!
NO RULE OF LAW!
ICE

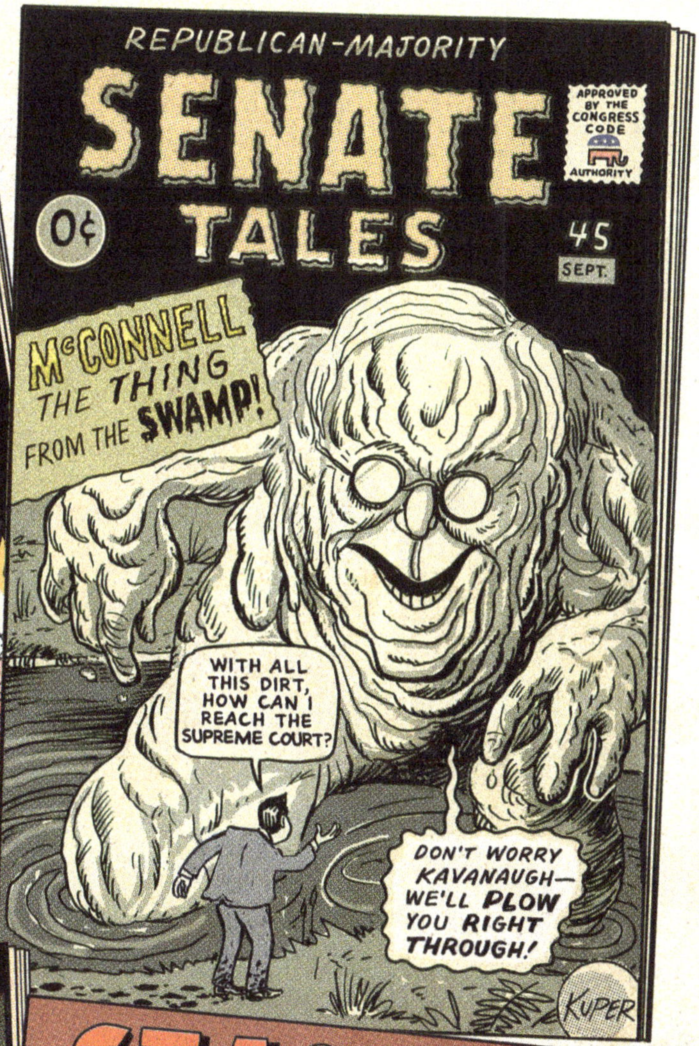

REPUBLICAN-MAJORITY
SENATE
TALES
APPROVED BY THE CONGRESS CODE AUTHORITY
0¢
45
SEPT.
McCONNELL THE THING FROM THE SWAMP!
WITH ALL THIS DIRT, HOW CAN I REACH THE SUPREME COURT?
DON'T WORRY KAVANAUGH— WE'LL PLOW YOU RIGHT THROUGH!
KUPER

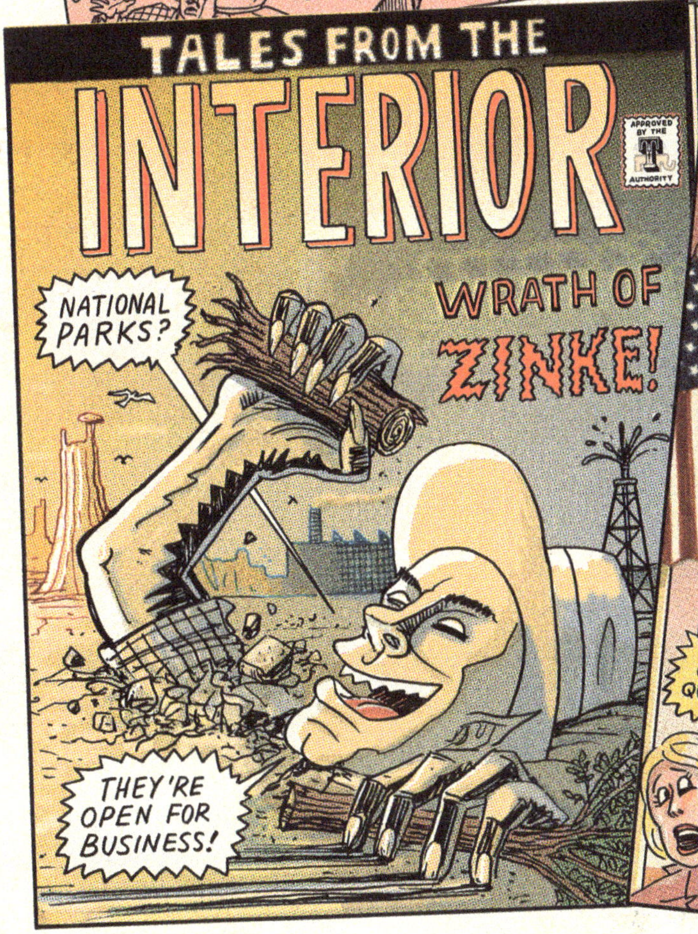

TALES FROM THE
INTERIOR
APPROVED BY THE T AUTHORITY
WRATH OF ZINKE!
NATIONAL PARKS?
THEY'RE OPEN FOR BUSINESS!

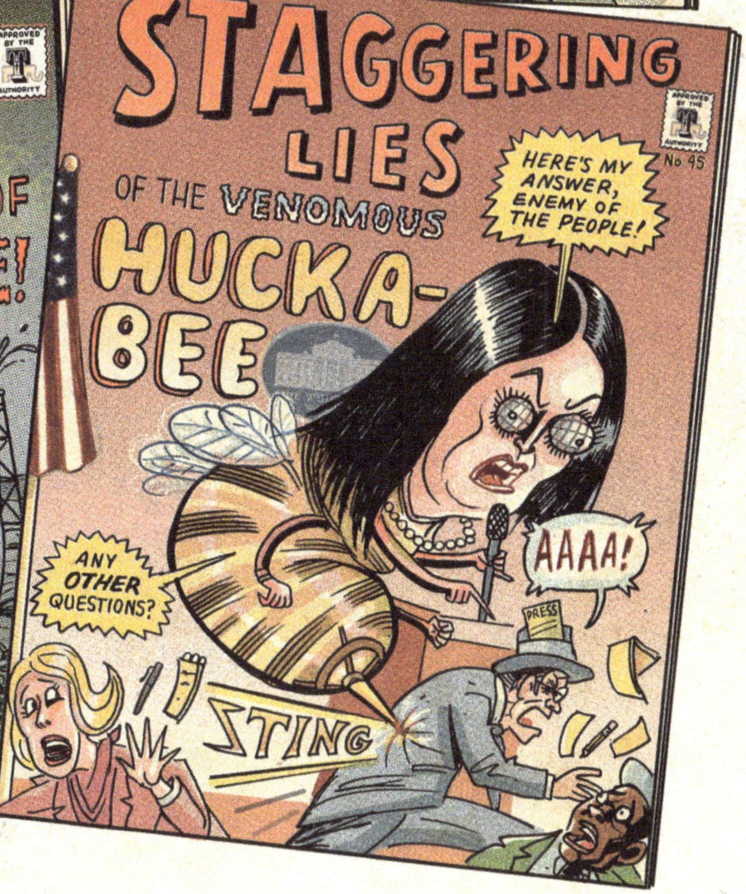

STAGGERING
LIES
OF THE VENOMOUS
HUCKA-BEE
APPROVED BY THE T AUTHORITY
No 45
HERE'S MY ANSWER, ENEMY OF THE PEOPLE!
ANY OTHER QUESTIONS?
AAAA!
PRESS
STING

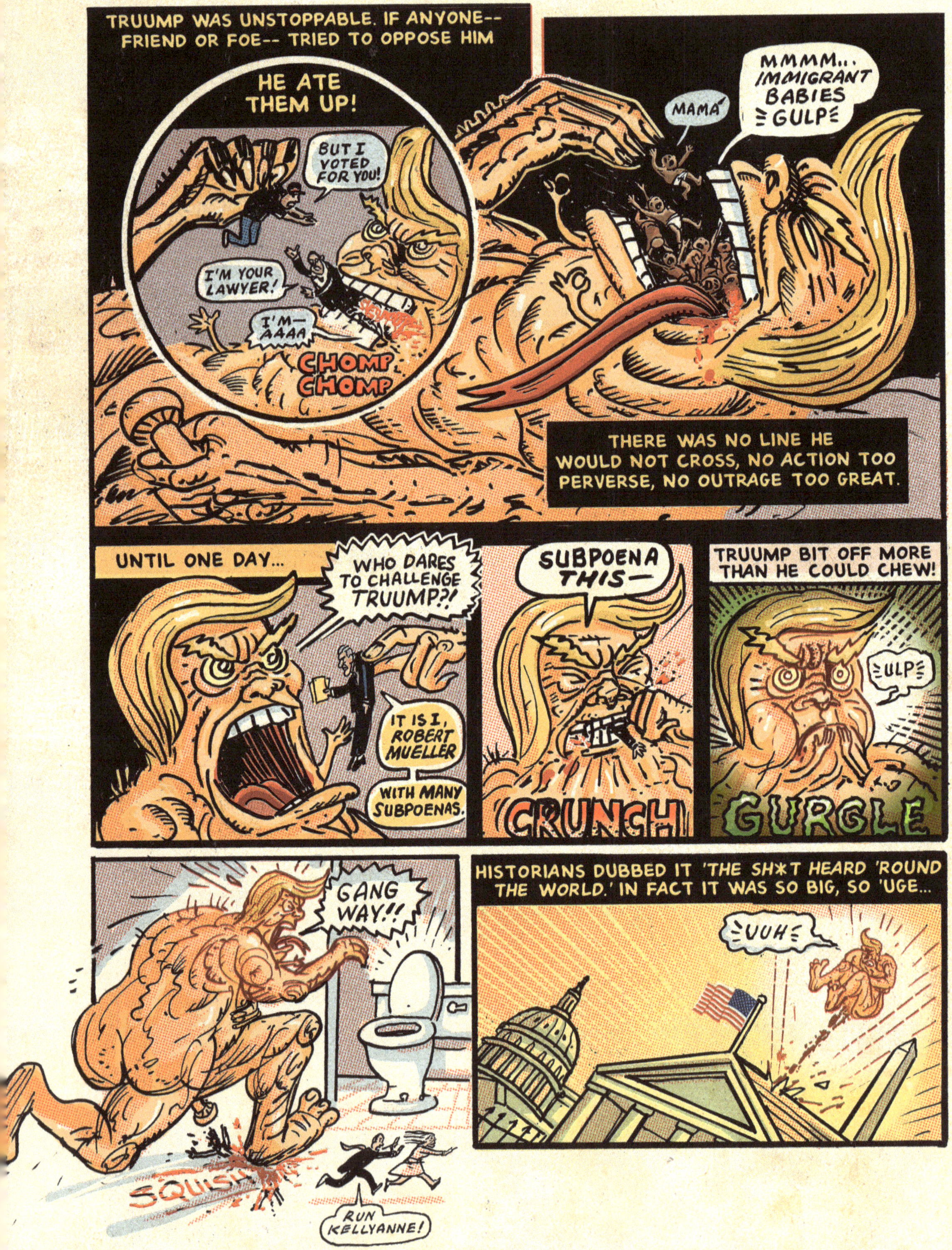
TRUUMP WAS UNSTOPPABLE. IF ANYONE-- FRIEND OR FOE-- TRIED TO OPPOSE HIM
HE ATE THEM UP!
BUT I VOTED FOR YOU!
I'M YOUR LAWYER!
I'M— AAAA
CHOMP CHOMP
MAMA
MMMM... IMMIGRANT BABIES
GULP
THERE WAS NO LINE HE WOULD NOT CROSS, NO ACTION TOO PERVERSE, NO OUTRAGE TOO GREAT.
UNTIL ONE DAY...
WHO DARES TO CHALLENGE TRUUMP?!
IT IS I, ROBERT MUELLER
WITH MANY SUBPOENAS.
SUBPOENA THIS—
CRUNCH
TRUUMP BIT OFF MORE THAN HE COULD CHEW!
ULP
GURGLE
GANG WAY!!
SQUISH
RUN KELLYANNE!
HISTORIANS DUBBED IT 'THE SH*T HEARD 'ROUND THE WORLD.' IN FACT IT WAS SO BIG, SO 'UGE...
UUH

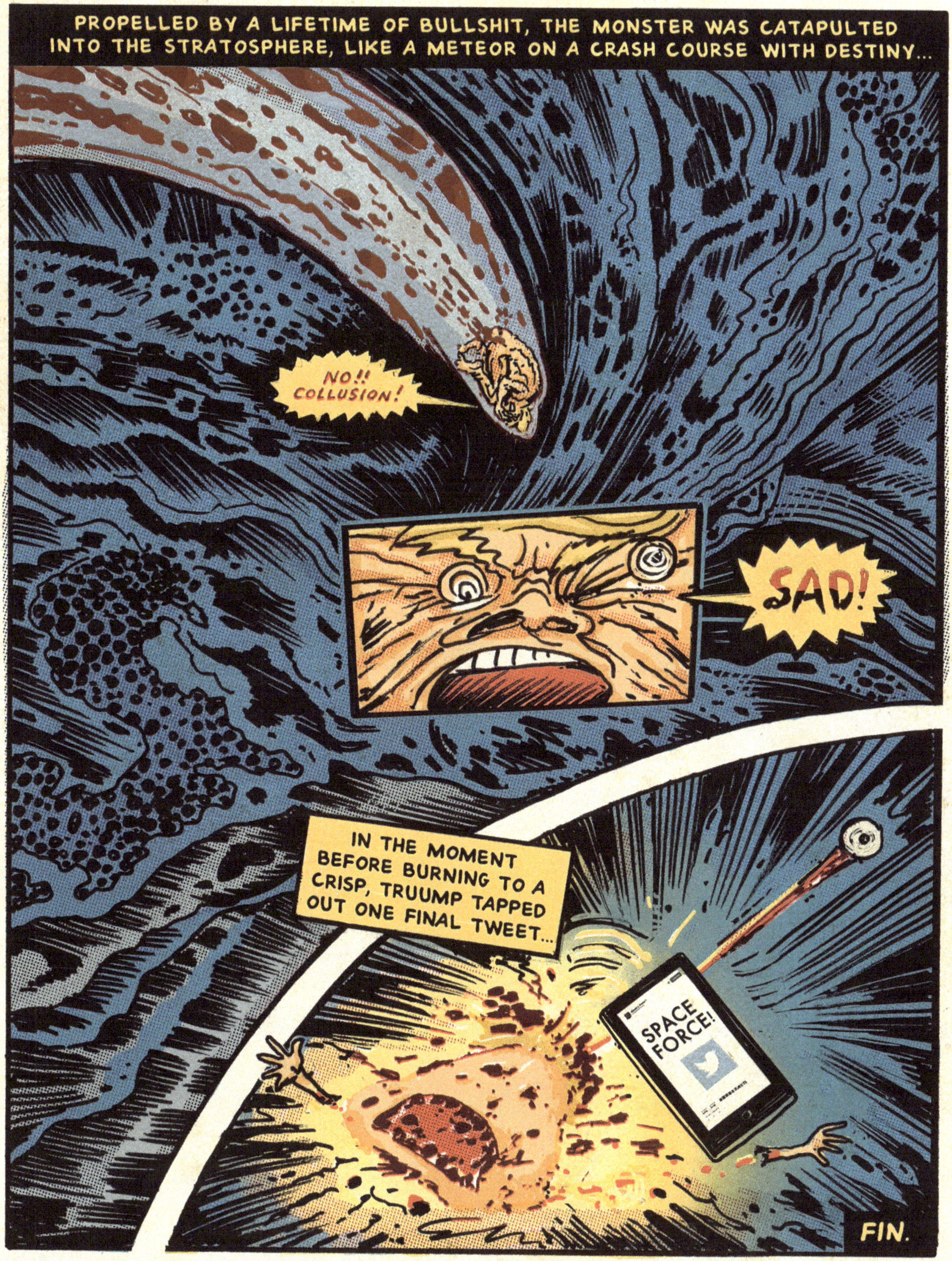
PROPELLED BY A LIFETIME OF BULLSHIT, THE MONSTER WAS CATAPULTED INTO THE STRATOSPHERE, LIKE A METEOR ON A CRASH COURSE WITH DESTINY...
NO!! COLLUSION!
SAD!
IN THE MOMENT BEFORE BURNING TO A CRISP, TRUUMP TAPPED OUT ONE FINAL TWEET...
SPACE FORCE!
FIN.

The Necroworld

What The Wars consisted of, how they started, or why they grew and continued, no one can say.

In all the known galactic civilizations surveyed by the biopolitigists of the InterSystem Consortium of Aaa, nearly every culture commemorates their dead with some form of memorial. In several million of the worlds that comprise Known Aaa Space, these take the form of physical locations for the interrment of the remains of the once-living. In most of these, the size or grandiosity of such monuments or memorial spaces, built to mark the final resting places of those who have passed on, reflect those individuals' relative status when alive. Those with access to power and resources are commemorated with grander tombs; those without, with less, or none. This is a consistent biopolitigistical principle from culture to culture, common even to civilizations separated by far-flung interstellar distances. But in all of Known Aaa Space there is only one planet where this principle has been taken to its ultimate conclusion: the silent, lifeless (except for a few strains of photosynthetic bacteria, all forms of life on this planet have been snuffed out in the long-distant past), and nameless sphere known formally among Consortium biopoligistical authorities as the Necroworld.

Third from its sun, orbited by a small moon and a vast artificial ring composed of the long-wrecked remains of orbital living-platforms, every part of the the Necroworld's surface (including seven continents, the icecaps, and—on elaborately-engineered floating constructions thousands of kiloUUMs wide—most of its five oceans) is covered by nothing but elaborate, grandiose structures designed to house and commemorate the dead. The average size of the former inhabitants (bipedal, four-limbed mammals, mostly hairless except for the topmost parts of their bodies, where their brains and sensory organs were located) was approximately 1.5 UUMs or shorter in height, but for each dead body there are, at a minimum, twenty times that amount of space devoted to the lavish architecture of its interrment; for particularly powerful or wealthy individuals these ratios go up drastically, in some cases covering several square kiloUUMs and rising to the height of hundreds of UUMs. Under such conditions, as you can imagine, an accelerating feedback loop is created as the deceased begin to outnumber the newly born, so it was not long before the space devoted to the dead by this civilization began to encroach on the area available for the living.

These memorial sites are filled with what the planet's inhabitants evidently considered luxuries: consumer technology, furnishings of the finest materials, architectural flourishes like spiral staircases or multi-levelled terraces and balconies, statuary and art of great cost and size, precious gems and metals, elaborately designed costumery, and other ostentatious displays of wealth, reflecting in each case the maximum amount of opulence that the deceased could afford. They are protected by highly sophisticated cybernetic automated-defense measures designed to insure the tomb's invulnerability to raiders and are, except in rare cases where looters managed to elude these deadly defenses, intact. Most importantly, they are also filled with caches of weapons—to this culture, one of the most highly prized of material possessions. For each and every one of the inhabitants of the Necroworld had died—prematurely, usually well before the midpoint of their natural lifespan, often only a few years into their adult maturity—in violent conflict with others of their own species, in what were known simply as "The Wars."

What The Wars consisted of specifically, how they started, or why they grew and continued unabated throughout the Necroworld's history, no biopolitigist can say. But this ongoing cycle of violence, which eventually subsumed all aspects of the Necroworld's planetary culture, seems to have been motivated by an intraspecies competitive instinct for the acquisition of more and more material

Todd Hanson *began working at* **The Onion** *in 1990, and has played TV's Dan Halen since 2005. He lives in Brooklyn.*

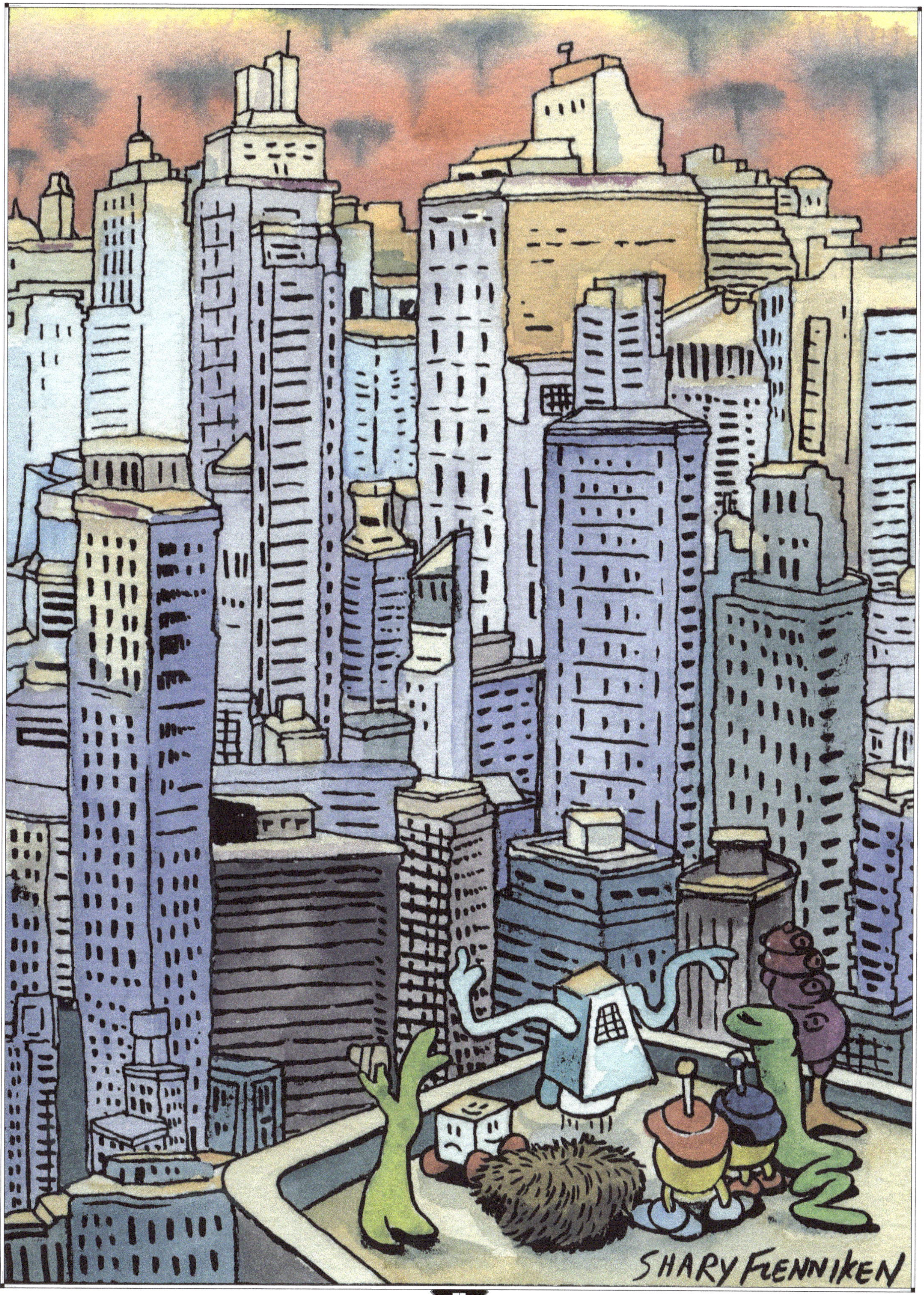
SHARY FLENNIKEN

goods and status. This vicious and fatal competition—which, by the end of Necroworld civilization, had consumed the entirety of its resources and population—was apparently motivated by an all-encompassing, universal goal: to acquire for one's self the largest and most costly possible tomb following one's inevitable murder by rivals.

Since an early death by violence was assured for everyone participating in The Wars, and since the ongoing dangers of The Wars prevented any peaceable enjoyment of the inhabitants' material status during their lifetimes, these memorial "Palaces of the Dead" represented the only means for the society's members to establish their accumulated status in a stable, lasting way. It is as if, denied by their culture any possibility of permanent glory while alive, they sought it in the only form available to them, the realm of eternal memory after death.

Over the course of millennia, as more and more of the planet's surface was devoted to the construction of these commemorative structures, the living population was eventually forced to migrate to orbital residential platforms above the planet's atmosphere. There, The Wars continued to escalate, as the dwindling population continued to compete for the remaining resources necessary for building and stocking the increasingly ostentatious final resting places they needed to construct on the planet's surface, in order to achieve social standing and legitimacy within their violence-based and materialistic society.

Within what most biopolitigists estimate must have been only a few hundred generations, all traces of the surface ecosystem of the Necroworld were completely wiped out, all indigenous wildlife habitats having been replaced by the cold, unmoving and silent expanses of increasingly expensive monuments to the dead. In time, when available planetary surface area ran out, the planet's sole moon (an airless craterscape inhospitable to life) was converted to this same purpose, eventually becoming covered by monuments as well.

It is not known what happened to the race of the Necroworlders in the end,

D. WATSON

but it is clear that some sort of final conflict destroyed the orbital-platform environments they had been reduced to, creating the vast debris-ring which orbits the Necrowold to this day. All that remains now of the efforts expended by this singular civilization's members in their deadly acquisitional struggle to outdo one another's wealth and status, are the endless, extravagant, sprawling mausoleums covering every centiUUM of the dead planet and its lifeless moon.

One might think that the sheer beauty and artistry of the funerary architecture left behind by the long-vanished Necroworlders, and the hoarded finery contained within it, might at least provide their planet with a certain dignity and respect in the eyes of those intragalactic tourists who visit it as a cultural oddity today. But this is not the case. Among almost all space-faring civilizations, the garish displays of the Necroworld's vast, gaudily decorated, utterly ruined surface are seen as a form of extreme kitsch—thus earning it the informal, comical nickname by which the planet is more commonly known: "Tacky-Land"—representing a cultural vulgarity and a lack of artistic sophistication unrivalled among the many and varied peoples of the InterSystem Consortium of Aaa.

B

A BIMONTHLY LITERATURE, ARTS, AND CULTURE MAGAZINE

POWERED BY THE BEVERLY ROGERS, CAROL C. HARTER BLACK MOUNTAIN INSTITUTE

THE BELIEVER

USE PROMO CODE

BYSTANDER

AT CHECKOUT TO RECEIVE 15% OFF

BELIEVERMAG.COM/SUBSCRIBE

NEW FROM FANTAGRAPHICS UNDERGROUND

"For 50-plus years, wherever the action, Mort's been front-and-center—a gimlet-eyed observer and artful insta-chronicler of our times, as fluent outside the box as, in our pages, drawing within it."

—**Emma Allen**
Cartoon Editor, *The New Yorker*

MORT GERBERG
ON THE SCENE
A 50-Year Cartoon Chronicle

Mort Gerberg's social-justice-minded—and bitingly funny—cartoons have appeared in magazines such as *The Realist*, *The New Yorker*, *Playboy*, and the *Saturday Evening Post*. And as a reporter, he's sketched historic scenes like the fiery Women's Marches of the '60s and the infamous '68 Democratic National Convention. Fantagraphics Underground is proud to present a 50-year career retrospective of this vital cartoonist, collecting his magazine cartoons, sketchbook drawings, and on-the-scene reportage sketches in one handsome volume.

AVAILABLE NOW AT FANTAGRAPHICS.COM

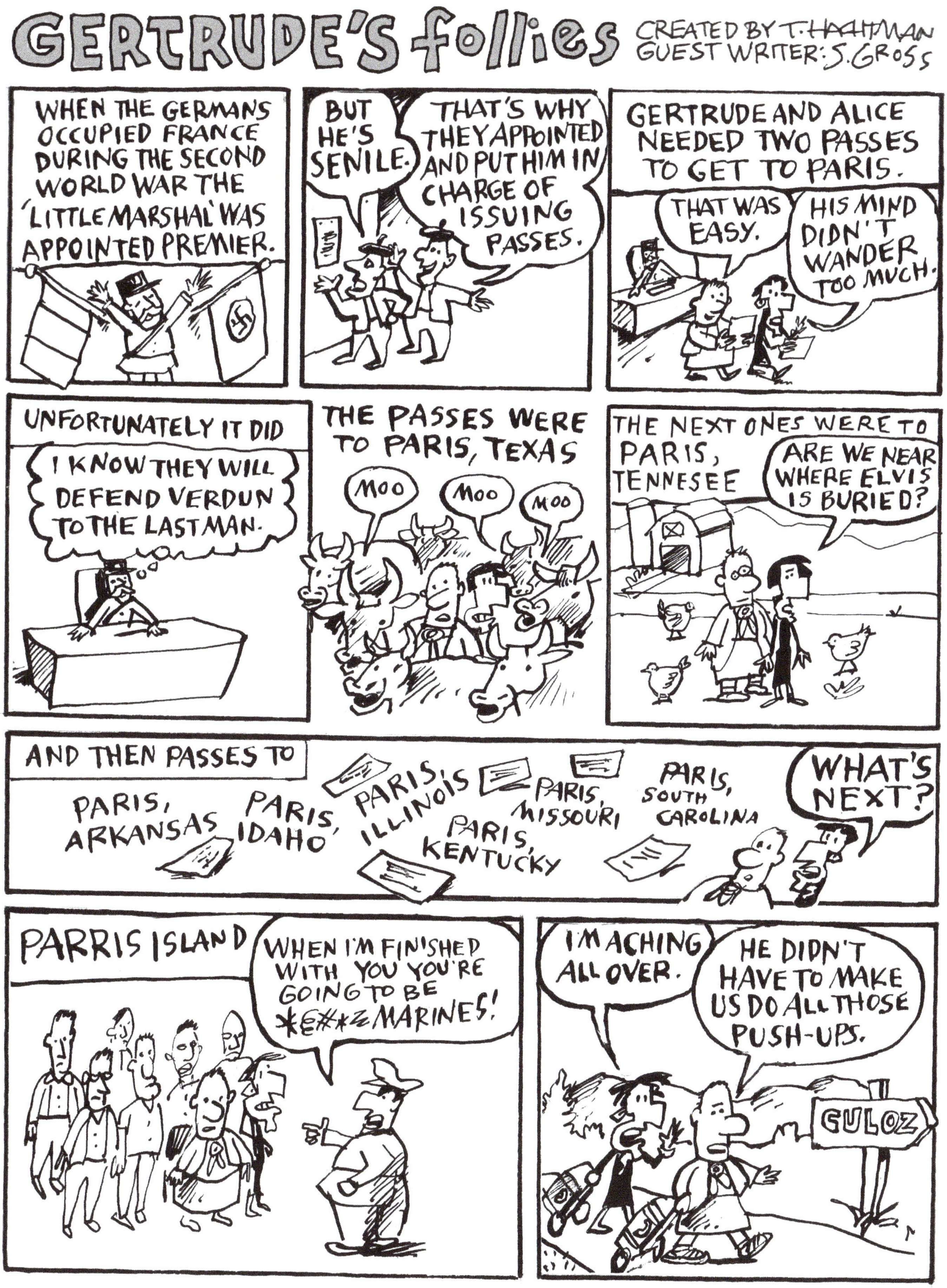
GERTRUDE'S follies
CREATED BY T. HACHTMAN
GUEST WRITER: S. GROSS
WHEN THE GERMANS OCCUPIED FRANCE DURING THE SECOND WORLD WAR THE 'LITTLE MARSHAL' WAS APPOINTED PREMIER.
BUT HE'S SENILE.
THAT'S WHY THEY APPOINTED AND PUT HIM IN CHARGE OF ISSUING PASSES.
GERTRUDE AND ALICE NEEDED TWO PASSES TO GET TO PARIS.
THAT WAS EASY.
HIS MIND DIDN'T WANDER TOO MUCH.
UNFORTUNATELY IT DID
I KNOW THEY WILL DEFEND VERDUN TO THE LAST MAN.
THE PASSES WERE TO PARIS, TEXAS
MOO
MOO
MOO
THE NEXT ONES WERE TO PARIS, TENNESEE
ARE WE NEAR WHERE ELVIS IS BURIED?
AND THEN PASSES TO
PARIS, ARKANSAS
PARIS, IDAHO
PARIS, ILLINOIS
PARIS, KENTUCKY
PARIS, MISSOURI
PARIS, SOUTH CAROLINA
WHAT'S NEXT?
PARRIS ISLAND
WHEN I'M FINISHED WITH YOU YOU'RE GOING TO BE *€#*Z MARINES!
I'M ACHING ALL OVER.
HE DIDN'T HAVE TO MAKE US DO ALL THOSE PUSH-UPS.
GULOZ

OUR BACK PAGES

WHAT AM I DOING HERE?

Our intrepid traveler finds the Vatican in the jungle • By Mike Reiss

The Wild, Wild West Africa

Arthur was skinny, middle-aged, pasty and hairless. He looked like the Pillsbury Doughboy after gastric bypass surgery. His new wife Shasta was a gorgeous African woman half his age. They were the kind of couple only online dating could create.

We met them at a New York party, just before Arthur quit his IT job and moved to West Africa to run his wife's chicken farm. "If you're ever in the Ivory Coast, drop in," he chuckled.

Never, EVER say this to my wife, even as a joke. Not long after, she booked us a Christmas vacation to West Africa: Ivory Coast, Ghana, Togo, and Benin. (If someone cursed my wife, "I'll see you in Hell!" she'd be on Expedia looking for flights). Our trip started in the Ivory Coast, a surprisingly dirty place considering it's named after two brands of soap.

When we dropped in on Arthur he didn't know who the hell we were. Still, he was excited to show us around his swampy, smelly chicken farm. "I'm going to turn all this into a boutique hotel!" he exclaimed, seeing things we could not see. "We'll serve fresh eggs, chicken, capybara…"

Capybara. The world's largest rodent.

"I'll import them from South America. They'll walk freely among the guests, but I also found some great capybara recipes online." He got his wife and giant rat recipes from the same place.

If the African heat had cooked Dave's brain, it had served to sharpen his wife's. She clearly realized she'd married an idiot. He'd been living in this French-speaking country for nearly a year, and hadn't learned a single word of the language. Not even *poulet*, of which he owned 1500. I could see how this would end—Shasta would tearfully tell police her husband had gotten lost in the jungle, when in actuality she had ground him up and fed him to the chickens.

We decided to abandon this West African production of *Who's Afraid of Virginia Woolf?* and head north to the Ivory Coast's one major tourist attraction: the Vatican.

Yes, the Vatican.

From 1985 to 1989, the Ivory Coast spent $175 million to build the Basilica of Our Lady of Peace. It was supposed to be an exact replica of the Vatican but just a little smaller, out of respect to Rome. Instead, by accident, it came out just a little bigger. Oopsie. It sits in the middle of the jungle, 200 miles from the nearest city. The Guinness book calls it the largest church in the world… and nobody goes there. My wife and I had the place to ourselves, and played Pope Horny and the Naughty Nun in the confessional.

In the middle of the West African jungle, we stumbled upon the Vatican.

The four countries of West Africa are shaped like four slender fingers, and next to the pointer of Ivory Coast is the upraised middle finger of Ghana. This is truly the Angriest Place on Earth, its name derived from the phrase "I'm Ghana kill you."*

We entered the country at a fishing village called St. James, populated entirely by supermen—they were huge and shirtless and more muscled than anything I've ever seen in a comic book. And they were all yelling at me for no apparent reason—I had to slip several of them five-dollar bills for my crime of existing. We stepped into the St. James gym where the only sport being practiced—no surprise here—was boxing. My wife insisted I pose for a cute photo, sparring with an eight-year-old boy. The kid proceeded to beat the crap out of me. And then I had to slip him a five.

I thought we'd be safe when we checked into our luxurious (for Ghana) hotel. But that night, I got up in the middle of dinner to use the rest room. "You can't leave!" screamed the *maitresse d'*. "You not pay!"

"I'm going to the bathroom," I whispered.

"Pay for meal first!"

"I'll be right back," I said. "I'm just using the rest room."

"Rest room?" she cried. "Rest room?"

"*Toilet!*" I hollered. "*I'M GOING TO THE TOI-LET!*" Every head in the restaurant swiveled to look at me. Americans—so rude.

I saw fistfights every single day I was in Ghana. Once, my taxi driver leapt out of the car to beat up a traffic cop; then he climbed back into the cab like nothing happened. Indeed, traffic may be a big part of everyone's anger—stoplights literally take five minutes to change, and even when they do, no one can move. The lights are purely decorative. A new brand of commerce has developed around this traffic, as vendors weave among the stopped cars. It's not just soda, ice cream and snacks—there are people selling shirts, shoes and bathroom scales. One guy even had a pile of end-tables stacked on his head. Plus, there are jugglers, acrobats and fire-eaters at every intersection. It's just like Amazon Prime, only the delivery is faster and the shows are better.

Ghana does have brick-and-mortar stores, and they put a lot of thought (and paint) into the names: My God is Able Plumbing Works, Blood of Jesus Electrical, I Am the Light and the Redeemer Stationery, and the vaguely troubling In God We Trust Fast Food. It's easy to mock these, but what's so great about boring names like Lowe's Hardware or Discount Shoe Warehouse? Let's not forget, we're

MIKE REISS is Intrepid Traveler for *The American Bystander*.

*Not really.

the home of Krispy Kreme Donuts: that's three misspelled words. And their donuts are neither krispy nor kremey.

Ghana's greatest commercial product is the quirky, adorable, candy-colored coffin. According to legend, a local chieftain ordered a wooden throne built in the shape of a lion. Sadly, he died before the throne arrived (it was probably stuck in traffic), so his tribe buried him in it. Though started by accident, Ghana now has a thriving business in fantasy coffins. They can be shaped like a sports car, a six-pack of beer, a pack of Marlboros, a Ghana Airways plane—presumably whatever killed you. I thought about buying a coffin shaped like an angry *maitresse d'*. But somehow I'd beaten the odds, and managed to finish the week in Ghana without being murdered.

Too bad. To be buried in a wooden powder-blue Porsche labeled "Little Bastard" is truly a death with dignity.

I headed off to Togo, a much more welcoming country. They clearly see very few Caucasians because everyone greeted me warmly: "Hey White Man!" and occasionally, *"Bonjour, Monsieur Leblanc!"* Giggling children would run up to me and run a finger along my arm, convinced I was a black guy painted white. Babies would look at me and burst into tears, wondering, "Jesus, what happened to you?" I loved it.

I was walking down a city street when a local man whispered to me, "Psst! Wanna see a nice orphanage?" This was the same technique used to lure me into Vegas strip clubs, and in both cases it worked. I entered to see sweet African orphans making handicrafts for sale. The man clapped his hands and the children assembled onstage and sang a sweet hymn in French. "Ordinarily, they would sing more, but they have to go home now."

"They don't live here?" I asked.

"No, their parents will be picking them up soon."

"Parents?" I said. "They don't really seem to be orphans. And this doesn't seem to be much of an orphanage."

"*Monsieur*, it is a very fine orphanage!" He handed me a donation form. "And it is supported by generous Christians like yourself."

I guess they hadn't seen many Jews before, either.

My wife and I visited some charity schools in West Africa, and they were scams too. Each had a model classroom they'd show to American donors. In one, the date on the blackboard was from two months earlier; the lesson for the day was the too-perfect "Democracy Good—Dictatorship Evil." The room was dusty, cobwebbed, and 100% kid-free. "We have other classrooms," boasted the principal.

"Can we see them?" my wife asked.

"No!" he snapped.

Denise dashed off and peered into the three padlocked classrooms: one was full of lumber, one contained bags of cement, and the third housed an old tractor.

"I don't know how that got in there," said the principal.

We'd been in Togo; now it was time to go to Benin. (Read that line again—the wordplay is delicious.)

Before we could enter Benin, I had to get a visa from The Most Imperious Man in Africa. He had a tiny office in a run-down strip mall, but he presided over it like a potentate. He wore leopard print pajamas and lounged on a sofa exploding with stuffing and springs. "Sit down," he commanded, yelling over an electric fan that provided lots of noise but no cooling whatsoever.

I took a seat on an office chair that canted dangerously to one side.

"Did I ask you to sit there?" he said.

"I did not."

I moved over to an even more busted chair. "I just need you to stamp our —"

"Did I ask you to speak?" he purred.

"I did not."

This powerless power trip lasted six hours, including his three-hour lunch break, but we were finally going to Benin. I was a man with a mission: this was the birthplace of voodoo, and I had an important question. I met with a revered witch doctor – he had a scraggly white beard, and was naked, save for a loincloth, beads and body paint. I sat on the dirt floor of his hut and said, "I have a play opening in September. Will it be a success?"

He began a twenty-minute ritual, chanting, humming, tossing bones, burning leaves. Finally, after a long silence, he said, "No."

And you know what? He was right.

He was right and I was wrong – Arthur and Shasta are still married. She's raising chickens in the Ivory Coast and he's doing IT work in Philadelphia.

P.S. MUELLER THINKS LIKE THIS

The cartoonist/broadcaster/writer is always walking around, looking at stuff • ***By P.S. Mueller***

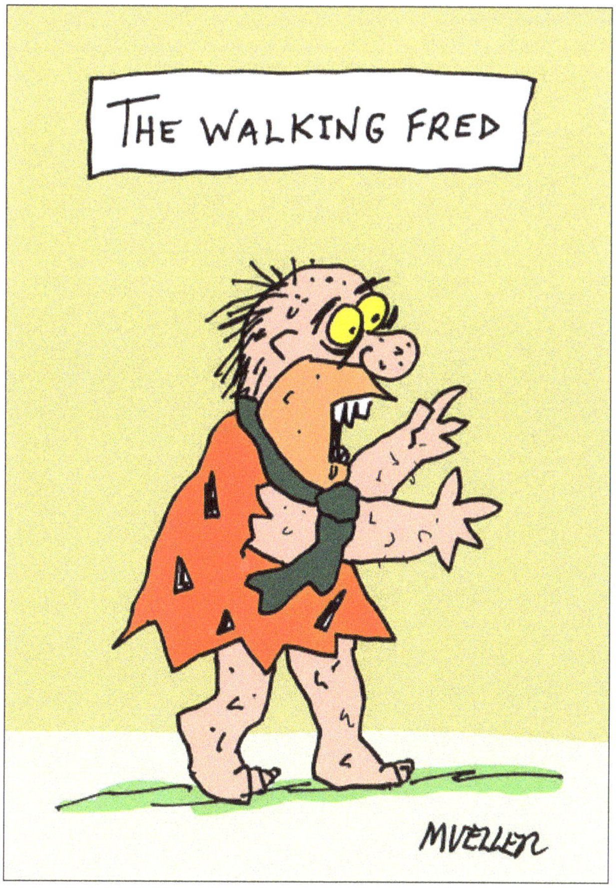
THE WALKING FRED
MUELLER

My Way

And now, my hand is here
Looks like my face, but I'm
uncertain
That hand, I keep it near
Just in case my mushroom's
hurtin'
I've grabbed a life that's stacked
I've combed it each and every
which way
And worse, much worse than
this
I wrecked it my way
Egrets, I've had a few
But in a stew I dare not mention
I hid what I hid from you
And deducted that exemption
I sold each quarterhorse
As primo steaks along the
highway
And worse, much worse than
this
I wrecked it my way
Yes, there were crimes, I'm sure you
knew
When I stuffed in more than you could
chew
But if I may, where there is clout
A strangled nation cannot shout
I grabbed it all, took Putin's call
And wrecked it my wayyyyyyyyyyyyyy

Nobody Dies in the End

But it gets damn ugly.

I was the next door neighbor of Art and Rita Langway. I had been carrying on an affair with Rita long enough to figure out why Art spent his evenings in the basement with feathers and fish-hooks, and I wanted out. My wife Mary has known about this all along and couldn't care less. She knits life-size horses.

While fishing with Art not long ago, he asked me if I trusted my wife. I told him, "Sure, she knits life-size horses." Art looked troubled and I asked him if he trusted Rita. He sat there, staring at his dangerous fishhook-covered hat for a long time before muttering, "Not sure." He went on to say Rita had become unusually quiet soon after they agreed to double their life insurance policies. He said they had both fallen into a kind of sidelong glance thing while watching CNN. He swore his couch was shrinking, until I told him the couch was fine, but his ass was fifty. He seemed reassured by this and stuffed his nightmarish head-wear into a strong, lockable tackle box and I rowed us home.

The very next night Art was at his golf club and Rita showed up at my back door, drunk. Really drunk. Mary was upstairs, deep inside the warp and hoof of her latest horse. So I got drunk, too. Not as drunk as Rita though. She was weird and confessional and all that—happy to have a listener, I guess. Then she wept about how things hadn't been the same with Art and her, ever since their son came out as solar. "And that ass! It's like the couch is shrinking or something for Chrissakes! Some days I just want him gone from my life oh God oh God I really mean that and...I'll be right back, gotta puke," she rambled. Or did she?

It turned out that Mary overheard everything upstairs while tricking out a pony with a glue gun and sequins. (By the way, Mary and I are both men and we don't really get into a bunch of identity stuff because it's just not relevant for us. Also, Art and Rita have never met Mary because Mary knits life-sizes horses and that's plenty for most people to simply hear about.)

Mary had a plan. A week later Mary anonymously called Rita from a phone at the airport. She asked Rita if she had any husband trouble she could do without. Rita was drunk again and immediately blurted "YES!" Mary, doing her amazing Humphrey Bogart impersonation, asked for one hundred thousand, half up front. Mary, and how's this for ballsy, told Rita to put the fifty thousand in her own garbage bin and wheel it to the curb. Everyone in the neighbohood rolled out bins for city pickup, always mid-evening the night before. At 3:00 a.m., I quietly walked

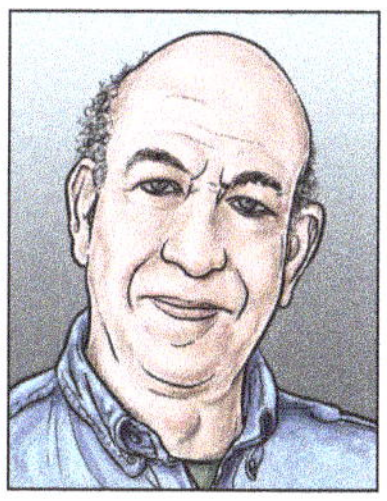

P.S. MUELLER is Staff Liar of *The American Bystander*.

OWN ORIGINAL CARTOON ART

Become the owner—or gift giver— of original artwork.

Sam Gross

"IT SORT OF MAKES YOU STOP AND THINK, DOESN'T IT."

P.C. Vey / George Booth

To enquire about your favorites please contact Samantha Vuignier:
SamanthaVuignier@CartoonCollections.com

or visit
CartoonCollections.com/originals

CARTOON COLLECTIONS
CARTOONCOLLECTIONS.COM

---

across the lawn and grabbed the money. I can't begin to tell you how cool this all was.

But my Mary took it further. She waited a night or two for Rita to go off and meet her secret Japansese robot lover. Then Mary put on a Donald Trump mask and let herself in through the patio door while Art was deeply involved with hooks and feathers downstairs. She even timed her descending creak on the boards perfectly as she raised a fake gun toward Art, who sat there, frozen. (Mary also bears a remarkable resemblance to Bogart) Then she said, giving it the old Humphrey, "It's nothing personal, pal. It's just a job," and began to take aim. Needless to say, Art yelled "Wait! I know Rita is paying you to kill me! I'll double that if you get rid of her, make her disappear!" Mary boldly instructed Art to leave his hundred thousand in the shed behind our place and the rest would be worked out later.

Then Mary returned to knitting stallions and I went fishing with Art. We let this go on for a few weeks before inviting them both over for a barbecue. The burgers were done and set out nicely on our picnic table under a tree by the shed. And then Mary came down to join us, going full-on Bogey with,"Hey, ain't I met you two around somewhere." I think the color that drained out of their faces fed our lawn.

Mary sat next to me and we held hands while Art and Rita gave each other some major side-eye. Mary laughed with than genuine Carol Lombard guffaw of hers and explained that, no, she wasn't going to kill anybody, but Art and Rita would liquidate everything they had and deposit it in a numbered account in some nameless country. Then she played them the recordings she made with her phone.

The last I heard of Rita, she was bussing tables at Fat Blabby's out on Route 25. Art supposedly moved into an uncle's cabin and accidentally put his nightmare hat on inside out while fishing drunk. Six months later and that hat is still on his head, and he is physically unable to tip it when passing ladies.

Mary and I sold our place and bought a fake ranchette with a little barn for Mary's upcoming Clydesdale series. We sit on the couch together and watch *The Voice* or old Andy Griffith shows. Mary can whistle the theme perfectly. I swear the harmonics make the room quiver sometimes. It's all good.

So why is she looking at me like that out of the corner of her eye?

BALLED EAGLE — SPARKS

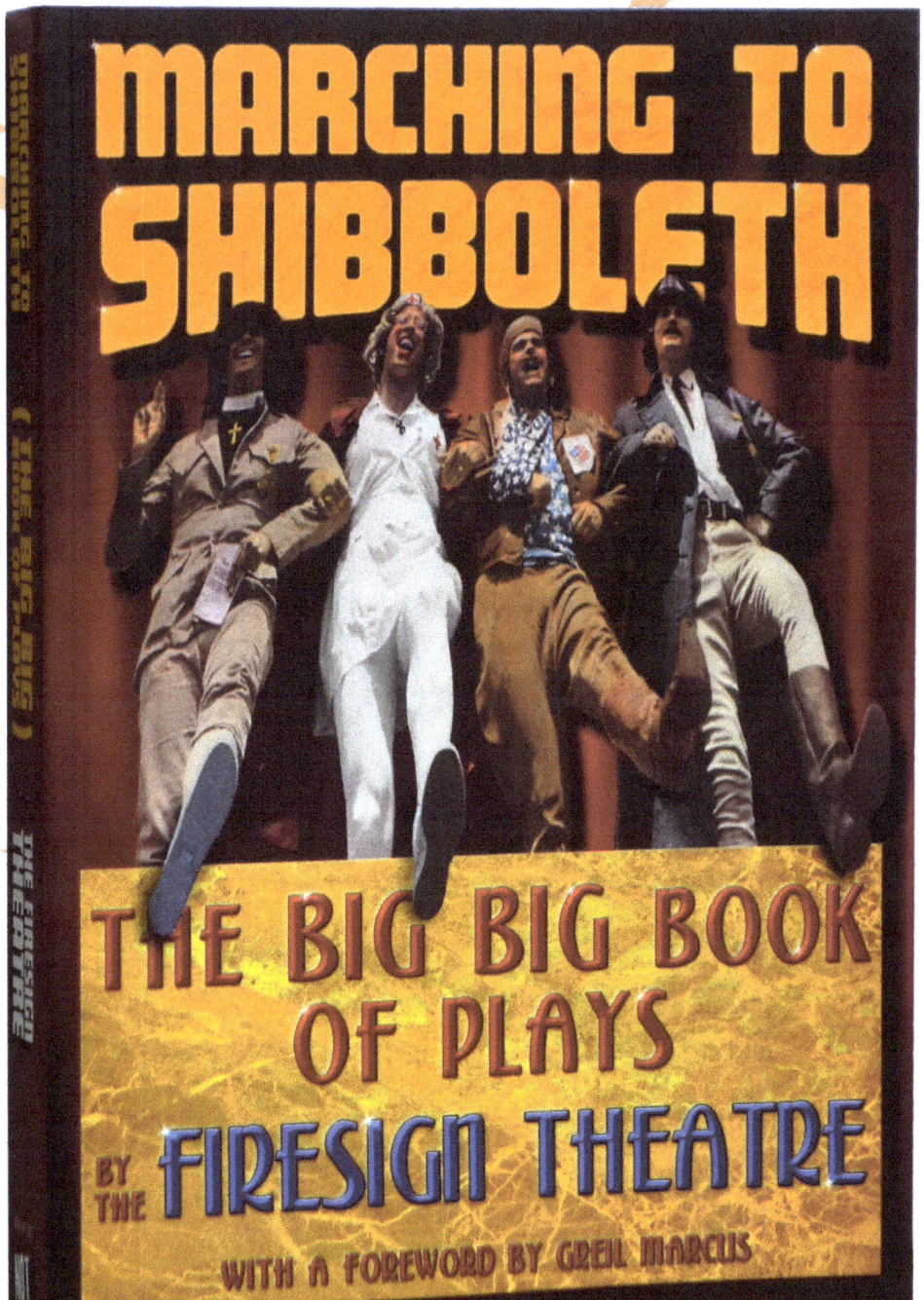

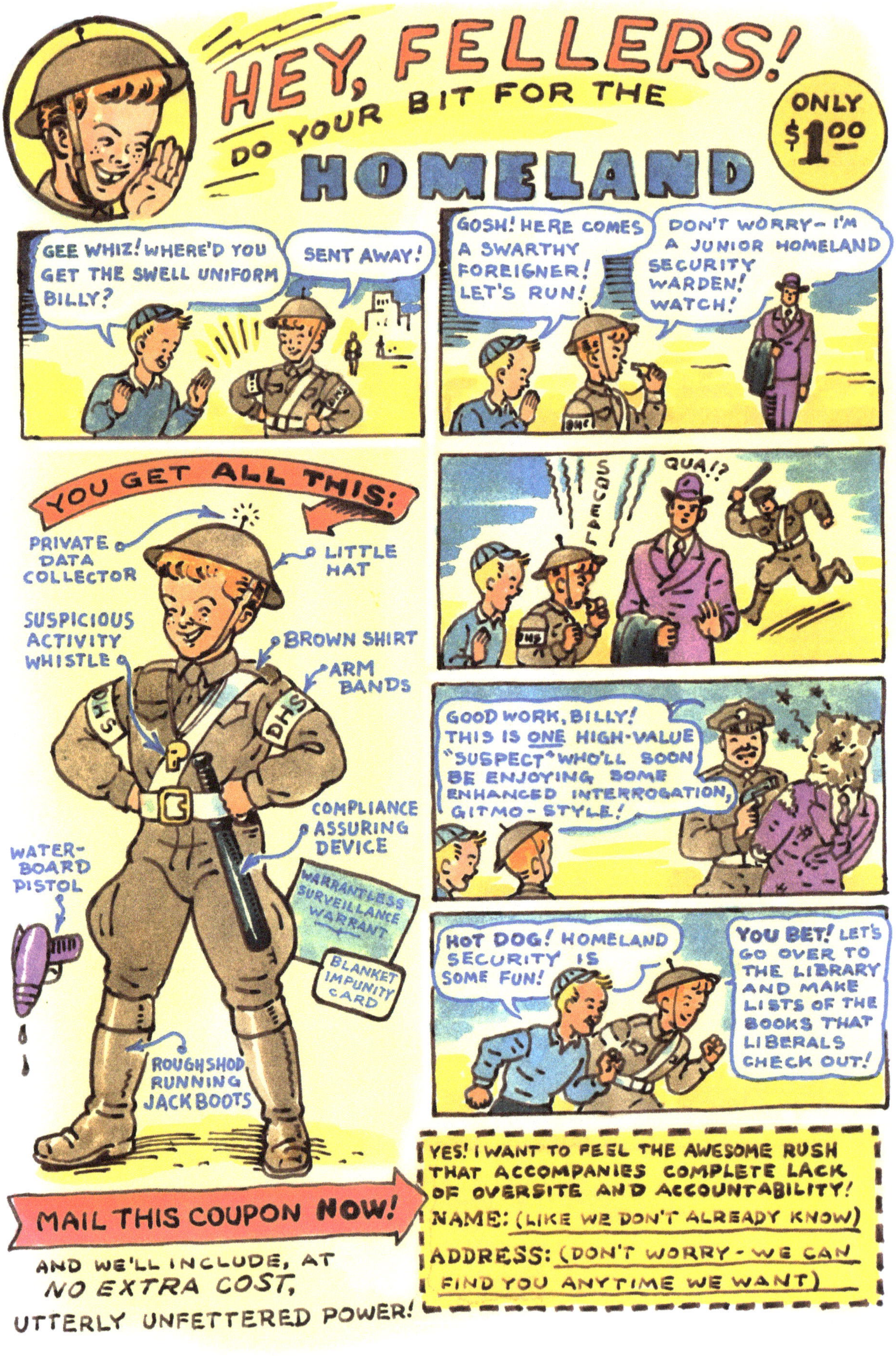
HEY, FELLERS!
DO YOUR BIT FOR THE
HOMELAND
ONLY $1.00
GEE WHIZ! WHERE'D YOU GET THE SWELL UNIFORM BILLY?
SENT AWAY!
GOSH! HERE COMES A SWARTHY FOREIGNER! LET'S RUN!
DON'T WORRY– I'M A JUNIOR HOMELAND SECURITY WARDEN! WATCH!
YOU GET ALL THIS!
PRIVATE DATA COLLECTOR
LITTLE HAT
SUSPICIOUS ACTIVITY WHISTLE
BROWN SHIRT
ARM BANDS
DHS
COMPLIANCE ASSURING DEVICE
WATER-BOARD PISTOL
WARRANTLESS SURVEILLANCE WARRANT
BLANKET IMPUNITY CARD
ROUGHSHOD RUNNING JACKBOOTS
SQUEAL
QUA!?
GOOD WORK, BILLY! THIS IS ONE HIGH-VALUE "SUSPECT" WHO'LL SOON BE ENJOYING SOME ENHANCED INTERROGATION, GITMO-STYLE!
HOT DOG! HOMELAND SECURITY IS SOME FUN!
YOU BET! LET'S GO OVER TO THE LIBRARY AND MAKE LISTS OF THE BOOKS THAT LIBERALS CHECK OUT!
MAIL THIS COUPON NOW!
AND WE'LL INCLUDE, AT NO EXTRA COST, UTTERLY UNFETTERED POWER!
YES! I WANT TO FEEL THE AWESOME RUSH THAT ACCOMPANIES COMPLETE LACK OF OVERSITE AND ACCOUNTABILITY!
NAME: (LIKE WE DON'T ALREADY KNOW)
ADDRESS: (DON'T WORRY - WE CAN FIND YOU ANYTIME WE WANT)
B

ROSS MACDONALD *(@brightworkillo) has contributed cartoons and humor to many fine periodicals, written four children's books, and created props for your favorite movie or TV show.*

www.ingramcontent.com/pod-product-compliance
Lightning Source LLC
Chambersburg PA
CBHW061754290426
44108CB00029B/2996